ABOUT THE AUTHOR

Mallika Basu is a writer, presenter and commentator on food, drink and hospitality, with a firm belief in the power of food as a force for good. A features writer and presenter for *Good Food*, she explores planet-friendlier eating and the links between food, people and the planet in her award-nominated newsletter, In Good Taste.

Mallika is the author of two Indian cookbooks, *Miss Masala* and *Masala*, a recipe writer and a regular speaker and chair at food events across the UK. She educates curious eaters about food systems and food writing at the British Library, and is a finale judge and co-presenter of the Guild of Fine Food's Great Taste Awards, reviewing entries for its ethical and sustainable bursary.

Alongside her food writing, Mallika has over 20 years of strategic communications and advisory expertise, having worked with organisations including Jamie Oliver Group and Waitrose. She also helped shape Borough Market's 2030 strategy. She has completed the Sustainable Food: Production and Processing programme at the University of Cambridge Institute for Sustainability Leadership (CISL) and holds a master's degree in journalism.

Born in Kolkata, India, Mallika lives in South London with her two teenage children.

For Leia and Noah,
because you deserve better

IN GOOD TASTE

**What Shapes What
We Eat and Drink –
and Why It Matters**

**Mallika
Basu**

CONTENTS

FOREWORD i
PREFACE 1
PROLOGUE 5
PLAYERS 43
PEOPLE 85
PLANET 121
POSITIVE, PRACTICAL CHANGE 161

APPENDIX 194
ENDNOTES 204
INDEX 225
ACKNOWLEDGEMENTS 235

FOREWORD

What goes through your mind when you're in the supermarket, trawling the shelves for your weekly essentials? Or at a market, jostling with the crowds to get the freshest food, hopefully straight from the producer? Or when you're in the kitchen, radio on, creating a new recipe? Maybe it's the appearance or smell, the price, the use-by date, whether it's gluten free or what it might best go with – perhaps that aubergine that's still lingering at the back of the fridge? Any of these, I imagine, and many more besides.

But you're probably not thinking about whether the farmer was paid a fair price, or if the soil that asparagus was grown in was depleted or healthy. I'm guilty of it myself – grab-and-go convenience, price over environmental concerns – despite all the knowledge I have about the negative impacts of how we produce and consume food. For many of us, these patterns are baked into our lives.

But what if we could do things differently? What if we could factor these other questions into our choices and make a positive change along with it?

Enter *In Good Taste*, a book that shows how our food system works, but also how to change things for the better – to create a food system that is truly sustainable, for people and planet.

Author Mallika Basu, a food writer, presenter and advisor, is also an alum of the Cambridge Institute for Sustainability Leadership's (CISL)

Sustainable Food: Production and Processing programme, a course which I led in design and development. With *In Good Taste*, Mallika matches her talent for writing and passion for food with academic rigour, and her first book on food sustainability is highly impactful.

Through my work at CISL I am well-rehearsed in the usual discourse about food sustainability. We often talk about the role of farmers, land use, government policy, plant-based diets or the power dynamics of large retailers. While all these topics are doubtless important to move the needle on food systems, we sometimes forget the fact that food is about so much more. Food is nutrition, yes, but it also holds cultural significance and brings joy to our lives when we source, cook and share it. Food can be intensely personal, can evoke powerful memories and can connect people to each other and to lands they may have long ago left.

In Good Taste holds the human connection with food front and centre. But its real success lies in linking this humanity to the discourse by helping the reader to both understand the challenges and identify with them on a personal, everyday level.

Mallika covers a lot of ground and reviewing this book was a pleasure. From start to finish, nuances and counterpoints are interwoven to create a comprehensive but remarkably concise diagnosis of the challenges with how we produce and consume food. But it doesn't stop there. *In Good Taste* puts a challenge to the reader from the start – to the foodies, the chefs, the influencers – to you – to take action to create positive change through the food you create and share.

In reading this book, you will find your own insights and meaning. Whatever you choose to take from it, I hope it inspires you to make positive changes and to encourage others to do the same, so that maybe next time you're doing the weekly shop or cooking an exciting new recipe, there are some different questions in your mind, ones which you not only know the answer to, but are actively trying to change.

Sarah Bailey

Sustainable Food Production and Processing Lead Course Designer, CISL

PREFACE

After much reflection on the political and sociological aspects of the table, I have realised that I am completely uninterested in food. My preference is for fodder that is cheap, quick and simple to procure and prepare, whilst providing the requisite nutrients to enable a person to stay alive.

**Eleanor Oliphant Is Completely Fine
by Gail Honeyman (2017)**

It's never been a better time to be a food lover. We binge *Bake Off*, follow foodie influencers, queue for trending hotspots and scroll endlessly for ideas on what to cook next.

But for all this appetite, how much do we really know about what goes on behind the scenes with our food? About the power that certain people have over it? The people growing it? The environment it depends on?

If we take a closer look, our epicurean world is full of contradictions.

* Why are apples flown in from halfway across the world during a successful British apple season?
* Why are rich, well-fed countries like the UK and US home to rising obesity rates, poverty, malnutrition and ill health?
* Why are the people growing and producing the food that we all need for our very existence often those who are struggling the most?

We don't usually have time to dwell on these questions. The answers are complex, confusing and often contradictory. Life is demanding. The cost-of-living crisis bites. We're lucky to be able to access what we need, when we need it – and that's fair enough. Wild weather, wars and hunger crises often feel distant. Besides, what can we really do to change things?

The truth is, how our food gets to us – and what we do with it – shapes our environment, our health and our future. Today's system runs on parched soil, exploited people, barrels of crude oil and acres of plastic. Built over centuries, it's global and political, but also fragile. And it's already affecting what ends up on our plates – and what doesn't.

Of course, none of this is top of mind when we sit down to eat with friends or enjoy a quiet dinner in front of the telly at the end of a long day. Most of us are far removed – physically and emotionally – from the people and processes behind our food. It arrives clean, portioned and packaged, ready to go.

But if you're reading this, you probably *do* care. As food lovers and as people working in and around the food industry, we are in the business of taste. We wear badges like 'foodie' and 'superfoodie' with pride, but those labels risk being synonymous with mindless greed and gluttony if we ignore where our food comes from or the impact it has.

Sure, we all have our Eleanor Oliphant moments when food is just fuel, but our love for food doesn't thrive in a vacuum. Loving food, or profiting from it, comes with responsibility. We are deeply invested in how food nourishes and delights us now, and into the future. But it can feel daunting, even overwhelming, to piece together the full story behind what we eat and drink.

That's where this book comes in. It's a guide to the issues shaping our edible world today. It's not exhaustive and it's not meant to be preachy. It's a starting point to help us see the bigger picture and find our place in it. This book distils a lot of complex, messy realities into a digestible guide, which inevitably also means the loss of some nuance.

Starting with a bird's eye view of how the food system works (and why it urgently needs transforming) in the prologue, the book then covers:

* **The players:** Who holds power, makes decisions and to what extent, and what food policy means for our everyday lives.
* **People:** How global trade, capitalism and the legacy of colonisation created inequality and continue to shape what we eat today – and who gets left behind.
* **The planet:** How we got here and what's at stake for nature, land, water and climate.
* **Positive, practical change:** The top 10 tangible ways food lovers can make an impact with what's on our plates and beyond.

As a proud member of the global majority, the South Asian diaspora and a British citizen living in London, I write with a global view and local references. For further ease, I've assumed that you're a curious eater like me: hungry for flavour, but also for context. Because we're not short on food content – we're low on food context.

If enough of us take an interest, we become powerful ingredients in shaping a fairer food world – we become tastemakers and change-makers. United by our passion for eating and drinking, we can play our part in what really matters in food and drink today.

HOW TO USE THIS BOOK

Despite undertaking the toughest summary job I've ever done, each chapter still comes with a generous helping of detail. You'll also find insights from expert contributors woven into the text and in sidebars. Feel free to read the book cover to cover or just dip in and out as you would a reference guide. If you prefer the grab-and-go option, each chapter ends with key takeaways: a top-line summary of the main points. Read these, along with the final chapter on small, practical steps, and you'll have a solid introduction to the issues and what you can do about them. If this whets your appetite, the books and reports quoted throughout and in the endnotes are a treasure trove of further reading.

PROLOGUE

An overview of the food system

'Earth is amazing! These are called "farms". Humans would put seeds in the ground, pour water on them, and they grow food, like pizza!'

The Captain, *Wall-E* (2008)

At first glance, it can seem like the magic of our meals is as simple as The Captain makes it out to be in *Wall-E*. But the truth is more complicated. What we eat, how we produce it and where it ends up are all part of something much bigger: a complex global network that transforms raw ingredients into what lands on our plates – and what doesn't. This network has a big job to do, feeding more than 8 billion people and counting.

What is the food system?

The food system covers the way we produce, process, distribute, market, eat and waste food.

So far, so straightforward. But the reality is far from it. This is where systems thinking becomes useful. Rather than looking at each element in isolation, systems thinking encourages us to see how everything is connected and how change in one area can ripple through others. These ripple effects are known as feedback loops.

Take rice, for instance, a beloved staple for more than half of the world.[1] When it's grown in flooded paddies it contributes to climate change, which in turn disrupts rainfall patterns and water availability where it's cultivated. As yields decline, pressure builds to grow more. Choosing to eat rice, how often we eat it or the type of rice we buy all plays a part in that bigger picture. Our food choices never exist in isolation.

Feeding us has always been a complex job, but with the global population set to hit 9.7 billion by 2050, the pressure on the food system is mounting.[2] Feeding everyone sustainably – in a way that protects the environment, supports people and doesn't harm the planet – is now considered to be one of the greatest challenges of our time.[3]

The food system has achieved much. Many of our daily needs are met with impressive efficiency. We can enjoy avocados from Mexico, asparagus from Peru and pineapples from Costa Rica all year round. Fruits grown in tropical areas, spices grown on balmy hillsides and sun-kissed vegetables from warm climes can be found on our supermarket shelves even in the depths of winter.

Journalist and food writer Joanna Blythman labelled this 'permanent global summertime',[4] a result of complex logistics, shipping and trade deals. We now expect to see strawberries in February and mangoes on demand. Most of us do a lot of our shopping in supermarkets, where products and ingredients from all over the world arrive just in time to meet our needs. It's a system designed for our convenience and our meals are more exciting because of it.

Every item on the shelf has made a journey, often a long and unexpected one. This journey is part of what's known as the food supply chain, the series of steps that move food from where it's grown to where it's processed, packaged, stored, transported, sold and eventually eaten. It's also called a value chain because value is added at each step, e.g. by transforming the food, extending its shelf life or getting it to the right place. Each step also involves different actors – farmers, factories, shipping companies, retailers – often scattered across multiple countries.

Take tinned pears. When UK conservationist Chris Packham shared their global journey in a post on X (previously Twitter) in 2021, it broke the internet. Grown in Argentina, packed in Thailand and shipped to the UK, those pears had travelled thousands of miles before reaching a kitchen table. The same goes for tinned artichokes from Peru, which might be processed in France or Denmark, then sold across Europe – an impressive feat of logistics.[5]

This is one of the defining features of the food system: it's inherently global and incredibly efficient. It's also a capitalist system. Private companies and corporations control much of the supply chain, driven by profit. Food is treated as a commodity to be bought and sold, not a basic human right. Every stage, from farm to factory to fridge, is shaped by market forces like supply, demand and efficiency rather than just making sure people are fed well. This sits in stark contrast to the UN's recognition of food as a basic human right.

In many parts of the world, the food system is also highly industrialised. Food is produced on a large scale in factories or on industrial farms, with an emphasis on speed, volume and efficiency. Much of this is mechanised, using machines rather than people to grow, harvest, process and package food.

How did the food system come about?

The food system didn't appear overnight. It evolved out of necessity, innovation and power, shaped by historical events, scientific breakthroughs and shifting human needs. Over centuries, the food system has adapted to feed more people, embrace new thinking and satisfy our lifestyles and growing appetite for food from everywhere.

Here's a whistlestop tour of some of the major milestones that brought us to where we are today. We'll take a deep dive into the controversies and consequences in later chapters.

Pre-agriculture and early cooking

Around 1.5 million years ago, our ancestors discovered how to control fire. This changed everything. Cooking made food easier to digest and nutrients easier to absorb. Harvard anthropologist Richard Wrangham has even linked the development of cooked food to the growth of the human brain, marking our departure as early humans from our primate relatives.[6]

Before freezers or vacuum packs, our early ancestors preserved food using fermentation, drying and smoking. This shaped early food culture, improving shelf life and helping communities survive lean times.

Early agriculture, trade and thinking about ecology

About 10,000 years ago, humans began farming, starting with grains. This shift from hunting and gathering to growing led to permanent settlements, the domestication of plants and animals, and the beginnings of agricultural economies. Staple crops varied by region: wheat and barley in the Middle East, rice in China, millet and sorghum in Africa.

Food surpluses allowed for storage and exchange, fuelling the growth of trade routes. These routes connected regions and enabled the sharing of ingredients, knowledge and culinary practices and traditions across cultures. Hundreds of years later, in the 9th century, African-Arab scholar Al-Jahiz introduced the idea of 'food chains', describing how plants, animals and humans are linked by who eats whom in nature. His work foreshadowed the ecological thinking that would become central to modern debates about biodiversity and food systems.

Global trade and land use

By the 15th century, European powers were expanding their footprint and their appetites. The early spice trade, along with cod and salt cod, drove maritime exploration and long-distance trade. Sugar, coffee, tea and more followed.

The Columbian Exchange, named after explorer Christopher Columbus, formalised the movement of crops, animals and food traditions between Europe, Africa, Asia and the Americas. This transformed diets and economies worldwide, but it also changed how land was used and who controlled it. You can find the terms we use to describe these geographical and societal shifts in the 'Who's Who in the World' section in the appendix.

Across Britain, shared or common land was enclosed for private use with parliamentary approval. Britons travelled overseas looking for opportunities, displacing rural and Indigenous communities, disrupting traditional food systems and establishing new agricultural systems across colonised lands.[7] These often took the form of plantation economies and monocultures (the practice of growing a single crop over large areas) to maximise productivity and meet European needs and demand. What began as a local shift in land use became a global pattern: moving from food grown for local sustenance to agriculture as a tool of commerce, control and empire-building.

Industrialisation and preservation

As cities expanded and empires stretched across continents, food needed to travel further and last longer for armies, sailors and growing urban populations. This pressure drove innovation. Exploration and warfare accelerated the development of processing methods like salting, drying, bottling and canning, all aimed at extending shelf life and moving food across distance and time.[8]

The Industrial Revolution happened alongside this. Tractors replaced human and animal labour. Synthetic fertilizers boosted agricultural yields. Steamships and railways connected farms to homes and factories to food from further afield. The arrival of mechanical refrigeration in the late 19th and early 20th centuries further transformed supply chains, allowing perishable foods like meat and dairy to travel across continents and into people's homes year round.

For the first time, large amounts of food could be grown in one place, processed in another and eaten somewhere entirely different.

Food rationing and resilience

During the First and Second World Wars, many nations introduced food rationing to ensure fair distribution and prevent shortages. In Britain, ration books limited access to staples like meat, sugar, fats and tea. People were encouraged to 'dig for victory' by growing their own vegetables, and resourcefulness in the kitchen became a necessity.

The wars also strengthened the role of government in managing food supply chains, fostering innovations in storage, preservation and nutrition science. Wartime food policies laid the groundwork for post-war agricultural reforms and shaped public attitudes towards self-sufficiency and national food security.

Grocery shopping

The modern supermarket emerged in the early 20th century, pioneered by American food manufacturers looking for efficient ways to sell processed, shelf-stable goods at scale.[9] With peacetime recovery, suburban growth and improved cold-chain logistics, supermarkets began to boom after the Second World War. This new retail model transformed the food landscape, offering low prices, long opening hours and one-stop convenience under bright fluorescent lights.

What followed was a wave of supermarketisation, gradually replacing traditional food markets, independent grocers and wet markets across much of the world. Further innovations in food retail, from bulk buying to online ordering and home delivery, have continued to reshape how we shop, stock and eat.

The Green and Gene Revolutions

In the early 20th century, scientific advances made it possible to produce synthetic fertilizers on a large scale, unlocking a new era of productivity in farming. This set the stage for the Green Revolution, which started after the Second World War as a global effort to increase food production and prevent hunger.

By the 1960s, new high-yield crop varieties, chemical fertilizers, pesticides and irrigation systems were being introduced in parts of Asia, Latin America and beyond. One of the most widely used pesticides at the time was DDT. Initially developed during wartime to combat insect-borne illnesses like malaria and typhus, it was later used to control pests and increase crop yields in agriculture.

These changes transformed farming in countries like India, Mexico and Pakistan, where wheat and rice harvests more than doubled in a matter of decades. The Green Revolution helped stabilise food supplies and address fears of famine in many regions.

This period also paved the way for the Gene Revolution: the use of biotechnology to modify crops for greater resilience and efficiency. Genetically modified (GM) plants, like pest-resistant maize and drought-tolerant wheat, were designed to thrive in difficult conditions and reduce the need for chemical inputs. Together, these two revolutions put science and technology at the centre of the global food system.

Globalisation and convenience culture

By the late 20th and early 21st centuries, global trade, corporate growth and supermarket dominance reshaped how we live, eat and drink.

Convenience became central – think frozen peas, washed and bagged salad and ready meals. For many, especially in urban areas, access to time-saving food meant more flexibility in work and family life.

For women in particular, convenience foods were often framed as tools of liberation, helping to ease the burden of unpaid domestic labour and support greater participation in the workforce. Urbanisation, packaging innovation and delivery services redefined what shopping and eating looked like.

Marketing, branding and fast food also became powerful cultural forces, shaping taste and aspiration across borders. American food companies, restaurant chains and marketing campaigns played a huge role, exporting not only products but a whole approach to eating that blended convenience and consistency with cultural aspiration. As incomes rose in many parts of the world, diets changed too, with a shift towards more processed foods, meat and packaged goods.

In recent decades, digital technology has added another layer of transformation. Online grocery shopping, app-based delivery services and social media trends have accelerated the speed at which new products, cuisines and food ideas spread around the world.

These changes have shaped who we are as eaters with three key patterns emerging, as analysis by Nesta shows. Businesses have found a way to sell us more food by adding calories from salt, sugar and fat. We have been moulded to be 'enthusiastic but passive consumers', less engaged with food itself. Finally, the way we shop has limited our interaction with people, which increases our likelihood of being unhealthy.[10]

What next?

The food system has evolved to feed more people, more efficiently, than at any point in human history and it's made our plates more joyous than ever. We can enjoy familiar tastes almost anywhere in the world, discover international flavours and experiment with creative cooking. Shops and restaurants offer something to suit almost every pocket, from budget basics to gourmet treats.

But this progress has come with a hefty price tag. Agriculture has become heavily dependent on synthetic fertilizers, pesticides and herbicides used to boost crop yields and control pests. These boost yields but affect biodiversity – the wide variety of living organisms around us – and disrupt ecosystems – the communities of plants, animals and microorganisms that interact with each other and their environment. Fewer wild pollinators like bees, birds and insects means fewer fruits and vegetables,[11] and worn-out soil can't grow nutritious crops.

The shift to industrial agriculture has also left many smallholder farmers behind. These family-run, community-based producers often lack the resources to compete with large-scale operations, even though they play a vital role in feeding local populations. At the same time, food corporations now shape much of what we eat, from seeds and fertilizers to the many jars, bottles and cartons we reach for on supermarket shelves.

These changes have deepened inequalities in how food is produced, who profits from it and who can access it easily, affordably and sustainably. We'll explore how things came to be this way and the continuing impact in more detail in the following chapters.

Getting the food system right is central to the kind of world we want to live in – and pass on. In 2015, the United Nations introduced 17 Sustainable Development Goals (SDGs) as a blueprint for a better, fairer future. Two focus directly on food – SDG 2: Zero Hunger and SDG 3: Good Health and Well-being – but at least 13 others are closely linked to what and how we eat, including climate action, clean water, life below water and life on land.

What we need now is a set-up that can nourish both people and the planet – today, and in the long term. Yet right now, our food system is more likely to be described as broken than achieving that goal.

CELEBRATING THE PROGRESS MADE BY THE FOOD SYSTEM

by Anthony Warner

It is a slightly uncomfortable truth for those of us who consider ourselves food obsessives, but perhaps the greatest miracle of modern life is that most of the time, we don't have to think about where our next meal is coming from. This freedom barely registers yet has changed everything.

For most of the history of humanity, hunger has been the most significant force holding back progress. Hungry populations do not develop vaccines, create new technologies or enhance our understanding of the world. When your children are crying out for food, you do not have the time or energy to produce great art, music or literature. When markets are empty and fields are barren, poisonous ideologies find places to thrive.

Yet when people are fed, democracy, fairness and innovation flourish. The freedom not to have to think about our next meal, once the preserve of a tiny elite, has allowed humanity to progress as never before.

This progress has mostly occurred over the past hundred years, largely because of our ability to develop a rational understanding of the world. Crop science has meant that we can now produce three times more food per unit of land than 50 years ago. Chilled supply chains have transformed the availability of fresh produce. Understanding of nutrition and food safety has saved millions of lives and alleviated untold suffering. During the 1960s, 50 per 100,000 of the global population died from severe famine each year. By the 2010s, due to advances in agriculture, transport, communication and trade, that number had fallen below 0.5 per 100,000, with large-scale famine events virtually eradicated. And over the past 25 years, the percentage of people suffering from chronic hunger has more than halved, despite the global population rising by over 2 billion.

We can certainly complain about aspects of our modern food system, and there is no doubt that we should act to improve it, but we must also appreciate that without it, we would live in a far harder, crueller and more difficult world.

Anthony Warner is a chef and author, often writing under the moniker of the Angry Chef. His latest book, Ending Hunger: The Quest to Feed the World without Destroying It, covers humanity's battle against hunger and how that fits within the need to eat sustainably.

Why is the food system described as broken?

For a food system to be considered sustainable, it must be profitable, it must support human well-being and it must have a neutral or positive impact on the natural environment, according to the United Nations. But today, the food system is under pressure from all sides. Growing populations, urbanisation, climate change and changing diets are all piling on. We need a complete overhaul of how we produce, sell and consume food.[12]

The signs that something is wrong are already in our bowls and on our plates:

* How did an unripe avocado reach our local supermarket all the way from Mexico?
* If there are more than 1,000 types of bananas, why do we find only one variety in most shops?
* If a jar of turmeric costs £1, what did the farmer who grew the plant earn?
* Why are products that are better for us more expensive than products that are likely to make us sick?
* What are ingredients like maltodextrin and calcium propionate, which we don't use at home, doing in our shopping basket staples like mayonnaise and bread?

To understand why the food system is described as broken, we need to take a closer look at four key, interconnected areas: environment and climate change; animal life; our health and nutrition; and inequity and inequality.

Environment and climate change

We rely on finite natural resources – water, land and fossil fuels – to feed people and livestock. We depend on and deplete these. The way we farm, fish and feed ourselves also impacts nature and, by extension, the quality of our own lives.

For millennia, these natural systems were able to manage themselves. Forests absorbed carbon, wetlands filtered water and soils replenished nutrients over time. In trying to produce more food more cheaply, we've altered the very landscapes that keep our climate in balance.

The atmosphere traps heat and filters harmful UV rays, but it's now overloaded with greenhouse gases (GHGs) such as carbon dioxide (CO_2), nitrous oxide (N_2O) and methane (CH_4). In 2024, global temperatures reached their highest levels since records began.[13] Food production is a major contributor, responsible for 25–30% of global GHG emissions.

One of the biggest drivers is land conversion, i.e. clearing forests, wetlands and grasslands to make way for farming. These areas are rich in life and act as carbon sinks – landscapes that absorb more CO_2 than they release. When they're cleared, stored carbon is released, habitats vanish, ecosystems are lost and the balance tips further out of sync. Between 2000 and 2018, agriculture drove almost 90% of global deforestation, especially in tropical regions like the Amazon and Southeast Asia.[14]

While much of this damage happens far from us, our eating habits are still connected. One of the drivers is meat, particularly the global demand for cheap chicken and pork. These animals are often fed on soya grown in Brazil and Argentina, where vast areas of tropical rainforest are cleared to plant crops to feed them.[15]

Ruminant animals such as cows, sheep and buffalo produce methane through their digestion and manure. Livestock are responsible for about 32% of human-caused methane emissions. Methane only stays in the atmosphere for about 12 years, but it's 84 times more potent than carbon dioxide over a 20-year period. Much of the heat it traps is absorbed by the deep ocean, where it continues to drive climate change long after the methane itself breaks down.[16]

On top of that, agriculture uses 72% of the global fresh water[17] and covers 44% of all habitable land.[18] A large amount of that water goes into food production. Most of it comes from groundwater, i.e. underground reserves that feed lakes, rivers and wells. These reserves are being drained faster than they can naturally replenish.

Data points to two major culprits: lower-than-average rainfall and intensive farming.[19] The Colorado River is shrinking, India's groundwater is being rapidly depleted and climate change is making droughts and wildfires more frequent. Yet water-intensive crops like cocoa and almonds are still grown in water-scarce regions.

The soil these crops are grown in is also deteriorating due to over-farming, monocultures and synthetic fertilizers. Up to 40% of the world's agricultural land is degraded, which reduces yields and accelerates desertification, where once-fertile areas turn barren. This affects the lives and livelihoods of 3 billion people.[20]

Meanwhile, manmade agrochemicals are used to help maximise the yield or output from a patch of land and to make monocultures more productive. While they help ensure that plants grow and pests are controlled, they also run off into streams, waterways and sources, polluting them and affecting aquatic life.

The prolonged use of chemicals has disrupted the foundation of what healthy farming relies on: the soil. Good soil isn't just dirt; it's alive with microorganisms that communicate, cycle nutrients and help retain moisture. Without this living network, growing productive crops becomes much harder, requiring more inputs and delivering poorer results over time.

It puts pressure on nature too. Chirping birds, fluttering butterflies and buzzing insects are all part of a delicate ecological balance that we often take for granted. In the US, butterfly populations have declined by 22%, in part due to changing insecticide use.[21] Bee numbers are also falling, which is a serious concern, as these and other pollinators are vital for around 75% of the world's food crops.[22]

The pressure on ecosystems doesn't stop on land. Marine degradation refers to the damage being done to oceans and coastal waters. Industrial fishing is weakening the ocean's ability to absorb carbon and support biodiversity. Since 1970, migratory freshwater fish populations have declined by 81%, driven by overfishing, habitat destruction and pollution.[23] Coastal ecosystems, like coral reefs and seagrass beds, are also being affected by agricultural run-off and rising ocean temperatures.

Fossil fuels are another natural resource that the food system depends on – and depletes – with devastating consequences for the climate and environment. Fossil fuels are compounds formed over millions of years from the fossilised remains of dead animals and plants buried deep under the ground and the seabed. They are used to produce chemical fertilizers for industrial agriculture. They also power the tractors in fields, the lorries that move produce and the manufacture of packaging that keeps food safe in transit and fresh at home. In fact, food production consumes around 15% of global fossil fuels, and that share is growing.[24]

Much of this packaging is plastic. Plastic helps protect food as it travels across the world and prevents it from spoiling early. It also pollutes rivers and oceans, entangles wildlife and breaks down into microplastics – tiny fragments that end up in the food we eat. According to the Break Free from Plastic campaign, the top five plastic polluters globally are food companies.[25]

The way food is produced, processed and delivered today is locked into a system that is deeply at odds with the health of our environment. Across soil, sea and sky, our methods of feeding ourselves are increasingly in conflict with the very environment we depend on.

Animal life

Most of the world's agricultural land is used to raise livestock for meat and dairy. By all accounts, we love consuming both. Global meat consumption per capita will continue to rise, albeit slower than it has in the past, reaching 35.4 kilograms per person annually by 2030. Chicken is expected to be a top choice due to its perceived health benefits and lower production costs.[26]

The animals we eat also need to be fed, watered and cared for, not least because they're sentient beings that can feel pain and emotion. Yet many of us live with what's known as cognitive dissonance: the discomfort of loving animals while eating them. We do this by detaching ourselves from how meat is produced or by imagining that the animals lived contented lives and somehow consented to their fate.[27]

That vision is far from the reality. While many meat lovers might prefer to picture animals roaming freely until the end, there simply isn't enough land to make that possible, especially as demand grows. Even so-called 'free-range' animals often spend much of their time indoors during bad weather, and climate change is making grazing land more arid.[28] From a business perspective, free-range farming is also less efficient – it requires more space, more time and produces less meat per animal.

That's why globally, most of the meat we eat today comes from intensive or factory farms.[29] Around 73% of land-based livestock are raised this way globally, rising to nearly 99% in the US. In intensive systems, particularly in the US, cattle are kept in feedlots, which are confined pens where they are fattened quickly on high-calorie feed before slaughter. In the UK, the picture is more mixed. Beef cattle usually graze outdoors for most of their lives, though some are finished indoors on grain. For pigs and chickens, intensive housing is more common, with animals kept in large sheds to maximise efficiency.

These operations allow producers to grow animals faster, with fewer resources and at lower cost, which makes meat cheaper for consumers. Price has always been a key factor in how we choose meat, with the most recent research showing that it's the most important factor for 78% of UK consumers.[30]

But cheap prices and productivity gains come at a cost to animal welfare. Animals in factory farms are often confined in conditions that bear little resemblance to how they would live naturally. Chickens, for example, are cramped, overstimulated and selectively bred for skeletal strength, disease resistance and body shape to grow faster than their bodies can handle. They now reach slaughter weight in just 35 days – up to four times faster than they did 50 years ago – earning them the nickname 'frankenchickens' among animal welfare advocates.[31]

Even free-range labels can be misleading. Many so-called free-range chickens are raised in enormous sheds housing up to 20,000 birds. Although they technically have access to the outdoors, many never go outside. Chickens are naturally reluctant to stray far from shelter, so when exits are far away or unfamiliar, they often remain inside. In these systems, free range can exist in name only.[32]

By contrast, slower-reared systems like those at Sutton Hoo Chicken paint a different picture. Their birds live for up to 12 weeks – more than double the lifespan of intensively farmed chickens – and are kept in small flocks with mobile sheds, allowing for outdoor access and natural behaviours like pecking, dust bathing and grazing. The food industry is signing up to a campaign called the Better Chicken Commitment or European Chicken Commitment for better welfare standards by 2026, evidence of which you may see appearing on labels soon.[33]

It delivers strong improvements in animal welfare and cuts antibiotic use by 80–85%, enhancing food safety, as concerns around medicines remain important. Overuse in some countries has raised fears of antibiotic resistance in animals and humans. While the UK, EU and many other regions, including China, have banned growth promoters and tightly restrict antibiotic use, preventative use is still common elsewhere. But slower-growing chickens are less feed-efficient, which raises carbon footprints. Production costs can also rise by up to 27%.[34] Better animal welfare is often linked to better environmental outcomes, but there are trade-offs everywhere.

Our oceans and waterways, meanwhile, are another source of food, including fish, seafood and seaweed. But warming waters, pollution and unpredictable weather are all affecting marine ecosystems and what's known as blue food. Fishing practices also raise serious concerns. Illegal, unreported and unsustainable (IUU) fishing threatens wild stocks and the role that marine life plays in carbon sequestration, i.e. the natural storage of carbon in the sea by marine life.

Fishing gear can be damaging in other ways. Large nets and lines don't just catch the fish they're meant to – they also trap other sea life like turtles, dolphins and seabirds, which are often injured or killed in the process. And when fishing equipment is lost or thrown away, it doesn't disappear. It drifts through the ocean as 'ghost gear', entangling marine animals and wrecking fragile habitats long after it's been abandoned.

We now produce more seafood from fish farms than from wild-caught fisheries, and this shift is only expected to grow. But not all aquaculture is equal. Farming fish, like salmon, trout and seabass (known as finfish), brings its own set of challenges. These species are often bred for fast growth, kept in crowded pens and treated with antibiotics. They can pass parasites like sea lice to wild fish and can contribute to declining stocks by consuming feed made from species that people in local communities also rely on for food. There are also growing questions around fish welfare, with strong evidence that fish, like mammals, can feel pain.[35]

The way we treat and eat animals has a direct impact on what ends up on our plates, what disappears from them and hides its true cost from the price we pay at tills. Whether on land or at sea, the choices we make ripple through the natural world, economies and the lives of other living beings.

CLIMATE AND AGRICULTURE: MENDING AN UNHAPPY MARRIAGE
by Thin Lei Win

One of the first stories I wrote after I started reporting solely on food issues was on the nexus between food and climate change, and a quote from an expert I interviewed became a key way of framing and understanding the crucial linkages between the two.

I already knew that modern-day hunger is a failure of political will, that being able to produce more food does not necessarily alleviate food insecurity if said food is not accessible or affordable, and that we are eating our way to illness, diseases and death. But I was just dipping my toes into the connection between what we're eating, how we're producing them and what's happening to our planet.

Andy Jarvis, who at the time was associate director-general at a major agricultural research institution, called the relationship between climate and agriculture 'an unhappy marriage'. '(They) are absolutely intertwined and completely connected to each other but actually pretty antagonistic (towards each other),' he told me.

You see, agriculture is extremely vulnerable to the vagaries of weather, whether it's a change in precipitation or temperature. Any slight variation in rainfall patterns could slash or boost yields since nearly two-thirds of the world's food production relies on rain-fed agriculture. A shift in seasons, say, summer starting earlier than normal, could also choke plants' growth and productivity.

Meanwhile, the ways we are currently producing food emit greenhouse gases (GHGs) that are heating up the planet. They include methane from ruminants and flooded rice fields, nitrous oxide from nitrogen fertilizer and animal waste, and carbon dioxide from running tractors and other machinery.

Andy's comment made me realise we won't be able to stop catastrophic climate change without looking closely at what's on our plates. It also convinced me that while so much of climate action is focused on energy and transport systems, food is the next frontier. Of course, it became my favourite, go-to analogy to describe what's wrong with our food systems.

Nearly two years ago, the comment got an update after I quoted it during a health and nutrition conference in Malawi. Rachel Bezner Kerr, Professor and Director of Graduate Studies at Cornell University, said the relationship is 'not just an unhappy marriage, but an unhappy marriage with an addiction problem'. She also expanded it beyond agriculture.

'The current food system is highly dependent on fossil fuels, whether it's synthetic fertilizer, the application of that fertilizer, pesticide use, the production of hybrid seeds, the transportation across thousands of kilometres across oceans, or the plastic packaging. The whole system is underpinned by fossil fuels,' she said. 'To get off it is going to require a significant transformation, but it's absolutely necessary. If we're going to survive ... we need to change the way we grow, produce and distribute food.'

Indeed, the world's food systems are responsible for a third of the total manmade GHGs, according to the most up-to-date data, which also showed that food-related emissions continue to grow in absolute terms. A significant amount (40%) of these emissions comes from the production of inputs such as fertilizers. Distribution accounts for 29% but it is growing and expected to continue growing.

Methane accounts for around 35% of food-system emissions in both developed and developing countries, mainly due to livestock production, farming (particularly rice farming) and waste treatment. And while we're at it, can I reiterate that livestock methane comes from the burps and not the farts?

Beyond pure emissions, our food systems are also a key driver of deforestation, biodiversity loss and pollution of our air, water and soil. It is also the largest user of fresh water and thus a major cause of water stress. Not only that, half of the world's habitable land is currently used for agriculture.

All of this perpetuates – and accelerates – the biodiversity crisis we have on our hands, which in turn messes up our ecosystems and climate. But it doesn't have to be this way. By rethinking not just what and how we produce food, but also how we harvest, process, transport, distribute, consume and discard it, we can be on a path where food and climate can end up in a happy marriage.

Thin Lei Win is a journalist and the author of Thin Ink on Substack.

Human health and nutrition

We've covered the health and well-being of animals in our food system, but what about our own? Here lies one of the great paradoxes of modern gastronomic life: despite having access to more food than ever before, many of us aren't healthier for it.

In wealthier parts of the world – and increasingly in lower- and middle-income countries – food abundance and economic prosperity have gone hand in hand with a rise in chronic diet-related illnesses, from obesity and diabetes to heart disease and certain cancers.[36] Our modern diets are often high in saturated fat, added sugar and salt, but low in fibre and whole foods. They're increasingly made up of pre-packaged snacks, sugary drinks, refined grains, processed meat and ready meals.

A lot of these products barely resemble what we might call 'real' food. Food industry research started engineering what we eat to appeal to our senses and override our natural hunger cues. Much of it was pioneered in the United States and adopted, adapted and expanded in other industrialised nations. In the 1970s, American market researcher Howard Moskowitz coined the term 'bliss point' to describe the perfect ratio of sugar, salt and fat that makes processed food more appealing.

Around the same time, a shift took place in how we talked about food itself. Nutritional value began to be broken down into component parts – calories, vitamins, protein – separating food from its cultural, social and natural contexts. Australian sociologist Gyorgy Scrinis later coined the term 'nutritionism' to describe this.

This reductionist way of thinking brought some benefits. It allowed food producers to fortify products with essential nutrients, e.g. iron, vitamin D and folic acid, which helped to tackle nutrient deficiencies in many countries. But over time, it also enabled highly processed foods to be marketed as healthy simply because they contained added vitamins or minerals, even if they were otherwise low in nutritional value.

These trends underpinned the rise of ultra-processed foods (UPFs) – products that are made primarily from industrial ingredients and additives not found in a home kitchen. In the 1990s, American nutritionist Barry Popkin linked this shift to broader economic and lifestyle changes in a concept he called the nutrition transition: the move away from traditional, plant-based diets to a global 'Western diet' that's calorie dense, nutrient poor and increasingly associated with ill health.[37] It was fuelled by industrial innovations in product formulation, packaging and marketing across the Global North alongside the consumer need for convenience, affordability and shelf life.

As multinational food corporations expanded into new markets and urban lifestyles took hold, the Western diet spread rapidly beyond its countries of origin. Local cuisines and cooking habits began to shift, often within a generation. In Brazil, the shift was noticeable. By the early 2000s, obesity rates had doubled while the sales of basic cooking ingredients like oil, salt and sugar were falling. Brazilian academic Carlos Monteiro and his team developed the Nova classification system to group foods by the level of processing, bringing terms like UPFs into global nutrition conversations.

In the UK, food writers like Joanna Blythman and Bee Wilson began shining a light on this world of preservatives, flavourings, stabilisers and thickeners, raising questions about what's really in our everyday food. In his book *Ultra-Processed People*, academic and TV presenter Dr Chris van Tulleken unpacks the science behind these products. He argues that UPFs are engineered to override our natural appetite controls, interfering with the brain signals that tell us we're full and nudging us to eat more than we need. He also challenges the idea that diet and weight are simply a matter of personal choice, pointing instead to the role of structural forces such as poverty, stress, product innovation and relentless marketing.[38]

These concerns have entered the mainstream, not least because of the growing evidence linking UPFs to poor health. A review of over 45 meta-analyses published in *The BMJ* found consistent associations between UPF consumption and higher risks of obesity, type 2 diabetes, cardiovascular disease, depression and early death. It also flagged potential links to cancer, asthma and gut health, though more research is still needed.[39] That said, scientists are careful to point out that correlation doesn't mean causation – in other words, just because two things happen at the same time or seem related doesn't mean that one causes the other. But the pattern is hard to ignore.

What we do know is that many UPFs are also high in added sugar, salt and fat, and low in fibre – a combination known to drive poor health outcomes. In the UK and US, UPFs now make up over 50% of the average diet, with even higher levels among children and people living in poverty.[40] The UK's baby food market, for instance, is awash with low-quality, poor-nutrition products with misleading names and on-pack messaging.[41] The result? In places where food is plentiful, illness and malnutrition are on the rise. Some of the most vulnerable members of society are compromised.

This is the other paradox of today's world of food and drink: you can be overweight and undernourished at the same time. Nutrient deficiencies, once associated with hunger, are now seen in people consuming too many calories, but not enough of the right kind.

Globally, more than one in eight people are clinically obese, a figure that surpassed 1 billion for the first time in 2022.[42] In the UK, over 63% of adults are overweight or obese.[43] In the US, at least one in five adults is living with obesity.[44]

While hunger is declining globally, it persists and continues to rise in much of Africa and western Asia. Around 673 million people worldwide go hungry, even though we already produce enough food to feed everyone on the planet.[45] Worse still, households globally throw away over 1 billion meals a day – the equivalent of 1.3 meals every single day for every person living with hunger.[46]

This inequality doesn't just reflect distribution; it's baked into the way the food system is set up. The industrialised food system has tended to prioritise crops for mass production and export, not necessarily nutrition. Nutrient-dense staples suited to local climes, like millets, legumes and leafy vegetables, were sidelined in favour of high-yield commodities with global appeal, like wheat, rice, maize and potatoes. Many of these are the raw ingredients that power UPFs, along with sugar, soy and palm oil. Even animal-based ingredients in UPFs often come from confined livestock raised on energy-intensive systems that rely on fossil fuels and chemicals like hexane, which is used to extract oils from crops.

Meanwhile, food that *should* nourish us is losing its quality. One major study found that rising levels of atmospheric carbon dioxide, combined with industrial farming and high-yield breeding, have led to an alarming decline in nutrients in common crops. Apples, oranges, mangoes, guava, bananas and vegetables such as tomatoes and potatoes have lost up to 25–50% of their nutritional density during the last 50 to 70 years. The effects of this include lower immunity, hidden hunger and widespread undernutrition, especially in developing and under-resourced parts of the world.[47]

So while some face an overabundance of unhealthy food, others go hungry or lack access to nutritious options altogether. These patterns aren't random – they follow deep-rooted lines of race, class, gender and geography. Health outcomes are shaped not just by what we eat, but by who we are, where we live and what we can access.

Inequity and inequality

Intensively farmed animals and land as well as highly processed foods were all developed to make food cheaper, but the trade-off has been high. But while cheap food comes at a cost, the need for cheap (even free) food hasn't gone away. We've been producing enough calories to feed the world since 1981,[48] yet millions go hungry. Meanwhile, one-fifth of all food produced – around 1.05 billion tons annually – is lost or wasted. Most of this comes from our homes, but restaurants and retailers also play a significant part.[49] It's hardly fair that so much food is wasted while so many go without.

This imbalance in the availability of food is unfolding against a backdrop of deepening global inequality. Since the start of the Covid-19 pandemic in 2020, the gap between rich and poor has only widened. We're heading for a world where the first trillionaire may appear within a decade,[50] while extreme poverty is rising again after decades of decline. Those who feed us are often the ones struggling the most: small farmers and agricultural workers, particularly in rural areas and among women.[51] Even though women make up 60–80% of the world's agricultural labour force, they still face limited access to land, finance, markets and decision-making.

Agriculture has one of the highest rates of poverty of any part of the food system. Smallholders – who produce much of the developing world's food – are often poorer and less food secure than even the urban poor.[52] Many of these communities depend on the global food trade for income, but the power imbalance between producers in the Global South and buyers in the Global North is stark.

This imbalance is rooted in centuries of globalisation, colonisation and capitalism. The Global South continues to grow much of the food consumed in the Global North, from coffee and cocoa to spices, grains and fruit, shaped by the demands of wealthier markets. Cash crops grown for export, such as soya, palm oil, sugarcane and maize, attract foreign investment but often come at a cost to local people and the planet. Expanding monocultures to meet global demand can reduce biodiversity, undermine food sovereignty (the right of people to control how their food is produced and consumed) and force communities to treat land and water as resources to be extracted, not protected.

Our foodie favourites have their own implications. In Mexico, illegal deforestation to grow avocados – a water-intensive crop – has depleted groundwater and left nearby communities short. As Daniel Wilkinson from Climate Rights International notes, 'You cut down the trees, and you deplete the water that's there underground, and then you install avocados, which is a plant that consumes as much as four or five times as much water as the natural vegetation.'[53]

Meanwhile, profits often flow elsewhere. The global coffee market is worth over $100 billion, yet smallholders – who grow 75% of the world's coffee – earn just 3% of the cost of a cup, according to the Fairtrade Foundation.[54] Cocoa farmers earn only 6% of the final value of a chocolate bar, often not enough to live on.[55] In some cases, child labour is used to make ends meet. Meanwhile, the global chocolate industry is valued at $130 billion by the World Economic Forum.[56]

The effects of climate change fall unevenly too. Rising temperatures, floods and droughts disproportionately affect the world's poorest farmers and fishermen and women, who have fewer safety nets and less adaptability.

Inequality doesn't stop at national borders. For centuries, people have migrated in search of opportunity, often as a direct result of systems that extracted land, labour and wealth from their homelands. Yet when they arrived in wealthier countries, they faced racism, marginalisation and systemic barriers to land, power and opportunity.

Today, wealthier countries' food systems depend on migrant labour, often from less wealthy regions. In the US, over 70% of farmworkers are migrants, many working in conditions that amount to exploitation or forced labour. In the UK, fruit and vegetable production relied heavily on EU workers; post-Brexit, the Seasonal Worker Visa Programme has expanded to other countries, but with increased risks of abuse.[57]

A system built on marginalised people, undervalued labour and struggling communities isn't just unfair, it's also unstable. It tips the balance in favour of big corporations, historical power brokers and the wealthy in a system that should work for all.

Prologue

Should we worry about food disappearing off our plates?

After everything we've covered so far, it wouldn't be surprising to answer the question 'should we worry about food disappearing off our plates?' with a resounding yes. A system this strained can only take so much pressure before it starts to buckle. But it's not just about whether there's enough to go around – it's also about whether it's nutritious, sustainable and fairly produced.

That's where the concepts of food security and self-sufficiency come in. Food security means having regular access to safe, nutritious food that supports our health, preferences and dietary needs. In recent years, the definition has broadened to include sustainability, how much is wasted and how much control or agency we have over what we eat. Self-sufficiency, on the other hand, is about whether a country can feed itself without relying on imports.

By these measures, the UK is not food self-sufficient. We currently produce around 60% of the food we consume, but this is under pressure from a long-term deterioration in natural resources like biodiversity, soil quality and clean water.[58] We import the rest, relying on global supply chains for everything from fresh fruit to fertilizer. This helps spread the risk, but it also makes us vulnerable to shocks and pressures further away.

The UK still ranks high on the Global Food Security Index – ninth out of 113 countries. However, that same analysis has warned that the global food environment has deteriorated for three years in a row, driven by conflict, climate extremes and economic uncertainty. The gap between the most and least secure nations has also widened, 'reflecting the inequity in the global food system'.[59]

We can rest easy that food isn't disappearing off grocery shelves en masse any time soon. However, there are some areas of concern, not just about what we eat, but also about how resilient, balanced and futureproof the systems that feed us really are. To understand where the risks lie, let's take a closer look at five interconnected factors that threaten our food security: market concentration, conflict, climate events, food retail, and household accessibility and affordability.

Market concentration

The food system thrives on efficiency, and that's a good thing. Bigger farms, larger processing plants and vast distribution networks can produce more for less, keeping prices low and shelves stocked. But efficiency often leads to market concentration, i.e. when a small number of companies, crops or transport routes dominate. This set-up works well until something goes wrong. You can see this concentration everywhere, from the seeds we grow to the supermarkets we shop in.

Since the early 1900s, we've been losing agrobiodiversity – the range of edible species, varieties and breeds we grow and consume. As farmers moved from local crops to high-yield, genetically uniform varieties more suited to large-scale production, 75% of plant diversity has been lost. Today, three-quarters of the world's food comes from only 12 plants and five animal species.[60] This makes our food supply more consistent, but it greatly reduces the variety we enjoy as part of our epicurean lives. It also makes our food more exposed to pests, disease and climate change.

Take apples, for example. While there are over 7,000 varieties worldwide, with approximately 2,500 in the UK alone, this abundance is not reflected in our supermarkets. Consumers typically encounter only six or seven varieties, such as Braeburn, Gala, Golden Delicious, Granny Smith, Jazz and Pink Lady.[61] These varieties are favoured for their high yields and uniform appearance, aligning with the demands of large-scale retail, not necessarily for their taste.

The same pattern is evident with avocados. While there are over 500 varieties globally, more than 80% of the avocados we eat are Hass, a variety favoured for its thick skin and long shelf life, not necessarily for its flavour or sustainability.[62] The same is true of bananas. The Cavendish variety now makes up 99% of global banana exports. It was chosen to replace the Gros Michel – a sweeter, larger banana wiped out by disease in the 1950s – because it travels well and stays green after harvest. But new strains of that same disease now threaten Cavendish bananas too, showing how genetic uniformity can become a liability.

Zooming out, the industrial food system relies heavily on just three staple grains – rice, maize and wheat – which provide nearly 60% of the world's plant-based calories and protein. Only a few countries specialise in growing these crops, and many other nations, especially lower-income ones, rely on them. Additionally, a handful of firms dominate trading in these commodities, buying and selling food like financial assets on volatile global markets.[63]

This kind of supply chain concentration – where food depends on a small number of firms, routes and varieties – creates pressure points. If one link in the chain breaks, entire supply networks can be disrupted. We'll look more closely at market concentration in agrifood corporations in the next chapter, but efficiency has come at the cost of resilience.

Conflict

Global food supply chains rely on stability. When tensions flare within or between nations, it's people who feel the strain first. Conflict disrupts lives, livelihoods, land and access to food, driving up prices and making it harder for communities to feed themselves. Alongside climate change, conflict is now one of the leading drivers of food insecurity, affecting both what food is available and who can afford it.[64]

In places directly affected by violence, food production itself is often devastated. In Sudan, conflict between rival military factions has crippled one of Africa's most agriculturally productive nations. In the Democratic Republic of Congo, meanwhile, a long-running humanitarian crisis has deepened: by March 2025, a record 28 million people were facing acute hunger as fighting displaced farmers, disrupted harvests and strained aid systems.[65]

The war in Ukraine brought these risks closer to home. When Russia invaded Ukraine in 2022, both agricultural giants, it sent shockwaves through global supply chains. Ukraine alone is among the top three wheat exporters in the world, and together they account for 60% of the global sunflower oil supply.[66] Known as 'the breadbasket of Europe', Ukraine's blocked ports and disrupted harvests caused international grain and cooking oil prices to spike.

As food security expert Jennifer Clapp notes, speculation on global commodity markets made this even worse.[67] Prices surged beyond already record highs, restricting food access for hundreds of millions of people, especially in countries reliant on Black Sea exports. In Ethiopia, over 80% of wheat imports came from Russia and Ukraine before the war. When supply chains collapsed, food insecurity worsened, compounding existing challenges like drought and internal conflict. Fertilizer shortages also disrupted planting and harvests across the region, making it harder for farmers to grow enough food.

The crisis wasn't limited to food. Russia's role as a major exporter of oil and gas meant energy prices also skyrocketed, raising the cost of everything from fertilizer to transport. These costs filtered down to our homes and kitchens. In the UK, sanctions on Russian fish imports even impacted the national favourite, fish and chips. Around 30–40% of white fish fillets used in UK chip shops came from Russia, and prices rose sharply when supplies were cut.[68]

Food isn't just a casualty of conflict. It is often deliberately weaponised. Recently, this is apparent in Gaza, where restrictions on humanitarian aid have created a hunger emergency. Under the blockade imposed by Israel, essential supplies like food, water and fuel have been prevented from reaching civilians. One in five people in Gaza – some 500,000 people – face starvation.[69]

The aftermath of conflict on people and their surroundings affects food at every stage and can last for years, long after the guns fall silent. Pollution from attacks on industrial facilities and scorched-earth techniques, including the destruction of agricultural infrastructure like canals, wells and pumps and the burning of crops, affect the livelihoods of communities and make them more vulnerable to food insecurity.[70]

Climate events

Climate change isn't just an environmental issue; it's also a food production and supply issue. Around the world, extreme and unpredictable weather is damaging harvests, pushing up prices and turning seasonal risks into structural ones. Droughts, heatwaves, floods, storms and frosts are now more frequent and intense, making food systems more fragile and volatile.

Wheat production in Argentina was already under pressure from prolonged drought when the war in Ukraine began. In Brazil, a freak frost wiped out coffee crops in 2021, triggering price spikes and panic buying. Buyers turned to Vietnam, only to find farmers there battling the worst drought in a decade. In response, researchers at London's Kew Gardens are working to futureproof coffee cultivation by exploring alternatives to the most grown species.

At the same time, climate disasters are pushing already vulnerable regions into deeper crisis. In war-torn Somalia, after years of erratic rainfall and one of the longest droughts on record, flash floods in early 2025 destroyed crops, killed livestock and displaced entire communities. The World Food Programme warns that over 1 million more people could face crisis-level hunger this year alone in a country already on the brink.[71]

When harvests are hit by weather extremes, governments often restrict exports to protect domestic supply, which has a knock-on effect on global markets. In 2023, Morocco temporarily banned tomato exports to stabilise prices at home, leading to shortages across Europe and contributing to a spike in UK food inflation.[72] That same year, India's tomato prices rose by 400% after unseasonal downpours wiped out crops. In 2024, India extended its ban on sugar exports following another erratic growing season. Together with drought-hit Brazil, this contributed to a 10.4% surge in global sugar prices.[73]

Climate change is hitting culturally significant foods too. Rice, which is central to diets and traditions across Asia, Africa and Latin America, is under pressure from declining yields, new diseases and rising temperatures. As chef JJ Johnson put it in *Time*, 'Rice is not just a food – it's the heartbeat of cultures ... a symbol of identity, heritage and survival.'[74] It contributes 12% of the world's methane emissions, making it both a victim and a driver of climate change.[75]

Olive oil – the 'liquid gold' of the Mediterranean – has also seen prices soar due to back-to-back droughts in Spain and Italy compounded by a tree disease thriving in warmer temperatures. It now joins cocoa, rice, soybeans and potatoes on the World Economic Forum's list of the most climate-vulnerable foods.[76] Brazil's orange harvest has been hit hard. Cocoa production in West Africa is under strain from shifting rainfall and temperature patterns.[77] Together, these changes are squeezing supply and pushing up the prices of everyday items.

Even well-resourced nations aren't insulated. The UK has faced unprecedented challenges. Record-breaking rainfall over an 18-month period led to England experiencing its second-worst harvest on record in 2024. In the US, many small fruit and vegetable farmers are struggling to find affordable insurance owing to escalating weather pattern risks from climate change.[78]

These weather shocks, driven by climate change, are making global food markets increasingly volatile, fragile and unpredictable, creating an environment of ongoing or 'perma' crisis that the food industry must navigate to keep our shopping baskets full.

Food retail

A full shopping basket at a local supermarket is a familiar scenario for many of us because these retailers dominate how we buy food and drink. They offer convenience, variety and year-round availability of almost anything we want, and most of us do the bulk of our grocery shopping there. In the UK, around 95% of food is sold through just 10 retailers, with the top four supermarkets controlling over 65% of grocery sales.[79] This kind of concentration fuels fierce competition, especially on price.

As the cost-of-living crisis bites, many shoppers have traded down from premium or branded products to own-label and budget options, intensifying the price war across grocery chains. While this can mean lower prices for shoppers in the short term, it can come at a cost elsewhere, which is often felt by suppliers, animals or nature.

The drive to keep costs down is baked into supermarket supply chains, which are built for scale and speed. They rely on a global food trade and what's known as just-in-time systems – models that ramp up or reduce stock based on consumer demand. That makes them efficient, but it also makes them vulnerable. Climate shocks, pandemics and geopolitical tensions can all cause delays or shortages. We've seen it firsthand – supermarket shelves stripped of tomatoes and lettuce during bad weather abroad, while local grocers still have stock.

These global supply chains don't just buckle under pressure; they also place it elsewhere. For smaller producers, meeting supermarket requirements around pricing, auditing and delivery schedules can be particularly tough. For supermarkets, the ability to trace, source and move vast quantities quickly often trumps seasonality or local availability. As Abby Allen, Farms Director at Pipers Farm, noted in an Instagram post during a bumper British apple season, supermarkets still continued to import apples from halfway around the world.

Of course, there are plenty of ingredients we can't grow in the UK, no matter how much we might want to. But even when we *can*, we often don't. The UK imports over 80% of our fruit and nearly half of our vegetables.[80] Our own growers are under increasing pressure. In a survey conducted in 2023, nearly half of farmers feared for the survival of their farms, and three out of four of them cited the way they are treated by supermarkets as a concern.[81]

Rising costs of energy, production and transportation have driven up prices across the board, contributing to a rise in food price inflation or the rate at which food prices go up in a given time. Even when prices don't rise, product sizes shrink. You might have noticed your favourite snacks or cupboard staples getting smaller. This is called shrinkflation, where prices stay the same but quantities quietly decrease. It's one tactic retailers and brands use to protect margins while trying to appear affordable, but the result is the same: shoppers get less for their money.

Then there's the bigger picture. Buying food in pristine packaging, uniform sizes and spotless displays reflects both supermarket systems and consumer expectations, but it distances us from how food is actually grown and harvested. It can make waste feel inconsequential and prioritise convenience over nutrition. It also limits our choices to what the supermarket decides to stock – and what it decides is worth paying for.

Accessibility and affordability

Everyone should be able to fill their shopping baskets with nutritious, satisfying food, but for millions that's out of reach. Food access isn't just about what's on the shelf; it's about whether people can afford to be in the shop at all. Income, geography and time shape what we eat, where we shop and how we nourish ourselves. In wealthy countries, nutritious food often comes at a premium, while cheap, ultra-processed options remain widely available. In poorer parts of the world, even the most basic foods can be scarce, with the current state of play driving up prices and pushing essentials out of reach.

In the UK, the cost-of-living crisis has put huge strain on household budgets. According to the Food Foundation's Food Insecurity Tracker, as of January 2025, around 7.3 million adults in the UK – equivalent to 14% of households – were experiencing food insecurity. Households with children, single parents, people on Universal Credit and those with disabilities were particularly affected. Alarmingly, 5% of households reported someone not eating for an entire day because they couldn't afford or access food.[82]

The Trussell Trust reports that one in seven people in the UK face hunger and hardship and have to turn to food banks.[83] As Cambridge neuroscientist Dr Giles Yeo puts it, 'Deprivation leads to poor choices or, more often than not, no choices.'[84]

In reality, healthy eating costs more. The poorest fifth of the UK would need to spend almost half of their disposable income on food to achieve the government's recommended healthy diet, according to the Food Foundation's 2025 *Broken Plate* report. For households with children, this rises to 70%. Healthier food is also twice as expensive per calorie as less nutritious alternatives.[85]

This hardship is not distributed evenly among communities. Black and minority ethnic households in the UK are 2.5 times more likely to live in relative poverty compared to white households.[86] Obesity rates are also higher among these communities, driven in part by poor access to affordable, nutritious food. A similar pattern is seen in the US, where the poverty rate for Black Americans, though at a historic low of 17.1%, is still more than double that of white Americans at 7.7%.[87] Factors such as structural racism and social exclusion continue to contribute to these gaps.

Assumptions about what people from lower incomes want to eat don't always match reality. The Food, Farming and Countryside Commission's National Conversation project showed that people from all walks of life want a healthier food environment with practical help.[88] And contrary to what people think, it is lower- and middle-income shoppers who are now the most frequent buyers of organic food and drink.[89]

Access is shaped by location as well as earning power. In low-income UK neighbourhoods, fast-food outlets far outnumber greengrocers and supermarkets. In the US, 76 counties have no grocery store at all, creating 'food deserts' that disproportionately affect rural and low-income communities.[90] Across the world, hunger remains a pressing challenge, with over 80% of the world's extreme poor living in rural areas,[91] with agricultural workers and their families among the hardest hit.

Globally, food isn't evenly distributed. Wealthy nations tend to have surplus, while many poorer countries face shortages. Infrastructure gaps, high transport costs and regional instability all play a role. The Food and Agriculture Organization (FAO) estimates that by 2030, nearly 600 million people will be chronically undernourished – 23 million more than if the Russia–Ukraine war had never happened. Africa is expected to bear the brunt.[92]

Children are especially vulnerable. Stunting from chronic undernutrition not only limits growth but can affect cognitive development and future earning potential[93] – a warning sign for the prosperity of the nation. Older people, too, are at risk when nutritious food is out of reach, with food insecurity linked to higher rates of illness and reduced independence.[94]

The consequences of food insecurity extend beyond nutrition. The Economics Observatory warns that hunger can drive everything from poor health outcomes to civil unrest and crime.[95] More and more, governments and researchers are recognising that food insecurity is a national security issue, not just a social one. As farming and food writer Jenny Jefferies puts it, 'The world thrives on charity because our political leaders have failed. Food lies at the heart of the struggle to break the cycle of hunger and poverty.'[96]

That old parental refrain – 'think of all the hungry children' – still rings true. But today, the solution isn't cleaning our plates. It's thinking about a system that determines who gets to fill and clear them.

Why we need to care

Justice and fairness should be at the heart of the food system, but the reality is far from it. Social and racial injustice, climate breakdown and animal exploitation are still baked in, shaping how food is produced, distributed and consumed around the world. The premise of the movie *Wall-E* – a sedentary, screen-obsessed society guzzling junk food on loungers while a single plant survives on a devastated Earth – no longer feels far-fetched. Many food system insiders admit that it's not transforming fast enough, and that the consequences are accelerating.

If this all sounds a bit heavy, it's because no amount of sugar syrup can make this an easier pill to swallow. Caring about each other, the planet and the set-ups we rely on isn't an optional extra; it's foundational to our societies and to our future. The EAT-Lancet Planetary Health Diet – a global framework linking what we eat to human and planetary health – reflects this shift. It reaffirms its earlier advice to eat mostly plants, while recognising local and regional realities around the world, and places justice and equity front and centre in the discussion.[97]

In 2015, social neuroscientist Dr Tania Singer proposed the idea of a 'caring economy', where prosperity was measured not just by wealth, but by empathy, relationships and well-being.[98] Since then, movements like #MeToo, Black Lives Matter and Stop Asian Hate have thrust inequality and injustice into the mainstream.

Companies were pushed to confront their own roles. They rushed to talk about equity, sustainability and purpose. But when politics shifted right, social and environmental policies were shelved and such commitments have been dismissed as 'woke' and used to stir division. Political polarisation is accelerating. In much of the Global North, left-leaning movements are increasingly aligned with the rights of minorities and marginalised groups, while the right positions itself as defending ethnically defined national identity. Elsewhere, democratic backsliding and authoritarianism are on the rise.[99]

Against this backdrop, sustainability and social impact budgets and initiatives are being slashed and stalled. Paul Polman, former Unilever CEO and global campaigner on climate and equality, calls this a colossal mistake. 'To say that this is a bad time to slow down is a profound, historic understatement,' he wrote in *Harvard Business Review*. 'The world's biggest challenges – climate change, inequality, biodiversity destruction – are getting worse.'[100]

The commercial case is clear. Diverse, inclusive organisations outperform their peers,[101] and transforming the food system could unlock $10 trillion in benefits annually for a fraction of the cost of doing nothing.[102]

We are more switched on too. Greenwashing and performative virtue signalling are increasingly called out, with new laws in places like the EU forcing greater transparency. Activism moves at the speed of social media. People are watching, and they're voting with their wallets, clicks and contracts. Boycotts, such as those targeting Israeli products, spread fast, and in a digital age, activism plays out in real time. Public figures and brands can find themselves 'cancelled', with real reputational and financial fallout.

This move isn't a flash in the pan – it's generational. As Danielle

Nierenberg, president of Food Tank, says, 'There is a new generation of eaters who wants the story of their food – where it comes from, who grew it, and its impact on the planet. Companies that can't pivot will not be around a decade from now if they don't change.'[103]

And change is coming – whether through pressure, principle or profit. The World Economic Forum has proposed a two-stage model for food system transformation:[104]

* Renovation involves incremental changes to recipes, packaging and supply chains that nudge public health forward.
* But reinvention is what's really needed: deep, systemic shifts in how food is produced, distributed and consumed (the radical overhaul noted by the UN).

It won't be easy, but it's possible. And there are some glimmers of hope. Half of us are reportedly eating healthier and nearly three out of four of us globally trust the food industry to 'do what is right', but this trust relies on transparency and honesty in claims and storytelling.[105]

Some of that change is already underway, from nature-friendly farming to cutting-edge food tech and investments to broaden where we get our protein. But progress won't come from one actor alone. It's going to take shared responsibility and co-ordinated action across the whole system, because the food system is like an onion: layered, interconnected and with the potential to make you weep.

Each layer – from policymakers and corporations to producers and eaters – plays a role. And to understand it, we need to explore how these layers fit together, where the pressure points are and who really influences the food we eat and to whose benefit. That's where we're headed next.

The big takeaways

1. **Food is part of a system:** It helps to look at the way we eat and drink as a system, because our choices aren't entirely in our control or made in isolation. Each element impacts another.
2. **Efficiency, but at a price:** The modern food system is global, complex and efficient, but this comes at the cost of diversity, resilience and fairness. Some 75% of the world's food now comes from just 12 plants and five animal species. For example, only six or seven types of apple are sold in supermarkets out of more than 7,000 varieties.
3. **Centuries in the making but not futureproof:** Our plates are shaped by history, from global trade and industrialisation to our lifestyles and the way we shop, but they need an overhaul to be able to sustain us in the future. While it has achieved much, the food system is often described as broken for its failings.
4. **Choice and convenience are relative:** Year-round strawberries, bananas and avocados are a triumph of logistics, but they detach us from seasonality, how food is produced and its impact.
5. **Pressure points affect our plates:** The system's drive for low prices and high yields puts pressure on nature, farmers, animals and our own health. It's having an impact on bees, birds and insects and the natural habitats that protect them. This means fewer fruits and vegetables and a decline in their nutritiousness.
6. **Global deterioration of our diets:** The rise of the 'Western diet', which is high in ultra-processed foods, refined grains, added sugars and fats, has reshaped food cultures and health outcomes, contributing to obesity, undernutrition and chronic disease.
7. **Food supply is under pressure:** While we don't have to worry about food running out, we can't take fully stocked grocery shelves for granted. Supply is being affected by market concentration, conflict, climate change, affordability and accessibility.

8. **Inequality is baked into the food system:** The food industry holds significant influence over what we eat. It's possible to be both overfed and undernourished, and people go hungry even when enough food is produced. Those who produce our food – particularly small producers and growers – are often the worst off.
9. **Change is possible and profitable:** Transforming the food system could unlock trillions in benefits each year. Diverse, inclusive and sustainable practices don't just build fairness; they also drive creativity, resilience and long-term stability.
10. **It's our future to shape:** Caring about each other, the planet and the set-ups that feed us is essential to building a food system that functions for everyone's benefit. It's a generational shift that is already underway.

PLAYERS

Key actors in the food system

'Nothing can hurt us as long as we're together.'

Mario, *The Super Mario Bros. Movie* (2023)

The food system is the ultimate multiplayer game. To understand why the food system can feel so dysfunctional, we need to examine who the players are, what roles they play and how their decisions shape our everyday lives. We'll look at government and policymakers; scientific and academic communities; big business; producers; manufacturers, processors and distributors; civil society organisations; media; and, of course, us.

Government and policymakers

Governments are responsible for shaping the availability, affordability and sustainability of the food we eat. They make policies that influence how food is grown, traded and consumed, and they have to do this by balancing domestic priorities, global supply chains, economic realities and public health concerns. Their decisions affect everything from our loaves of bread to our access to nutritious food, as food policy commentator Gavin Wren notes in his piece later on.

National governments also participate in political and trading blocs like the EU as well as multilateral organisations such as the World Trade Organization (WTO) and the United Nations (UN) to respond to global food challenges. But despite these collaborations, food policy is often fragmented. The voices of those most affected, from small farmers and fishermen to food workers, are rarely heard in the rooms where decisions are made.

That's why food policy needs to be more inclusive. It needs to be informed by lived experience and grounded in justice. Governments have many levers at their disposal to make this happen, from subsidies and tax incentives to labelling laws, advertising rules, public health campaigns and how they spend public money. In many countries, subsidies favour commodity crops like wheat, corn and soy, which are the building blocks of ultra-processed foods (UPFs), while healthier crops like fruit and vegetables receive far less support.

But some governments are taking action. Around 43 countries and territories have taxed sugary drinks or HFSS (high in fat, sugar, salt) foods. Over 130 countries have introduced front-of-pack nutrition labelling schemes, ranging from voluntary traffic light systems to Chile and Mexico's mandatory warning labels. Mexico leads the way, with one of the most comprehensive national food policies globally.[1]

Local authorities are increasingly stepping in too:

* In Copenhagen, over 90% of the 70,000 meals served daily in public kitchens are organic.[2]
* Amsterdam's food strategy promotes more plant-based eating and healthier food environments.
* The Milan Urban Food Policy Pact brings together over 250 cities worldwide to build more sustainable urban food systems.
* More than 14 global cities, including London and Los Angeles, have committed to aligning their food strategies with the EAT-Lancet Planetary Health Diet, which proposes a way to eat that connects our health with that of the planet.[3]
* In the UK, cities like Bristol and Birmingham have launched local strategies to tackle food inequality, waste and access.

The UK's status quo is mixed. At least 13 different departments and public bodies have a hand in it – and that's not including the Treasury, which funds the National Health Service (NHS). Obesity and excess weight now cost the country an estimated £126 billion a year, including £12.6 billion in NHS treatment and £30.8 billion in lost productivity.[4]

The irony? Hospital vending machines and canteens often sell unhealthy foods, despite the staggering cost of the UK's obesity crisis. Stronger public procurement standards for better school meals, healthier hospital food and sustainable sourcing could help change this.

There has been some progress. The government has introduced mandatory calorie labelling in restaurants and takeaways, and has restricted where HFSS foods can be promoted in supermarkets. A sugar tax on soft drinks introduced in 2018 led to a 46% drop in the average sugar content between 2015 and 2020.[5] Some argue the government should go further and promote healthy food more actively, penalise harmful practices and create a level playing field for businesses. Others cry 'nanny state' at the mere suggestion of more intervention.

Food policy is often shaped less by health and more by political pressure. Governments may hesitate to tax cheap, low-nutrition foods for fear of voter backlash. Public health campaigns rarely match the scale, spending or celebrity star power of commercial food marketing. And behind the scenes, corporate lobbying plays a major role in shaping food governance.[6]

Political cycles disrupt long-term planning. In the UK, Brexit and a change from a Conservative to a Labour government in 2024 exacerbated uncertainties. For example, the UK's National Food Strategy, initially developed by Henry Dimbleby for the Conservative government in 2019, was shelved. The new government has now launched its plans for a 'Good Food Cycle' to improve the nation's relationship to food.[7]

Farming and food production also carry political weight, especially where environmental responsibilities sit uncomfortably with commercial realities. For example, despite the environmental concerns surrounding salmon farming in Scotland, it's called 'pink gold' for its economic value. In the Netherlands, farmer protests against livestock emission rules sparked the rise of a new political party, BoerBurgerBeweging (Farmer–Citizen Movement), which won 15 out of 75 senate seats in 2023.

The EU's Green Deal, introduced in 2019, set out ambitious targets for sustainable agriculture, emissions reduction and biodiversity protection. However, farmer protests in France, Germany and Poland forced a rethink. Many farmers argued that strict environmental regulations, rising costs and cheap imports threatened their livelihoods. In response, the EU scaled back certain Green Deal measures, weakening climate policies to ease tensions with the agricultural sector.

Despite these concessions, the EU has continued discussions on sustainable food systems. It reached a consensus with key stakeholders – including Copa-Cogeca, the influential European farming lobby – on the need to reduce meat consumption to tackle climate change. Meanwhile, the EU Deforestation Regulation

(EUDR), designed to curb imports of products like palm oil and soy (linked to over two-thirds of EU-driven deforestation), has been postponed due to industry unpreparedness.[8]

This delay also highlights the complex dynamics between producer nations and global markets. Asia-Pacific and Latin American countries have pushed back against EUDR, warning it could divert trade to China. US President Donald Trump's proposals for sweeping import tariffs have added to this uncertainty, signalling a shift away from multilateral co-operation towards more protectionist trade policies. This could disrupt supply chains, increase costs of everyday staples and put new pressure on developing nations that rely on exports.

Amid the turmoil, multilateral organisations play a critical role in trying to keep the system stable. The World Trade Organization (WTO) exists to prevent trade wars, mediate disputes and ensure that food trade flows fairly, especially when political tensions are high. Without the WTO, powerful nations could impose their own rules, making global trade even more unpredictable.

The United Nations (UN) also plays a key role. Its agencies – including the World Food Programme (WFP), the Food and Agriculture Organization (FAO) and the World Bank – provide emergency aid, fund agricultural development and support national strategies for food and nutrition. The UN Food Systems Summit, held every two years, brings together countries, producers and civil society to set global goals and track progress.

In summary, governments and policymakers face multifaceted challenges when it comes to making decisions about food. They must balance national interests, economic pressures and global commitments, always with people and planet in mind.

WHAT IS FOOD POLICY AND WHY DOES IT MATTER TO US?

by Gavin Wren

What does food policy mean?

Food policy is simple: it's when people agree to manage food in a given way. Of course, the word 'policy' sounds very officious, like something that governments create. However, any person, group, organisation, charity or business can create a policy, even you and your family at home. Food policy is any agreement regarding the production, organisation, management or use of food, from the individual all the way through to the global scale.

If you decide to begin using a compost bin at home for your food waste, that would be a food policy. At the other end of the scale, if the government provides vouchers for pregnant people and new parents to buy healthy food such as fruit, vegetables and milk, that is also a food policy. If multinational businesses plot how to voluntarily reduce sugar in their food by 10% in the next year, that, too, would be a food policy.

Even though anyone can create a policy, governments are the only entities that have the power to enforce policies using the law by passing a policy into legislation and making it a legal requirement.

To create a policy, all that is required is some form of agreement between a group of people that any subject relating to food will be managed in a particular way in the future. A school could have a food policy; so could an office or an entire town. Once you've made the decision and everyone involved has agreed, then you've created food policy.

How does food policy manifest in our day-to-day life?

A loaf of sliced white bread is one of the most obvious signs of food policy in daily life. On the surface it's simply a loaf of bread with a brand name on the pack and an ingredients list. However, everything from the way the bread is made through to the specific information on the pack is governed by policy.

Packaged foods - especially fresh foods that go off quickly, such as meat, fish and dairy - must conform to a range of policies under the Food Information to Consumers (FIC) Regulation No. 1169/2011. Here are some of the policies that determine how bread is packaged and sold:

* The name of the food must be stated. For example, you can't sell bread and say that it's cake – it needs to be clearly stated that it's bread.
* You must list the quantity of food in the packaging using units such as grams or number of items (e.g. six bread rolls).
* There must be an expiry date, either 'use by' or 'best before'.
* If the product contains more than two ingredients, there must be a list of those ingredients on the pack, listed in order of weight, which means wheat will be listed first on a loaf of bread.
* Any ingredients that are allergens need to be highlighted.
* There must be a list of the nutritional content of the food.

There's still a lot more, but we're getting into the weeds now. Bread is one of the few food products with a food policy that requires vitamins to be added by law to support people's health. These are calcium, iron, vitamin B1 and B3, as set out in the Bread and Flour Regulations 1998, and you'll find these added to every loaf of white bread. Adding these vitamins has proven to be a great success.

There's more. Even the outer packaging, which might be plastic, could fall under the UK Plastics Pact, which is a voluntary policy agreement between some of the biggest businesses in the world to reduce unnecessary plastics. If you dig around, you'll find that everything we eat is subject to many different policies all the way from the farm through to waste.

In an ideal world, what would a great food policy look like?

The aim of food policy is to ensure everyone has access to the food they need for a healthy and active life, befitting their culture and circumstances. That means all our food should be safe, healthy and readily available. Food policy also needs to support everyone, including people on low incomes, in affording to buy healthy food and not having to rely on unhealthy, high-fat, high-salt or high-sugar foods.

Policy also needs to be equitable, meaning it should benefit as many people as fairly as possible, with as few trade-offs as possible and with as little negative impact as possible. Sometimes, this is hard to achieve. For example, for the government to invest in food production, it often needs to raise funds elsewhere, e.g. through taxes.

Because policy can cover anything from social media advertising to the wildlife on farms, it's a broad area of study. Good policy should always aim to support healthy people and planet.

Gavin Wren is a food policy commentator, content creator and coach.

Scientific and academic communities

The scientific and nutrition communities have played a defining role in shaping what we eat and how we understand food for centuries. From early ideas of food as medicine to advances in food safety, industrial agriculture and public health, their work has transformed diets, farming and policymaking around the world.

In early industrial societies, scientists and medical professionals became more involved in food systems, responding to concerns around hunger, malnutrition and sanitation. The isolation of vitamins and nutrients in the late 19th and early 20th centuries gave rise to the idea of nutritionism, which we covered in the previous chapter. While this unlocked progress in tackling deficiency diseases, it also helped lay the foundation for today's highly processed and industrialised foods, which were often marketed as healthy because they were fortified.

Scientific breakthroughs also powered agricultural productivity, from chemical fertilizers to synthetic pesticides like DDT. Once celebrated for its ability to control insects and boost crop yields, the optimism soon faded. By the 1960s, concerns began mounting over the environmental and health impacts of DDT, most famously documented in Rachel Carson's book *Silent Spring*. DDT was eventually banned in many countries and became a turning point in public awareness of the darker side of industrial agriculture.

In its wake, a wave of scientists, writers and campaigners began to expose the social, environmental and health costs of industrial food, pushing for new ways of thinking about sustainability, justice and human well-being.

Today, science remains central to the food system, but it's not without controversy. Debates continue over corporate influence, transparency and how science is used to justify or challenge dominant food narratives. Whether in climate research, nutritional science or the development of alternatives to meat, the role of science is evolving. The question is: who does it serve – and who gets left out?

The politics of nutrition science

Nutrition science is moving fast, but it's not without complexity. Professor Susanne Gjedsted Bügel at the University of Copenhagen is leading an international effort to refine the Nova system. Recognising its limitations, like lumping nutritious breads or rye loaves with junk food, her group is working on a 'next-generation' classification. They aim to incorporate factors like nutrient content and the food matrix rather than just processing level and have brought together experts from around the world to reach agreement.

The rise of UPFs isn't just a nutritional issue. It's also a story of power and influence. Dr Giles Yeo, an obesity researcher and science communicator, has been vocal about the need for more balance in the UPFs debate. But he is keen to clarify that he is not funded by the food industry. His sensitivity speaks to the historic and often insidious links between the scientific communities and corporations that confuse rather than help consumers.

Gyorgy Scrinis, who coined the term 'nutritionism', has spent years exposing the corporate takeover of food science. He argues that companies influence nutrition research by funding studies that favour their products – and avoiding those that might reveal harm. 'Manufacturers of ultra-processed foods have had little interest in funding research that measures the detrimental effects of their products,' Scrinis notes. 'Which may explain why this research was neglected for 50 years.'[9]

This influence goes beyond funding. In the US, the Academy of Nutrition and Dietetics has accepted millions of dollars in donations from food corporations – and has even held stock in them.[10] In the UK, a 2024 *British Medical Journal* investigation found that 11 out of 17 members of the government's Scientific Advisory Committee on Nutrition (SACN) had financial ties to the food industry.[11]

When SACN reviewed UPFs in 2023, they acknowledged that these foods are typically energy-dense and high in saturated fat, salt or free sugars, which have all been linked to adverse health outcomes. But they advised caution against relying solely on the Nova system, citing concerns about its clarity and reliability. They noted that the link between UPFs and health could be due to their nutrient profile rather than processing per se. In the end, no changes were made to UK dietary guidelines.[12]

As Dr Chris van Tulleken wrote in a post on X, 'Despite two decades of work from a conflicted SACN, we've seen an explosion of suffering and death from diet-related disease in the UK.' The conclusion is clear: we need independent, rigorous science to shape food policy that puts health before profit.

Others are more sympathetic, noting that government committees like the Scientific Advisory Committee on Nutrition (SACN) operate under political, economic and evidential constraints. Either way, we need independent, rigorous science, protected from commercial influence, to guide food policy in the public interest.

What weight loss drugs mean

While science is refining how we define and measure ultra-processed foods, it's also closing in on ways to treat the damage they can cause. Drugs like Ozempic, Wegovy and Mounjaro were originally developed to treat diabetes, but are now being prescribed at scale for weight loss. These drugs work by mimicking GLP-1, a natural hormone that helps regulate appetite and blood sugar. By targeting GLP-1 receptors, they slow digestion, curb hunger and alter how food is experienced.

The implications are huge. Demand continues to grow as medical use broadens, pill formats emerge and global adoption increases. Morgan Stanley forecasts a US$150 billion market by 2035.[13] We could see major shifts in what and how people eat. Early reports suggest GLP-1 users are buying fewer snacks, sugary drinks and other ultra-processed options, and even ordering less in restaurants. In the UK, weight loss drugs are set to be available on the NHS following a government deal.

But the drugs also raise deeper questions. Are we medicalising the consequences of a broken food system rather than addressing the root causes? Will these drugs become a privilege for the wealthy while low-income communities remain trapped in unhealthy food environments? Will they simply create a new market for 'GLP-friendly' products and smaller portion sizes without changing the system that made people sick in the first place?

Food companies are already responding. Some are testing new formats or reformulating products for this new wave of appetite regulation. For example, Nestlé has launched Vital Pursuit, a frozen ready-meal range high in protein and portioned to suit GLP-1 users' reduced appetite. But without systemic reform, GLP-1s risk becoming a pharmaceutical sticking plaster on a deeply unhealthy and unequal food landscape.

As science evolved, so did the players that stood to profit from it. What began as discovery and innovation soon became the foundation of powerful industries. Nowhere is that more visible than in the rise of big business in the global food system.

Big business

Big business plays a dominant role in shaping the global food system. This isn't to say that big business is inherently bad. Large companies often bring real benefits, including efficiency, scale and innovation, and they employ lots of people. They help keep supply chains running, offer an affordable range of products and invest in better outcomes for people and the planet, from improving working conditions and reducing emissions and waste to sourcing more responsibly.

Across the agri-food chain – from seeds and fertilizers to farming, processing, trade, retail and consumption – a growing share of control sits with only a handful of powerful corporations. But when too much power is concentrated in too few hands, it can distort priorities, putting shareholder value and return on investment above social and environmental outcomes. This concentration of market power also influences food governance, consumer choice and the livelihoods of farmers, fishers and small food businesses around the world.

Jennifer Clapp notes a clear pattern across the global food system: at nearly every stage, a handful of firms dominate. Clapp is part of IPES-Food, a coalition of 25 global experts advocating for sustainable food systems. Their report, *Tipping the Scales*, illustrates how corporate consolidation reduces competition and centralises power in a few hands.[14] The term 'Big Food' is often used critically to describe these large commercial players, whose influence can lead to adverse economic and social outcomes.

Consider seeds, the very foundation of agriculture. The push to grow more from the same amount of land has led to the widespread use and commodification of 'scientifically improved', genetically modified (GM) seeds. These often need specific 'proprietary' pesticides and fertilizers to thrive. This has created a highly profitable interdependent system.

Over time, mergers and acquisitions have resulted in a global seed and agrochemical oligopoly. Today, just four firms – Bayer, Corteva, Syngenta and BASF – control over 50% of the commercial seed market and more than 60% of the agrochemical market. The UN General Assembly has warned, 'This high concentration of corporate power allows a relatively small group to restrict people's access to seeds, and to shape markets and innovation in a way that serves the ultimate goal of shareholder profit maximisation and not the public good.'[15]

This concentration of control threatens farmer autonomy, biodiversity and food sovereignty – and it extends to labour across the food chain. Many agricultural and food-processing workers endure low wages, unsafe working conditions and limited labour protections. Smallholders, particularly in the Global South, are locked into contract farming models that shift production risks onto them while corporations set prices and quality standards. Many grow crops for export markets, where prices are volatile and the power to negotiate is limited. This makes them especially vulnerable to food price shocks and economic insecurity.

Furthermore, the global grain trade is dominated by four powerful companies: Archer Daniels Midland, Bunge, Cargill and Louis Dreyfus, collectively called the 'ABCDs'. Together, they control an estimated 50–60% of the global trade in key agricultural commodities like cereals, oilseeds and protein crops (COPs). While they once focused on transport and storage, research for the European Parliament notes they are now expanding into animal, pet and human nutrition, raising concerns about 'vulnerabilities created by few dominant traders'.[16]

The power of Big Food extends beyond agriculture and trade. Just a few global food and beverage companies dominate processed food markets worldwide. These giants shape global diets through extensive marketing, mass production and control over thousands of everyday brands. In the UK, the 10 biggest food and drink manufacturers – Coca-Cola, Danone, Ferrero, Kellogg's, Kraft-Heinz, Mars, Mondelez, Nestlé, PepsiCo and Unilever – have more than 240 brands and over 5,300 products between them.[17] While they are investing in healthier product lines, reformulating recipes, supporting sustainable farming and reducing environmental impact, critics argue that they exert disproportionate influence over what we eat and fuel the overconsumption of unhealthy products.[18]

A similar pattern of consolidation is seen in food retail. In Canada, five companies account for over 75% of grocery sales, prompting a 2023 competition watchdog report calling for more market diversity.[19] In Australia, two supermarket chains control two-thirds of the sector, triggering demands for regulation to prevent supplier exploitation.[20] In the UK, major retailers have faced allegations of unfair practices, including last-minute contract cancellations, tight supplier margins and misleading consumers with fictional farm names.[21] Meanwhile, digital platforms and e-commerce giants like Amazon are reshaping how we buy food, adding another layer of corporate control, fuelled by consumer data.

Beyond market control, Big Food exerts political influence through lobbying and the 'revolving door' phenomenon, where government officials take roles in the food industry and vice versa. For instance, in the US, the Food and Drug Administration (FDA) and United States Department of Agriculture (USDA) have faced criticism for close ties with the food industry, with former executives from major food corporations moving into regulatory positions. This undermines trust in regulation and raises concerns, like those voiced by Chris van Tulleken.

While corporate concentration in the food system has clear drawbacks, it also has notable advantages. Large-scale food businesses benefit from their size, which reduces production and transportation costs. These efficiencies in turn allow supermarkets to offer a wide range of affordable products, making food more accessible to consumers.

Investment in research and development (R&D) by food corporations has driven innovations in food safety, packaging and preservation. Companies have introduced foods with added nutrients like iron, iodine or vitamins to tackle nutritional deficiencies and have made high-profile sustainability pledges in response to growing public concern. Developments such as these fortified foods and alternative proteins stem from corporate R&D, addressing global challenges like malnutrition and environmental sustainability.

Supermarkets and large food retailers also play a key role in shaping consumer behaviour, with many nudging shoppers towards healthier choices through promotions, product reformulation and clearer labelling. They also support millions of jobs across the supply chain – from farming and logistics to retail – and increasingly invest in local communities and diverse talent. Moreover, their extensive logistics and distribution networks ensure food reaches both urban centres and remote populations efficiently.

While size has its advantages, it raises understandable concerns about fairness, transparency and power imbalances. In the apt words of Raj Patel, research professor at University of Texas and IPES-Food panel member, 'When the number of companies controlling the gateways from farmers to consumers is small, this gives them market power over the people who grew the food and the people who eat it.'[22]

Producers

Those who produce our food are businesses too, of course. They are responsible for our meals at their source. They have deeply specialist roles in making sure we don't go hungry and that we have enough of the right kind of food. We'll look at three groups that are particularly relevant to the challenges facing the food system: farmers; fishermen and fish farmers; and alternative protein manufacturers.

Farmers

Farmers are the foundation of food systems across the world. They sow seeds, raise animals, manage soil and ecosystems, and carry generations of knowledge. Their role is more than just production – they are also stewards of animal welfare, environmental health and rural economies. But it's a gruelling gig, and it's getting harder every year.

Across the world, many farmers are being relentlessly squeezed on all sides. Climate change is wreaking havoc with harvests. Floods, droughts and unpredictable seasons make growing food increasingly risky. Costs are increasing, labour is in short supply and the prices farmers receive are often dictated by powerful buyers such as supermarkets and manufacturers. Add to that shifting government policies and subsidies, and many are left uncertain, exhausted and ready to give up. It's no surprise, then, that farmers have taken to the streets to protest reforms to inheritance tax relief on farmland. It's yet another threat to a way of life and survival in a precarious sector.

Meanwhile, it's an ageing sector marked by inequity. The average age of a farmer is 55.[23] At the government's last count, only 3% of farmers were under 35, with over a third of them over the age of 65.[24] For young people, the barriers to entry are steep, from sky-high land prices and the allure of city-based jobs to the perception that farming is low status, hard graft and financially unrewarding. The overall number of farms worldwide is predicted to drop by half between 2010 and 2100, driven by consolidation and urban migration.[25]

Gender inequality is also rife. Women make up around 43% of the agricultural workforce but own less than 15% of the land. They also face significant disadvantages compared to men when it comes to their land rights.[26]

Then there is the gap between the Global North and Global South. In wealthier nations, agriculture is often more mechanised, consolidated and industrial in scale. In the US, for example, larger farms dominate, often specialising in monocultures with limited biodiversity. This is where the regenerative agriculture movement – a push to restore soil health and biodiversity after decades of intensive farming – is starting to take hold. (There's a full list of agriculture terms from IPES-Food in the 'Climate Solutions in Agriculture: Some Definitions' in the appendix.)

In contrast, most of the world's farmers live in the Global South. Over 84% of the world's 608 million farms are smallholdings. Many are under two hectares, often family-run and passed down through generations. These farms are especially concentrated in countries across Africa, Asia and Latin America, where they form the backbone of rural economies.[27]

It's estimated that these smallholders produce around one-third of the world's food and are vital to rural economies. Yet they remain among the world's poorest people and are the ones affected the most by climate events, despite often holding the knowledge and practices needed to farm in ways that support biodiversity and climate resilience. For example, crops like millet and sorghum, native to Africa and India, are attracting attention globally for their ability to thrive in heat and drought and to help fight food insecurity.

In the UK, farmers manage around 70% of the land, yet they receive less than 1% of the profits from the food they produce.[28] The cost of land and equipment is eye-watering, and aspiring farmers are priced out by investors who treat land as merely an investment asset. Seasonal income means winters can be especially tough – farmers can't afford to pay workers when there is no work. And for those relying on migrant or casual labour, labour shortages only add to the pressure.

Jeremy Clarkson's foray into farming made great television, but it laid bare the stark financial reality that without subsidies, many farms simply can't survive. Some have diversified by adding farm shops, glamping facilities or event venues, but that takes money, time and skills that many don't have access to.

On top of all that, political uncertainty clouds future support. Plus making the shift to regenerative or low-impact systems often means short-term drops in yield, and most farmers are already operating on a knife edge.

This begs the question of where we go from here. Precision fermentation and lab-grown meat are being touted as the future of food. Writers like George Monbiot[29] champion them as a solution to meeting the growing demand for more without trashing the planet. But critics, like Chris Smaje in his book *Saying No to a Farm-Free Future*,[30] argue this vision ignores the cultural, social and environmental role of farming.

We won't feed the world with kitchen gardening and window boxes, but neither should we rely solely on tech giants to feed us. Somewhere between industrialised agriculture and bioreactor food lies a middle ground, and farmers are very much a part of it, with many players working together and in harmony with nature. But they need support, security, investment and respect, because the people growing our food are as critical to our survival as the food itself.

Fishermen and fish farmers

Not everything we eat comes from the land. Fishermen and fish farmers are the guardians of our waters, sourcing what's known as 'blue food' from oceans, rivers, lakes and farmed waters. From wild-caught fish to shellfish and seaweed, these foods are vital to diets, livelihoods and environments around the world. Rich in protein, omega-3 fatty acids and essential micronutrients, seafood sustains billions of people and supports local and national economies alike.

The ocean covers 70% of the planet but provides just 5% of our food. The UN sees this as an opportunity for sustainable expansion.[31] With care and consideration, the ocean could nourish far more people while also restoring ecosystems and supporting those who depend on it.

Globally, 33 million people are directly employed in wild-capture fishing,[32] while more than 60 million people work directly in fisheries and in aquaculture, i.e. fish farming.[33] The vast majority are based in the Global South, and most work in small-scale or artisanal operations. These are the blue food equivalents of smallholder farmers: low-tech, family-run and locally embedded.

As with land, the pressures on our waters are intense. Climate change is warming oceans and making them more acidic, affecting fish migration patterns and disrupting the delicate balance of marine ecosystems. On the positive side, 64.5% of marine fish stocks are now fished at sustainable levels, but 35.5% remain overfished, a figure that has stayed stubbornly high.[34]

For small-scale fishermen and fish farmers, these pressures mean dwindling catches, declining incomes and growing uncertainty about their ability to sustain their livelihoods or feed their communities. The strain is compounded by the growing dominance of industrial fishing fleets – which are often heavily subsidised – that increasingly encroach on coastal waters.[35] In regions like West Africa and the Pacific, these large-scale operations push out small local fishermen, taking fish that coastal communities have relied on for generations.[36]

These fleets don't just deplete resources – labour abuses, corruption and environmental damage are also inherent in this model.[37] In fact, much of the seafood we eat is processed thousands of miles from where it was caught or farmed, often in countries where labour protections are weak and wages are low. This distance masks exploitation and removes us from the plight of the people who actually handle and prepare our food.

The global seafood industry is also highly concentrated. A handful of multinational corporations, including Thai Union, Mowi, Maruha Nichiro and Nippon Suisan Kaisha, dominate everything from fishing fleets and aquaculture farms to processing plants and retail packaging. Their size gives them huge influence over prices, policies, supply chains and small-scale producers.

Beneath it all lies a familiar pattern: open ocean resources have been claimed, privatised and controlled by a few. In 1982, UNCLOS (United Nations Convention on the Law of the Sea) granted countries Exclusive Economic Zones (EEZs). Extending 200 nautical miles from their coastlines, they gave governments special rights over the marine resources within them. These rights are often allocated through fishing licences and quotas, frequently favouring large industrial fleets that are seen as more efficient and profitable. But this approach concentrates market power and often sidelines Indigenous, small-scale and subsistence fishermen.

And just like farmers, fishermen face a steep inequality gap, but it plays out differently around the world. In the Global North, small-scale operators are struggling with shifting fish stocks, warming seas and climate legislation that can favour larger, more industrial fleets. Small producers in the Global South face similar climate pressures but with fewer resources and weaker safety nets, making them especially vulnerable.[38]

Women, too, are largely invisible in global seafood systems. Despite making up nearly half of the post-harvest workforce – in drying, processing and trading fish – women are often excluded from formal decision-making and denied access to finance, quotas or infrastructure. This affects their ability to adapt to and recover from environmental and economic shocks.[39]

Still, these same fishermen often hold the key to nature-friendly food production. Their work is deeply tied to local diets, seasonal knowledge and care for the oceans. In Asia and Africa, small-scale fisheries remain a vital safety net against poverty, gender inequality and food insecurity. Their methods, from selective gear types to community-led marine protections, support biodiversity and resilience at a time when both are under threat.

Fish doesn't just come from the wild, of course. The farming of fish, shellfish and seaweed now supplies half of all the seafood consumed globally.[40] Aquaculture is one of the fastest-growing food-production sectors in the world. When done well, it can ease pressure on wild stocks, support rural economies and even improve marine environments. Seaweed farming, for instance, helps to clean water and capture carbon, provides a nutritious, renewable food source and creates economic opportunity for coastal women.

But like its land-based counterparts, aquaculture is shaped by how it's done and who controls it. Poorly operated and poorly regulated fish farms can cause more harm than good by polluting surrounding ecosystems, spreading disease and threatening wild species. Many depend on feed made from wild-caught fish, raising further sustainability and equity concerns, particularly in origin countries. For instance, Norway, the world's largest producer of farmed salmon, relies heavily on fish meal and oil sourced from West Africa, where these local fish stocks are crucial to the diets of coastal communities.[41]

Globally, around 12 million tons of wild fish – roughly 15% of the total wild catch – are ground into fishmeal and oil each year to feed farmed fish and shrimp.[42] A recent study estimates that it can take up to 6 kilograms of wild fish to produce just 1 kilogram of farmed salmon, and 1.5 kilograms for every kilogram of shrimp. The demand is unsustainable, and it's already driving critical declines in wild fish stocks that will only worsen with climate change.[43]

In many regions, aquaculture is geared towards export markets. While this can bring jobs, infrastructure and tax revenue, the benefits don't always flow evenly to local communities. In some cases, environmental damage and resource use can leave locals worse off.

Off the coast of Turkey, for example, industrial farming of sea bass and sea bream has quadrupled production, with three-quarters exported to supermarkets and restaurants across Europe. Meanwhile, locals are finding it harder to access anchovies and other small wild fish that have long been part of their diets. Many of these smaller species are caught to make feed for farmed fish. With local stocks depleted, Turkish firms are now fishing off the coast of West Africa, where small fish are also in sharp decline, affecting food supply and livelihoods for coastal communities there.[44]

But a different kind of fish and seafood farming is taking shape. Some producers are using nature-friendly methods that grow several species together, like seaweed, shellfish and fish, in ways that mimic marine ecosystems. This approach, known as integrated multi-trophic aquaculture (IMTA), helps reduce waste and improve water quality. Others are building vertical ocean farms, where species are grown at different levels in the water, or raising climate-resilient species that can survive in warming seas. These ideas are being championed by a mix of scientists, Indigenous coastal communities and pioneering producers ranging from seaweed farms in Indonesia and East Africa to regenerative ocean farmers in Norway, Canada and the US.

In the UK, taking back control of British waters has proved more complex than promised post-Brexit. Fishing quotas – the mechanism that determines how much can be caught, and by whom – remain hotly debated, and the spoils are unevenly shared. Today, the most lucrative quotas are concentrated in the hands of a few large operators, including multinational corporations that often control not just the catch, but also the price, from 'sea to plate'.[45]

Small-scale and low-impact fishermen continue to play a vital role in the UK's food system, often working seasonally, landing a variety of native species and sustaining local economies and cultural ways. Yet they struggle for fair access and visibility and work with patchy infrastructure. While small vessels under 10 metres make up nearly 80% of the fishing fleet by number, they are in decline.[46]

Meanwhile, supermarket supply chains continue to favour a narrow range of imported, mass-market fish, largely reflecting demand from shoppers. Cod has been central to British fishing since the 15th century and is the most popular white fish in Britain. We are the world's biggest cod market, spending £350 million a year on it. But local stocks have long been overfished, so 90% of our cod is imported from Russia, Norway and Iceland.

As with farmers, the future of our food from the sea depends on who gets to produce it, under what conditions and with what support. And as with the land, the story of our oceans isn't just about food – it's about fairness, access and survival.

Alternative protein manufacturers

If farmers are the stewards of our land and fishermen are the guardians of our waters, then there are engineers of a new kind of food – one that seeks to decouple protein from animals entirely.

The case for doing so is rooted in science, but also in culture, climate and health. Protein has long been prized for its role in human evolution and is foundational to the smooth running of our bodies. It's made up of 20 amino acids, nine of which the body can't produce on its own. These nine 'essential' amino acids are found most completely in animal products, but also in soya and some other plants. Traditionally, cultures around the world have paired grains with pulses – rice and beans, dal and roti – to source complete proteins from plants.

But in many parts of the world, especially since the 1980s, protein has become synonymous with meat.[47] Global greenhouse gas emissions from animal-based foods are roughly twice those of plant-based foods.[48] While red meat gets the most attention, fish is also a major protein source globally, especially in the Global South, but rising demand and overfishing are putting pressure on fish stocks. In addition, high consumption of red and processed meats is linked to increased risks of heart disease, cancer and diabetes; wild meat can carry zoonotic risks (diseases passed from animals to humans); and intensive livestock farming contributes to deforestation, water scarcity and antimicrobial resistance.[49]

This is where alternative protein steps in. Often grouped together as 'alt-protein', it includes everything from plant-based meat substitutes (known as meat analogues) to mycoprotein (fungus-derived protein), algae, insect protein and laboratory-led developments, as outlined by Catherine Tubb in her piece later on. Many of the most successful plant-based meat analogues rely on ingredients like soy, pea protein and mushrooms, along with added ingredients, to replicate the texture, succulence and appearance of meat.

These products are improving rapidly, both in taste and in how closely they mimic conventional meat, with advances in food science and sensory technology. Fermentation, for example, a method as old as human civilisation that makes things like yogurt and kimchi, is being repurposed as a precision science.

The idea of alt-proteins is simple: feed people protein without the environmental cost, cruelty or inefficiency of farming animals.

Imitation meat is not a new phenomenon. In China, it has existed since the 6th century thanks to Chinese Buddhists ingeniously creating vegetarian versions of their favourite meats.[50] Products like Quorn (launched in the UK in the 1980s) and Tofurky (a US invention from 1995) have been around for decades. However, the current wave of innovation is tech-driven, investment-backed and scaling fast. When Beyond Meat and Impossible Foods entered the market in 2009, they didn't just target vegans – they were aimed squarely at meat eaters, with slogans about changing the system from the inside.

In 2016, long-time animal rights campaigner Bruce Friedrich founded the Good Food Institute (GFI) to help formalise the movement. GFI acts as a global think tank and advocacy group, supporting the development of plant-based, cultivated and fermentation-derived proteins. It describes plant-based meat as a way to 'make meat more efficiently by skipping the animal and turning plant ingredients directly into meat'.[51]

These developments have attracted over $18.6 billion in investment since 2016[52] and are being framed as the 'second domestication of plants and animals', where we've gone from mastering macro-organisms to micro-organisms.[53] A mix of food tech start-ups, biotech firms and global food giants, including meat and dairy companies, such as Nestlé, JBS, Eat Just, Meati and Perfect Day, are investing in the space, all hoping to secure a foothold in the protein markets of the future.

In countries like Singapore, where 90% of food is imported, cellular agriculture is part of the national food security strategy.[54] It became the first country to approve cultivated meat – specifically chicken – for sale in 2020, followed by limited approvals in the US. The UK has so far approved it only for pet food, although the Food Standards Agency has committed to putting cell-cultivated meat on human shelves by 2027.[55]

While cultivated meat is no longer science fiction, it's still a long way from supermarket shelves. Costs are high and regulations are slow. Meanwhile, the taste, texture and 'clean label' credentials of plant-based meat substitutes don't yet match consumer expectations. Some companies have already folded. And there's pushback. The meat and dairy industries, especially in Europe and North America, are resisting everything from product naming rights ('is it meat if it's grown in a tank?') to shelf space and subsidies.

There's also growing discomfort around how centralised and tech-heavy the alternative protein industry is becoming. Critics argue that replacing one kind of industrial system with another – even if it's lower-carbon – still risks leaving power in the hands of the few. Others worry about ultra-processing, lab dependency and the loss of culinary tradition.

Research also highlights a 'great deal of diversity in nutritional profile' among processed plant-based meat. Many are classed as ultra-processed foods (UPFs), with some high in saturated fat, salt and sugar.[56] Replacing well-reared meat, produced responsibly and eaten in moderation, with these kinds of UPFs brings its own health risks.[57]

Most innovation is concentrated in high-income countries, raising questions about global access, affordability and food sovereignty. Will alt-proteins serve the people most vulnerable to climate-linked food insecurity or simply create new markets for the already well fed?

And then there's culture. Meat has meaning in many food cultures, whether as an aspirational centrepiece for celebrations, a marker of hospitality or a daily anchor in countless cuisines. It can signal prosperity and care, with its preparation tied into recipes, rituals and memories. It provides key nutrients, while livestock farming also plays a central role in rural economies and landscapes. Simply replacing it with high-tech alternatives isn't a silver bullet.

There are other sources of protein to consider. Insects, for instance, are eaten in many parts of Africa, Asia and Latin America, from mopane worms in southern parts of Africa to chapulines in Mexico. Insect protein is increasingly being used in pet food. But creepy crawlies still face a 'yuck factor' in much of the Global North, where cultural bias often overrides their nutritional or environmental benefits.

For now, alternative protein remains a fast-moving, imperfect solution. It's full of promise, but also full of questions. What it can offer is a chance to consider how we produce protein: who controls it, who benefits from it and what kind of system we want to feed the future.

WHAT THE NEXT 20 YEARS COULD LOOK LIKE FOR FOOD

by Catherine Tubb

The way we produce and deliver food is changing fast, with the past 50 years bringing some of the biggest advances in food and farming technology we've ever seen. Innovations like genetic engineering, high-tech farming and improved refrigeration have made it possible to produce food with fewer resources, in harsher climates and with higher safety standards than ever before.

Looking to the next 20 years, even bigger changes are on the horizon. Some of the most exciting - and controversial - advances are focused on taking animals out of the food chain. New technologies are being developed to make animal products like meat, milk and eggs without using animals at all. Here are some of the most promising developments in this space.

- **Cultivated meat:** Cultivated meat, also called lab-grown meat, involves growing muscle and fat cells in a tank instead of a living animal. The goal is to make meat that's nearly identical to what we eat today - like steaks, burgers and chicken - without needing to raise or slaughter animals. While it's still expensive, costs are

coming down, and a few countries have even approved it for sale. This approach could one day offer us a way to enjoy real meat with a much smaller environmental impact.
- **Precision fermentation:** Precision fermentation is a process that uses tiny microbes, like yeast or bacteria, to produce specific proteins. This method is already used to make medicines like insulin, and now it's being used to create proteins found in foods like milk and eggs. Since proteins play a key role in giving foods their texture and taste, this technology is especially promising. By programming microbes to produce these proteins, we can make foods that act just like animal products but without the animals. For example, Impossible Foods uses this technique to make a protein that gives their burgers a meaty taste.
- **Alternative protein mimicry:** While plant-based burgers and other meat alternatives have become common, new techniques are making these products more realistic. Technologies like 3D printing and special freezing methods are giving plant-based ingredients a texture closer to actual meat. At the same time, there's increasing interest in alternative protein sources like algae, insects and lesser-known crops that are packed with nutrients and easy to produce.

It's easy to dismiss these new technologies as niche or futuristic. But costs are falling, flavours are improving and they offer real advantages in terms of sustainability and efficiency Many of these technologies are also finding uses beyond food, like in materials, cosmetics and medicine, which helps them grow and develop faster. Imagine baby formula made with human milk proteins, or collagen supplements that come from human cells instead of animals.

Of course, these advances are just part of a larger picture. The entire food system is being transformed, with new innovations in packaging, delivery and even personalised nutrition. Each of these developments is shaping the way we produce, access and think about food, helping us prepare for a more sustainable future.

Catherine Tubb is an analyst, director of research and the co-author of 'Rethinking Food and Agriculture 2020-2030: The Second Domestication of Plants and Animals, the Disruption of the Cow and the Collapse of the Industrial Livestock Industry', published in the Industrial Biotechnology journal.

Manufacturers, processors and distributors

We don't simply eat the food that comes out of the ground, from the water or from a lab. Food manufacturers, processors and distributors play a vital role in turning raw ingredients into the food we find in shops, cafés, restaurants and takeaways. They wash, chop, mix, cook, preserve, package, store, transport and market it, shaping not just how food tastes, but how it fits into our lives.

They must also make the numbers work. That means striking a balance between production costs, profit margins and what people are willing or able to pay. Margins are often wafer-thin. Rising energy prices, supply chain disruption, staffing shortages and inflation all add pressure, especially in sectors where contracts are fixed months in advance. And there's only so far prices can go before shoppers walk away, particularly when our household budgets are already stretched.

While global multinationals dominate headlines, much of this work is done by mid-sized or regional businesses such as co-packers, ingredient suppliers, frozen food manufacturers and logistics companies. These players are critical links in the chain, often working behind the scenes to keep food moving and available. In the UK, firms like Brakes, 2 Sisters Food Group and Greencore supply major retailers and caterers every day.

Food manufacturers and processors have also played a defining role in creating new ways – and times – to eat. The rise of 'snacking' as a fourth mealtime is a manufactured category, one created and promoted by processed food makers. From breakfast bars to protein bites and low-calorie snack packs, entire product lines have been built around the promise of grazing. By focusing on single nutrients like fibre, protein or fat, the concept helped to mask the reality of highly processed foods in the interest of corporate profit rather than public health.

How these companies formulate, promote and price their products has come under increasing scrutiny. From campaigners to clinicians, a growing chorus is asking how food manufacturing contributes to the triple challenge of diet-related disease, inequality and ecological breakdown.

Processing itself isn't inherently bad. It has made food more portable, shelf stable and cheaper to transport. Dehydrated noodles, individually wrapped snacks and long-life ready meals are easier to ship and store than fresh or perishable foods, making life more convenient for us and helping manufacturers expand globally. This has supported affordability in some cases by lowering the cost of food.

The Chorleywood process, for example, developed in the late 1950s, transformed how bread was made. It allowed cheap, fluffy loaves to be produced quickly and at scale using lower-protein wheat, enzymes, emulsifiers and intensive mixing. Although it was initially developed to help small bakers compete with industrial giants, it was soon adopted by large commercial bakeries and ended up putting many smaller ones out of business.[58] It made sliced bread affordable and widely accessible, but it also rewired how we view bread. Like many other staples in our weekly shop, it deepened our reliance on centralised, highly processed supply chains.

Marketing of the more highly processed products, which are also nutritionally subpar, is part of the problem. A global review of food and drink advertising found that the tactics used to promote unhealthy products were 'aggressive, insidious and everywhere'. From celebrity endorsements and sports sponsorships to school tie-ins and influencer campaigns, the reach is vast. Children are particularly vulnerable. Unable to distinguish ads from entertainment, they absorb subtle messages that shape food preferences and social norms early on.[59]

Low-income communities[60] – and in the US, people of colour[61] – are disproportionately affected by UPF marketing and pricing strategies, as they are often cheaper than their whole-food counterparts. With access to quality food limited by geography, cost and time, the result is a food system where the most nutritionally poor products are often the ones that are the most readily available and most aggressively promoted.

The pressure on manufacturers to change is real and rising. Public awareness of UPFs is growing. Government policies and procurement standards are evolving. Retailers are trialling everything from reformulation and repositioning to gamification, education and price incentives. There's commercial opportunity here too: Mintel found that 68% of UK consumers and 74% of Canadians say they eat healthily all or most of the time, despite financial concerns.[62] Demand for healthier, more sustainable food isn't a niche. It's a shift.

Many businesses are responding to this, investing in people and the planet. Larger manufacturers are making moves, from reformulating products to investing in regenerative supply chains. Saying that, progress is uneven and often complicated by cost pressures. Across the UK and globally, a growing number of independent, artisanal and craft food brands are showing that it's possible to build businesses rooted in ethics. They focus on transparency, ingredient integrity, fair supply chains and flavour, often avoiding the mainstream norms and prioritising sustainability, provenance and purpose instead.

Take Hodmedod's, who source UK-grown pulses like fava beans and lentils while regenerating soil and reviving local supply chains. Or Tony's Chocolonely, the Dutch chocolate company on a mission to end slavery in cocoa farming. Karma Cola partners with small-scale farmers in Sierra Leone, sharing profits and putting Fairtrade into fizzy drinks. Wildfarmed has successfully brought bread made with regeneratively farmed wheat to supermarket shelves.

These are values-driven businesses working to create products that don't just taste good, but do good. They're often nimble, close to their communities and more transparent. But the key challenge for them is how to grow without compromising their principles, otherwise they may remain too small and niche to make a significant impact

The path to growth isn't easy. Independent brands face steep challenges in securing shelf space, scaling production, managing costs and weathering supply chain shocks without the cushion of deep pockets. Many are squeezed by supermarket demands, overshadowed by louder voices and bigger budgets, and challenged by consumers not always recognising their value. Yet they persist, showing that a different kind of food system is possible, one jar, bar or box at a time.

Behind all these manufacturing and processing companies are distributors and logistics providers: the quiet engine of the food system. They manage cold chains, route planning, customs paperwork, shelf-life tracking and just-in-time delivery across regions and borders.

Their work becomes even more critical during crises. During the Covid-19 pandemic, grocery distributors played a critical role in keeping shelves stocked despite panic buying, border delays and shifting demand from food service to retail. Warehouses operated 24/7. Drivers rerouted goods from shuttered cafés to supermarkets. Emergency food hubs popped up to support vulnerable households. It wasn't perfect – many small producers lost out – but for a system built for efficiency, not resilience, it largely held together under extraordinary pressure.

Behind the shelves and supply chains are millions of workers: pickers, packers, drivers, cleaners and line operatives. Many are migrants or from marginalised backgrounds. During the pandemic, they were rightly hailed as essential, but that status was short-lived. These workers saw their 'essential' label quietly dropped once restrictions lifted and life returned to normal. Their labour, like the food they produce, is too often taken for granted unless a major disruption affects us. In a world where food moves faster than most of us realise, it's easy to forget how many hands make that possible – until something breaks.

Civil society organisations

Civil society organisations (CSOs) are the campaigners, researchers, charities, unions, social movements and citizen groups that advocate for change, often where governments and markets fall short. They challenge harmful narratives, share knowledge, hold power to account and step in when systems fail.

CSOs range from think tanks and academic institutions to grassroots alliances, professional bodies and public-interest non-governmental organisations (NGOs). They connect communities to decision-makers, bring lived experience into policy debates and fight to keep justice, health and equity on the agenda. Their presence in rooms, around tables and at global summits helps to represent the voices of those who are often left out.

Yet they're often excluded from the most powerful spaces. Costs, accreditation hurdles and lobbying by corporate or political interests mean that CSOs, particularly from the Global South, are routinely shut out of decision-making. Take COP, for instance, where the 198 signatories of the UN Framework Convention on Climate Change meet annually to review progress and set targets. At COP28 in Dubai, fossil fuel lobbyists outnumbered most country delegations, while many farmer and Indigenous groups were reportedly given limited access to formal negotiations.[63]

At COP29 in Baku, Azerbaijan, the repression of dissent and CSOs was even more overt. Local NGOs were shut down, critics were jailed and silenced,[64] and international observers reported sky-high accommodation costs and restricted access to negotiations.[65] The UN Climate Bureau has held crisis talks about the soaring cost of accommodation for COP30 in Brazil's Belém, which will affect poorer nations and marginalised groups.

CSOs raise their voices in different ways, but they aren't immune to influence, of course. Funding can shape priorities and agendas. Yet they often join forces to take a stronger stance. When the EU Deforestation Regulation (EUDR) was delayed in 2024, over 200 organisations from 40 countries issued a joint statement expressing their dismay. In the same year, when the EU considered changes to commercial seed laws, 139 CSOs from 23 countries signed an open letter warning that new rules could threaten crop diversity and undermine the rights of farmers to save and share seeds. While the rules are still under review, campaigning is keeping farmer-saved seeds and heritage seed varieties on the policy agenda.

Some CSOs are rooted in broader social movements, fighting to democratise land, strengthen ties between people and nature, and challenge entrenched power structures. La Via Campesina, a global movement of peasants and Indigenous food producers, puts frontline communities at the heart of debates on food security, farming, climate and trade. They advocate for food sovereignty (explained in the following sidebar) and for the rights of women, small-scale producers and rural workers.

Their UK chapter, the Landworkers' Alliance, envisions a food and farming system with more jobs, better livelihoods and access to affordable, ecologically produced and culturally appropriate food. As director Deirdre (Dee) Woods says, 'Food is about people, but in a tired, capitalist system, it has become about the profits. The task of CSOs is to be disrupters, bring lived experience, collaboration, social solidarity and the rights of people to the front and centre of public policy.'[66] That's what many organisations do, and often without the resources or platforms of their private-sector counterparts.

Public policy advocacy is central to many CSOs. Some focus on research, evidence and systems thinking, providing the data and analysis that governments need to act. For example, IPES-Food produces rigorous, independent research and policy recommendations with a global reach. 'We work closely with civil society organisations by collaborating on research, policy advocacy, and public campaigns for sustainable food systems,' says Robbie Blake, communications manager at IPES-Food. 'It's about amplifying grassroots voices, sharing knowledge and building coalitions that drive change.'[67]

In the UK, initiatives like Bite Back 2030 – a youth-led movement founded by Jamie Oliver – are challenging junk food marketing and demanding better food choices in schools, shops and communities. The Food, Farming and Countryside Commission (FFCC) is another organisation helping to shift the national conversation. Their Food Conversation project brought together over 2,000 people across the country, many of whom felt unheard and locked out of food decisions.

CSOs have had to adapt. The combined shocks of Brexit, Covid-19 and the cost-of-living crisis pushed many away from policy into frontline response, tackling hunger, inequality and community breakdown in real time. According to Rachael Durrant, an academic at the University of Sussex who studies the evolving role of CSOs, 'The net effect of all this is a shift from focusing on big multi-sector partnerships ... to a situation where you're either working to plug holes in the failing regime or you've given up and are trying to build something new.'[68] Her research shows how CSOs are increasingly stretched between responding to crisis and reimagining what comes next.

But there are powerful examples of what's possible when CSOs are given a seat at the table. Brazil's National Council for Food and Nutrition Security (CONSEA) has been widely credited with major progress in reducing hunger and improving nutrition.[69] In meat-loving Denmark, CSOs like the Vegetarian Society of Denmark (DVF) helped push through a national commitment to plant-based and sustainable food systems. By building coalitions across scientists, farmers and policymakers, they helped secure €170 million in government funding for organic and plant-based production.[70]

In a system where many feel voiceless, CSOs amplify what matters and can be instrumental in driving positive change.

WHO HOLDS THE POWER? FOOD SOVEREIGNTY, CONTROL AND THE RIGHT TO FOOD

The themes of power and control come up time and time again in conversations about today's food system – and both are deeply connected to people and planet. At the heart of the debate is a simple question: who gets to decide how food is produced, distributed and eaten, and to whose benefit?

On one side is the push for local agency and diverse, small-scale agricultural practices. On the other side is the growing centralisation and commercialisation of food systems by corporate entities.

Food sovereignty, according to IPES-Food, is 'a movement for more local control of the food system by people who produce, distribute and consume food (in contrast to global corporations)'.[71] It prioritises local, healthy and culturally appropriate food, produced through ecologically sound and sustainable methods. It also supports the right of countries and communities to define their own agricultural and food policies without being undermined by trade deals, exports or 'dumping' from more powerful economies.

An example of dumping is when subsidised surplus milk powder from the EU is exported to West Africa at low prices, thereby undercutting local dairy farmers and forcing them out of business.[72] Another is the continued production and export of hazardous pesticides, banned in the EU for health and environmental reasons but still sold to Africa and other regions.[73]

Closely linked is the idea of the 'right to food', which is the basic human right to have regular, reliable access to enough nutritious food that respects cultural traditions and supports a healthy, dignified life.[74] It's also known, more simply, as the right to 'good food for all'. That may sound obvious, but it means ensuring that everyone can eat enough, eat healthily and meet their basic needs with dignity.

Right now, the global food system is failing to uphold either food sovereignty or the right to food for millions. Activists, CSOs and not-for-profit organisations are calling for a fundamental rebalance of power: one that puts people, communities and food producers back in control of how food is grown, shared, consumed and governed.

Media

From specialist podcasts and investigative exposés to food hacks and glossy recipes, media is omnipresent in our gastronomic adventures. It influences what we eat, how we feel about it, who we trust and what we believe is possible. And like the rest of the system, it's shaped by commercial pressures, political influence and competing interests.

The way we get our daily updates about wars or politics also shapes how we stay updated about our love for food – and how we consume news is changing fast. The Reuters Institute's annual *Digital News Report* is a useful barometer for tracking developments. Smartphones are now the dominant device for accessing news globally. Video, especially the short-form kind on TikTok and YouTube, is rising. But interest in news overall is falling, with nearly 40% saying they avoid it altogether. Many cite exhaustion or feeling bombarded by content.[75]

Podcasts and newsletters have offered a new route in. Interestingly, the shows we hear are also the videos we watch, blurring the lines between media, entertainment and community. Younger audiences are tuning in to partisan commentators, influencers and content creators on social media platforms rather than a traditional newsroom as a by-product of scrolling. As they do, trust is waning and concern about misinformation is growing, with TikTok and X flagged as the least trustworthy platforms.[76]

This has big implications for how food issues are seen and understood. Mainstream media tends to focus on what's visible and immediate: food prices, food shortages, climate-linked weather events or political flashpoints. The deeper structures – who controls land, who sets prices, who benefits – are often the domain of niche titles, independent journalists or academics.

Investigative journalism has played a vital role in exposing what lies beneath. From modern slavery in supply chains to the power of the seed industry, longform media has helped surface hidden stories. Journalists like Joanna Blythman, Jay Rayner, Sheila Dillon and Leyla Kazim have consistently connected the dots between what's on our plates and the systems behind them, while Bee Wilson's feature on ultra-processed food in the *Guardian*[77] helped spark wider interest and inspired Chris van Tulleken's book *Ultra-processed People*.

Food media is also shaped by who gets to speak. Sponsored content, product placements and brand partnerships can steer coverage while editorial budgets shrink. Meanwhile, the pressure to present 'both sides' of an issue that makes journalism trustworthy can downplay the scale or urgency of systemic problems with climate and health. Mainstream food media still often centres white, middle-class and Eurocentric voices, though progress is being made in platforming more diverse perspectives.

Social media has both cracked open the conversation and complicated it, but the democratisation of writing and content creation has made space for new voices. *Vittles* changed UK food writing by platforming overlooked writers and stories. Gavin Wren uses TikTok to explain UK food policy. Tim Spector popularised gut health with Instagram and data. Thin Lei Win's *Thin Ink* newsletter brings independent, global analysis of food and climate to readers outside traditional media channels.

Social media platforms have turned chefs, home cooks, nutritionists and lifestyle creators into powerful tastemakers, often with more reach than traditional food media. A single post can sell out a product, revive a bakery or trigger backlash. From mukbang feasts of live excessive eating to 'what I eat in a day' reels, food is increasingly about performance and entertainment. Algorithms can amplify both creativity and misinformation. The same reach that sells sourdough can also spread fad diets or conspiracy theories.

In a space where lines between paid partnerships, personal opinion and actual qualifications often blur, trust is easily stretched. A survey of 53 top nutrition misinformation 'superspreaders' found the three most common types are those who use the title 'Dr' for faux authority, those who push anti-establishment conspiracies and those who wrap bogus health claims in slick marketing to sell products and programmes.[78] Meanwhile, artificial intelligence (AI) is adding a new layer of uncertainty and untrustworthy content.

In short, used well, social media builds connection, visibility and understanding, but used irresponsibly, it distorts, distracts and deepens divisions. For all the voices that get heard, many still go unheard. In the food world, who tells the story shapes real-life outcomes. What's visible gets attention. What's missing can get forgotten. In a world of instant information and shrinking attention, media is one of the most powerful players in the food system, whether we realise it or not.

We, the people

People are the beating heart of the food system. At the FAO's last count, 1.23 billion people were employed in global agrifood systems, from production to processing, packaging to retail, home kitchens to street stalls.[79] Almost half of the global population lives in households linked to these systems. In many low-income countries, especially in Africa, agriculture and food remain the main source of income and employment.

We are both the hands that produce the food and the mouths that consume it. We are part of the supply chain and the driver of demand. Our choices matter, especially for those with privilege and purchasing power, yet they can only go so far without structural change. That said, how we shop, cook, eat and waste food still makes a difference. In the words of the UK's largest grocery retailer, every little helps.

There are signs of a shift in what shapes what we eat and drink. People, particularly younger generations, are increasingly willing to pay more for sustainable products across 28 countries,[80] while environmental concerns like polluted rivers and seas, plastic waste and global warming are increasing in the UK.[81] Many of us expect businesses to lead – not just reduce harm, but actively do good.[82]

Saying that, price, taste and nutrition still reign supreme. We only care about sustainability if it aligns with these.[83] Behaviour change often stalls in the messy middle between intent and action, the so-called 'say–do' gap. For many, daily food decisions are shaped more by time, cost and convenience than ideals. The uncomfortable truth is that the more comfortable among us rely on the exploitation of other people elsewhere to make convenience, choice, abundance and even our health and well-being possible.

The Landworkers' Alliance has highlighted the exploitation of migrant farm workers in the UK and Europe.[84] Meanwhile, banana workers in tropical regions face low pay, toxic exposure and precarious contracts, and similar stories echo across cocoa, coffee and tea. These products, which are central to the economies of the Global South, have been shaped by a long history of colonialism and unequal trade. Power continues to rest unequally, dictating what's grown, who benefits and at what cost.

These inequalities don't just exist between nations, but within them, shaping who eats well, who goes hungry and who gets overlooked. Across all societies, it is the most vulnerable – women, older people and children – who suffer most when food systems fail. Older people are increasingly food insecure. They can be overlooked in policy and vulnerable to diet-related illness, loneliness and poor access to services.

Children – who will inherit this inequitable system – are among the hardest hit. Hunger-related illness remains the leading cause of child deaths globally,[85] while obesity is climbing even in low- and middle-income countries.[86] In the UK, one in 10 children is obese by the time they start school.[87]

Food education is either missing or patchy across state schools, with lessons often limited to making sugary fairy cakes or pizzas. The scrapping of A-levels in Food led to a further drop in food teaching at secondary level, leaving many young people with little understanding of health, nutrition or the basic life skills needed to eat well.[88] Poverty is fuelling shorter stature, poorer health and fewer life opportunities.[89]

Climate change adds another layer of injustice. A 2023 UNICEF report found that nearly half of the world's children live in countries at extreme risk from its impacts.[90] Overconsumption in the wealthiest countries is accelerating this crisis, while children, who have contributed the least, suffer the most.

Yet we are not just victims of the system. We are also participants, culture-makers and change agents. In their book *Citizens: Why the Key to Fixing Everything Is All of Us*, Jon Alexander and Ariane Conrad call for a shift in our identity from being passive consumers to active citizens.[91] Citizens are people who take responsibility, shape their communities and imagine something better. They ask not just 'what do I want?' but also 'what can we do?'

Many food lovers already are. From food banks and mutual aid groups to online farmers' markets and community farms, people are stepping in where the system falls short. Others are campaigning, organising and resisting – demanding better school food, fairer wages or stronger food rights. Food writers, educators and communicators help make the food system more accessible – for example, by translating complex issues into everyday language, building caring communities, learning and action. Through newsletters, books, podcasts and supper clubs, they're starting new conversations to spotlight how food connects us to everything from floods and wildfires to identity.

As cooks, growers, storytellers and eaters, we keep food culture alive. We pass on knowledge, preserve rituals and create connections through meals. Whether reclaiming lost ingredients, resisting junk food or feeding our families with care, we shape food culture – and it shapes us. When that knowledge fades, we lose more than recipes; we lose a part of who we are.

But structural inequalities – in wealth, representation and power – still shape what people eat, how they live and whether they're heard. The next chapter explores this further, diving into power structures that were established centuries ago, the societies and communities they forged and the impact they have on the world of food, drink and hospitality that we love.

OTHER INFLUENCERS IN THE FOOD SYSTEM

Not every influence on the food system is front and centre, loud and visible. These players still help shape what we eat, how it's made and who benefits.

- **Finance and investment:** Private equity, venture capital and pension funds are increasingly active in food, from buying farmland and water rights to funding agri-tech and alt-protein start-ups.
- **Tech and data platforms:** Smart fridges, tech platforms and recipe, food delivery and nutrition apps now influence everything from what we cook to what we crave.
- **Packaging and waste management:** The packaging and waste sectors preserve food and drink, shape its design, aid shelf life and affect environmental footprint. For example, disappearing, edible and reusable packaging are addressing waste.
- **Culinary education:** From high-tech facilities and farms on site at universities to training chefs in schools and prisons, culinary education and kitchen confidence is a new form of food power.
- **Chefs and restaurants:** From fine dining to high-street chains and pubs, chefs and restaurants shape what's aspirational, desirable and plated up. They are important markets for great produce and products, influencing sourcing, seasonality and sustainability.

The big takeaways

1. **The food system has many players:** Governments, corporations, scientists, farmers, fishermen and fish farmers, media, civil society and people all shape what ends up on our plates.
2. **Policies set the rules:** Subsidies, taxes, labelling laws, public health campaigns and even what schools, hospitals and public bodies buy decide much of what we eat. There are great examples of positive progress, but food policy can be fragmented, politically driven and prone to conflicts of interest.
3. **Science drives progress and controversy:** From nutrition guidelines to weight-loss drugs, research underpins change, but commercial influence can distort findings and delay public health action.
4. **Corporate power concentrates control:** A handful of global firms control seeds, grains, processing, brands and retail, bringing efficiencies and benefits but also price power, market dominance and reduced choice.
5. **Farmers and fishermen are under pressure:** Climate change, rising costs, policy shifts and industrial competition threaten livelihoods. Smallholders and smaller fishing fleets remain vital to food security and biodiversity around the world.
6. **Alternative proteins are redefining possibilities:** They promise progress but raise questions about the evolution of the way we eat and drink and who controls the next food frontier.
7. **Manufacturers and processors shape diets:** Product formulation, marketing and pricing, with ultra-processed foods dominating advertising and shelf space, influence our choices, but values-driven brands and businesses are emerging.

8. **Civil society pushes for fairness:** NGOs and activist groups amplify unheard voices and fight for better, healthier systems, although their work is moulded by funding and determined by access to decision-making spaces.
9. **Media and social platforms frame the narrative:** Investigative reporting can expose hidden harms, but misinformation, commercial influence and algorithm-driven trends also distort public understanding.
10. **Change needs us too:** We may not be able to change the system single-handedly, but our food choices, stories and everyday actions can still make a difference.

PEOPLE

Culture, power and identity behind our plates

'Did you say chocolate hummus?
Do you know what you just did?
You just insulted my grandmother.
Yeah. F-ck your lineage.
To hell with your culture.'

'Lo siento. I did not know that hummus was Mexican.'

Mo (Netflix)

Food is more than what we put in our mouth. It's a cultural artefact and a vessel for identity, memory, tradition and belonging. Every bite tells a story.

The rich variety of meals we enjoy today, from spice-laden curries to fiery jerk, fragrant pho to sizzling stir-fries, is inspired by communities across the world. But the legacies of trade, empire and exploitation still shape who grows our food, who profits and whose cuisines are celebrated or misrepresented. Understanding these historic and ongoing power dynamics, especially when working with the food of the global majority, helps us to rebalance them and better reflect the world we live in today.

Who held power and how was it used?

Food commodities have been historically valuable as currency. As European appetites grew, so did the drive to trade in them and claim their sources. By the 15th century, English expeditions were already underway to find cod to salt and dry for the growing market in Europe.[1] Spanish and Portuguese traders were growing sugar off the coast of West Africa and in the Canary Islands. Around the same time, spices became the must-have symbols of wealth in Europe, making their way west via Arab merchants. But European empires wanted more than trade – they wanted control.

Exploration to colonisation

The hunger for exploration and commerce led to conquest and control. In 1493, Christopher Columbus carried the first sugarcane plant to the Caribbean, mistakenly thinking he'd reached India and so calling it the 'West Indies'. His voyage also marked the beginning of the Columbian Exchange: the widespread transfer of plants, animals, culture and people between the Americas, West Africa and Europe.[2]

Tomatoes, potatoes, maize, cocoa, chillies and peanuts travelled from the Americas, while wheat, rice, sugarcane, coffee and livestock (animals kept for gain/profit) moved in the other direction. This included enslaved labour, laying the groundwork for centuries of exploitative practices in the global food system.

One of the devastating effects of the Columbian Exchange was the spread of infectious diseases. Deadly pathogens swept through and devastated Indigenous populations in the Americas, who had no natural immunity.[3] This mass depopulation weakened resistance to colonisation and made conquest easier for European powers.

Five years after Columbus, Portuguese explorer Vasco da Gama set sail for India, hoping to tap into the spice riches of the East.[4] By the late 1500s, the Spanish and Portuguese had established sugar plantations across parts of the Caribbean and South America, powered by the brutal, forced labour of enslaved West Africans. These early systems set the foundational template for monoculture farming and exploitative global supply chains.

Meanwhile, Dutch traders were seeing huge returns from the spice trade, with fleets delivering 400% profit to private investors over four years by 1599.[5] Not to be outdone, the British launched the East India Company (EIC) in 1600 to establish direct maritime routes with spice-producing countries.[6] In 1657, further powers were handed to the EIC to help it grow its presence through law enforcement, conflict and colonisation – an early example of corporate control in the food system.[7]

As Europe's tastes changed, spices took a back seat to cotton, silk, sugar, coffee and tea. Sugar became cheaper as the transatlantic slave trade expanded,[8] entering the diets of Britain's poor in copious amounts.[9] By the 18th century, tea was booming. What started as a luxury drink powered factory workers in the Industrial Revolution and became a national, sugary obsession in Britain – and a highly profitable one.

To fund its tea imports from China, Britain began trading opium illegally, fuelling addiction and sparking the Opium Wars when China pushed back. The EIC was at the heart of it all. Its monopoly over the tea trade led to the Tea Act of 1773, which granted it tax exemptions in the American colonies. This triggered the Boston Tea Party, a protest that helped ignite the American Revolution.

Exploitation and empire building

Many European powers were involved in colonialism, but the British Empire became the largest in the world, spanning continents and centuries. At its peak, it controlled one-quarter of the Earth's land surface and more than 458 million people were under its rule.[10] Central to this dominance was the spirit of entitlement, the control of land and the subjugation of Indigenous people, a strategy aligned with wealth-building and extractive practices. But it's important to note that many of the societies they encountered already had their own hierarchies, conflicts and forms of exploitation.

The British approach was an extension of the Enclosure Movement in Britain from the 15th to the 19th centuries, which transformed rural lives and livelihoods.[11] Landowners became more efficient and profitable, while dispossessed farmers and rural workers were forced into cities, providing labour for the Industrial Revolution, or overseas. Intensified domestic agriculture, the expansion of the railways and cheap imports from the colonies helped feed the new urban workforce.

Meanwhile, the model was exported across the Empire. Lizzie Collingham notes in *The Hungry Empire: How Britain's Quest for Food Shaped the Modern World*: 'Ideas about land ownership, farming and the right and proper way for a society to acquire its food were central to the ideology of Britain's first Empire.' Irish pastoralism was rejected as barbaric, and while the English refused to recognise North American clearings in the forest as farms, they had to turn to those same Indigenous methods to avoid starvation.[12]

Colonisers imposed a worldview where 'land' was seen as separate from 'nature' and from the people living on it.[13] This view was entrenched by what one scholar has called 'unmatched corporate violence':[14] systems of exploitation, extraction and taxation that alienated colonised peoples from their land, livelihoods and rights.

Chattel slavery, the treatment of people as personal property, was a central tool in the making of British food systems, as the Food Matters *Sankofa Report* highlights.[15] For 150 years, three times as many Africans left their native lands on British ships for the New World as Europeans, according to the report. As Sathnam Sanghera explains in *Empireland*, slavery was 'an aspect of the British Empire'.[16] Britain may not have started the transatlantic slave trade, and the regions they drew enslaved people from weren't initially British colonies, but they were sent to British territories where they powered imperial profit.

By the time slavery was abolished in 1833, Britain had transported over 3 million Africans to the Americas,[17] part of a system that saw more than 12 million people abducted and/or forcibly removed from their homelands by European powers.[18] But abolition didn't mean freedom. Newly freed people were tied to land through debt and unfair tenancy contracts. The Empire turned to a new source of cheap labour: indentured workers, primarily from British India, but also from China and other parts of Asia. Over 2 million Indians[19] and 250,000 Chinese labourers[20] were shipped to colonies in the Caribbean, Latin America, Africa, Mauritius, Malaysia and Singapore to replace enslaved labour in the 19th century.

Control over food production and provisions often went together with colonial power. When famine hit, the results were catastrophic. During the Irish Famine in the 1840s, 1 million people died and another 2 million fled, a number that continued to grow into the 20th century.[21] Yet British food exports from Ireland continued even as its people starved.[22] In Bengal in 1943, up to 3 million people died in a famine linked to Churchill's wartime policies.[23]

Food and land became tools of conquest during the so-called Scramble for Africa, a period in the late 19th century when European powers raced to claim and divide up African territories. Drought and famine had already left many communities vulnerable to invasion, making resistance nearly impossible. As Gary Oswald notes in *Africa during the Scramble*, 'Portugal in Angola, Britain in South Africa and Italy in the Horn of Africa all launched their most serious attacks after or during existing drought-caused famines.'[24]

War and invasion only deepened the crisis, destroying crops and livelihoods and turning hunger into a weapon. With weakened resistance, colonisers were once again able to seize control more easily, often justifying their actions under the guise of bringing 'order' or 'civilisation'.[25]

Sanghera's books and commentary in recent years have done much to lift the lid on a British past that can be difficult to digest, though he stresses that the stories of food within it are often full of complexities and contradictions. The legacies of that era linger in who controls food production today, whose labour feeds us and who gets left behind.

But this era of extraction also set the stage for something else: the development of cuisines and cultural foodways. The same movements of people, plants and power that built empires also gave rise to new ingredients, dishes and cultural exchange. Created in struggle, these were often marked by joy.

As Josina Calliste explains in her piece below, the legacy of land ownership and colonial systems still shapes who gets a say in food and whose voices are ignored.

CONNECTING THE STRUGGLES FOR LAND, CLIMATE AND RACIAL JUSTICE

by Josina Calliste

Land is ultimately about power. Those who own the land decide what to do with it, who can access it and how they are allowed to behave on it. Historically, the more land you owned, the more political clout you had in Parliament, the more wealth you could accumulate and, perhaps, the more desire you had to acquire greater swathes of land at home and abroad. The accumulation of land and power led to the mass enclosures (a process whereby common land is taken into private ownership) in the UK from the mid-18th century (although informal practices of enclosure had been taking place for hundreds of years before). These brought more and more of the country out of common ownership and into private ownership, forcing people off rural land and into the towns and cities to fuel the burgeoning Industrial Revolution.

At the same time, the colonisation of land abroad, and the violence towards the Indigenous populations often involved, brought more and more of the Earth's surface under British control (alongside other European colonial powers). Extraction of resources, 'improvement' of the land to make it yield ever more goods, and the capture and use of human beings to generate bigger profits through enslavement are all deeply interwoven processes.

Racial injustice that persists today has its roots in the colonisation and enslavement of peoples across the world by the ancestors of many living in the UK today. Over time, the exploitation of the land and those forced to labour upon it, using the deeply damaging agricultural practices of the plantation, harmed ecosystems, ruined soils and continue to have devastating climate implications today. If we want to repair and transform the harm that has been done to the land, to the climate and to racialised peoples, we need to connect struggles for land, climate and racial justice.

Josina Calliste is a health professional, community organiser and co-founder of Land in our Names (LION), a Black-led collective addressing land inequalities in Britain. Extracted from her piece in the fourth issue of the New Economics Zine with her permission.

The tastes and flavours that evolved out of struggle

The complex layering of forced migrations, impoverishment, hunger, resilience and resistance have given us tastes, flavours and recipes that are deeply embedded in the complicated histories of the global majority. (The appendix includes an explanation of terms like *diaspora*, *immigrant* and *refugee* in 'The Language of Food and Identity' section.) As chef Marie Mitchell says in her cookbook *Kin: Caribbean Recipes for the Modern Kitchen*, 'The most important form of preservation practised by our forebears ... is self-preservation.'[26]

Mitchell reflects on how, during the era of plantation slavery, markets were one of the few places where enslaved people could share ideas, swap news and sustain culture. African agricultural knowledge played a crucial role in the community's survival. The ground provisions that became staples in Caribbean diets – starchy root vegetables and fruits like yam, cassava and green banana – were often grown in the small plots available to the enslaved. Boiled in salted water, served as sides or in soups, these dishes were both nutritious and resourceful.

Mitchell and other food writers have also traced the journey of ingredients across continents through the transatlantic slave trade. Across the African continent, crops and techniques introduced through trade and colonisation fused with Indigenous knowledge systems. In East Africa, Indian and Arab influences shaped dishes like pilau and samosas. In West Africa, cassava and maize – introduced via the Columbian Exchange and later expanded under colonial rule – became integral to dishes like fufu and kenkey.

Plantain and banana, for instance, arrived in the Caribbean via West Africa, having previously been introduced to the continent through Asian trade routes. Slave ships carried staples of the African diet: rice, okra, tania, black-eyed peas, cassava, yams, kidney beans and lima beans.[27] These ingredients not only fed enslaved people, but they also shaped the cuisine of the lands they were taken to.

Culinary traditions travelled too. Historian Jessica B. Harris explores how African food culture formed the bedrock of many American dishes in her book *High on the Hog*, which became a landmark Netflix series.[28] Caribbean rice and peas, for example, is said to trace its roots to waakye, a dish made by the Akan people of West Africa.

Ackee and saltfish is another example, highlighted by food writer Riaz Phillips, author of the cookbooks *East Winds* and *West Winds*. He explains, 'It's Jamaica's national dish, created to reflect its diverse history. Ackee is a fruit from West Africa, where many Jamaicans trace their ancestry, while saltfish (preserved cod) was imported from Northern Europe to overcome food preservation challenges in the Caribbean.'[29]

Phillips also points to the role of Indian indentured labour in shaping Caribbean flavours. Workers from India brought with them dishes and spices that fused with African traditions. Trinidad and Guyana in particular became hubs of Indo-Caribbean cuisine. The 2012 film *Dal Puri Diaspora* documents the journey of a lentil-stuffed flatbread from Eastern India to the Caribbean and eventually to North America, where it became known simply as roti.

Chinese indentured labourers also left their culinary mark, especially in Trinidad, Jamaica and Mauritius, where stir-fries, chow mein and fried rice became part of the everyday food landscape, blended with Caribbean flavours and ingredients. One example of this cultural layering is oxtail stew. With roots in African cuisine, oxtail was once considered an unwanted cut and was slow-cooked into rich, comforting stews by enslaved Africans. In Jamaica, the dish evolved further, often braised with soy sauce, ginger and scallions, 'a nod to the Chinese influence in the islands', as Keshia Sakarah writes in her cookbook *Caribe: A Caribbean Cookbook with History*.[30]

The culinary transformation wasn't limited to recipes. In India, the British presence reshaped food habits, often in complex and contradictory ways. The Hindi word 'chamcha', which means 'sycophant', literally translates to 'spoon', referencing Indians who adopted British table manners to curry favour during the Raj. It set the stage for a lingering Westcentric disdain of eating rice and curried food with fingers. It also altered our tastes. As Sathnam Sanghera notes, 'terrible imported British food developed social cachet in the colonies',[31] creating a taste for European products, ingredients and recipes that still lingers today.

Colonised communities adopted and adapted ingredients introduced by the British, such as chillies, potatoes and tea. Masala chai is a perfect example: a spiced tea blend that emerged from colonial trade routes, now a global comfort drink. The widely used phrase 'chai tea' is an irritating tautology for the community, but it also hints at how flavours transcend borders, identities and languages.

Meanwhile, the Empire's legacy profoundly changed British cuisine itself. Rum arrived in Britain from the Caribbean as a by-product of sugar production. First popular among sailors and soldiers, it later gained prestige in high-society punch bowls. Historian Lizzie

Collingham explores how South Asian food transformed British tables in her book *Curry: A Tale of Cooks and Conquerors*.[32] From chutneys and pickles to kedgeree and the iconic gin and tonic, many British favourites have been shaped by colonial encounters.

Collingham highlights how curry powder – a British invention designed to mimic Indian spice blends – became a staple of colonial kitchens and remains a fixture in many UK households today.[33] 'Curry' rose to become the UK's most popular cuisine. Though likely derived from the Tamil word 'kari' (which means 'sauce'), it became a generic label for a wide range of South Asian dishes, often bearing little resemblance to the originals.

The culinary transformation didn't stop at home kitchens. In post-war Britain, migrants from South Asia, the Caribbean, China and East Africa created new food cultures from limited resources, adapting traditional recipes to local ingredients and palates. These were dishes born of entrepreneurial zeal and necessity – affordable, flavourful meals that became staples on British high streets.

Indian takeaways and curry houses, many run by Bangladeshi families from the Sylhet region, served dishes that were created for British working-class palates – think chicken tikka masala or balti. Chicken tikka masala isn't available in India and the word 'balti' means 'bucket'. Chinese takeaways also created menus tailored to local tastes, often with no direct equivalent in China. These cuisines became deeply embedded in British culture, frequently being mistaken for the cuisines of origin nations or dismissed for being smelly, greasy or foreign. Yet these offerings went on to define the nation's comfort food cravings and what British food means today.

These were more than meals – they were cultural offerings, acts of resilience and enterprise. Migrants built livelihoods through food, creating comfort and familiarity for their own communities while serving up something new for others to enjoy. Their lives, experiences and social status were forged against a backdrop of racism, struggle and determination. Today, their influence continues in everything from halal fried chicken shops to roti wraps and bubble tea bars, a legacy of culinary creativity, identity and adaptation that continues to grow.

As chef and food writer Maria Bradford says, Africa is the final frontier of food.[34] A new generation of African food entrepreneurs like her are fine-tuning the narrative. From Michelin-star fine dining to Nigerian suya grills, Ghanaian street food stalls and Afro-vegan pop-ups, British-African communities are enriching our culinary experiences with bold, joyful flavours that are rooted in tradition but evolving with every bite.

One of the most vibrant examples of a community coming together to celebrate its food culture is Black Eats LDN, the UK's first and largest platform to champion, showcase and celebrate Black-owned food and drink businesses. It's become a platform for chefs, pop-ups and food businesses from African and Caribbean diasporas, showcasing everything from jollof rice to plantain waffles while creating space for cultural expression, ownership and visibility. As with the discovery of other diasporic cuisines, these developments are shaped by ingenuity, resourcefulness and deep pride, even when recognition and visibility still lag behind.

How does the past affect us today?

The ideas established during Empire didn't disappear; they evolved. It fostered a belief in exceptionalism and Eurocentrism – the idea that Europe was the architect of world history and the pinnacle of human progress and development.[35] That mindset still influences thinking and fuels discrimination today.

Over time, this worldview was extended to include the United States, Canada, Australia and Japan – countries where Europeans settled or aligned to its cultural, academic and economic systems. America rose to become the global cultural superpower in food. Fast-food chains have transformed eating habits, from supersized portions and bottomless refills to the grab-and-go culture of fast food and takeaway coffee. These icons of American culture have become shorthand for modern eating across the world.

The same belief in white superiority created hierarchies and perceptions that continue to govern how we view cuisine, medicine, our bodies and cultural traditions today. For example, Ayurveda is the oldest documented medical system in the world, developed in South Asia over thousands of years. 'Colonial authorities believed local medical practices were inferior to Western medicine and repressed them,' says Ayurvedic doctor and Oxford researcher Eeshani Bendale.[36]

Today, Ayurveda is still labelled as 'alternative medicine', often misused in the wellness world by unqualified voices. It's also dismissed because it doesn't always align with Western scientific models. Its personalised, holistic approach doesn't easily fit into standardised clinical trials, and poor regulation in some markets has further undermined its credibility, even though its practices are rooted in generations of experience.

Other cultural ingredients and traditions are routinely dismissed or demonised. Plantain, mustard oil, coconut oil and white rice have all been cast as 'unhealthy' by Eurocentric dietary models. Nutrition scientist Dr Kera Nyemb-Diop, known as The Black Nutritionist online, challenges this thinking. 'Everything we've learned about healthy eating is not just incomplete, it's culturally biased,' she says. 'We urgently need nutrition models that reflect the full diversity of human food traditions.'[37]

Even health measures used today have exclusionary roots. The body mass index (BMI) is based on 19th-century research on the 'ideal body weight' drawn from white, male participants.[38] It reflects racialised ideas of health and beauty emerging from the eugenics movement, a pseudoscience that sought to 'improve' the human race through racist, fatphobic and ableist beliefs. Researcher Sabrina Strings argues, 'BMI is a continuation of white supremacist embodiment norms, racialising fat phobia under the guise of clinical authority.'[39]

Strings traces how fatphobia, particularly in the West, grew out of colonial anxieties about the bodies of African and East Asian women – sexualised, pathologised and contrasted against white European ideals of physical build and restraint. These ideas didn't just shape medicine and public health – they spilled over into views on food cultures too.

Chinese food, for instance, has faced long-standing racism and cultural aversion in the West. TV presenter and botanist James Wong, along with food writer Mimi Aye, have written and spoken passionately about the demonisation of monosodium glutamate (MSG), a naturally occurring flavour enhancer. Their work debunks 'Chinese restaurant syndrome', a term now renamed 'MSG symptom complex', as thinly veiled xenophobia.

In fact, MSG was identified and patented by Japanese chemist Kikunae Ikeda in 1908 and became widely used across Asia and the US. By the 1950s, it was in everything from baby food to tinned soup. Suspicion of MSG also exists within parts of East and Southeast Asia, often linked to concerns about processed foods rather than racial bias. Cheryl Chow, writing in *Pit* magazine, points out that MSG was inexpensive, added umami and made plant-based food more satisfying. Yet fears about its safety in the West disproportionately targeted Chinese food, with no scientific basis.[40]

Chinese cuisine has contributed far more to global food culture than it's often credited for. Food writer and Chinese cuisine specialist Fuchsia Dunlop highlights that fake meat, often framed as a Western innovation, was invented in Buddhist monasteries in China as far back as the 10th century. And while the French are widely credited with inventing the restaurant, formal dining establishments existed in China some 600 years before their earliest European counterparts.[41]

These legacies of suspicion and supremacy also shaped our ideas of culinary excellence. French food became the gold standard for fine dining, but who decided that? As historian Annie Gray jokes in *Delicious* magazine, 'Essentially, the French did, then persuaded everyone else to agree.'[42] Behind the humour is a deeper history. As Gray explains, it was British colonial elites who helped export the idea of French food as aspirational, drawing on 18th- and 19th-century ideals. Ironically, much of what spread globally was not French food itself, but British notions of it.

Gray notes a conscious deification of French 'greats' like Marie-Antoine Carême, the first celebrity chef, who codified haute cuisine for aristocratic courts, and Auguste Escoffier, who popularised it through grand hotels and modern restaurant kitchens across Europe and America. The influence of French cuisine persists in chef training, prevails in the names of dishes we love to cook and eat, and even in the way we assess the quality and standards of restaurants that don't serve French food.

From French brigade kitchen hierarchies to the Michelin Guide, the benchmarks of excellence in food and hospitality were defined by the West. Today, rankings like the World's 50 Best Restaurants continue to favour European palates and dining experiences. Food policy expert Professor Krishnendu Ray, author of *The Ethnic Restaurateur*, argues they reflect the tastes of affluent, often white Anglophone men and disadvantage Asian, African and Indigenous cuisines.[43]

This shapes who gets ahead and gains recognition in the food world. In a fiercely competitive and commercially tough environment, the career aspirations of chefs and food writers are also affected more broadly. Ray also notes that 'there is a tendency to "ghettoise" Chinese, Mexican and Indian American chefs into cooking "their own food", whereas white chefs tend to find it easier to cross boundaries, and are seen as "artistic" when they do.'

Food writers and media personalities often feel pressure to 'whitewash' their work to make it more palatable to mainstream, white-majority audiences, which can come at the cost of cultural compromise. It's often only when ingredients or recipes are taken up by the white majority that they enter the limelight, usually stripped of their context and reframed through a Western lens. Turmeric, matcha and ashwagandha are all cases in point.

This legacy of colonial thinking persists in some parts of the Global South. In South Asia, for instance, chefs and diners alike often prioritise Western-style food, ingredients and dining formats over traditional ones. As one chef remarked, 'The biggest hangover of colonisation is the idea that West is best.'[44] Generations of imperial rule left many communities with internalised doubt about the value of their own traditions. With corporates exploring global markets, the evidence is visible in fast-food chains, shiny supermarkets and the slow erosion of local, seasonal food cultures.

But cultural reclamation is underway, often in the quiet, everyday acts that resist internalised shame. Food and travel writer Chaitali Verma captured this in a post on Threads: 'My small everyday act of cultural rebellion and reclamation (especially while travelling) is to eat rice with my hands even in the swankiest restaurants. Nobody bats an eyelid when I pick up a slice of pizza or a burger with my hands, but I do feel a lot of puzzled and often judgmental eyeballs on me the moment I scoop rice with my hands. The colonialists deemed everything in our culture as uncouth and uncivilised – our eating, dressing, talking – and we foolishly listened to them.'

Today, people like Verma and American politician Zohran Mamdani are flipping the chamcha script, using food to reconnect with pride, dignity and cultural confidence. Because reclamation isn't only about resistance. It's about sharing the food that shaped you and serving what once made you feel ashamed with pride and purpose. Food offers nourishment in every sense of the word – and when that is honoured, it becomes a powerful act of self-celebration.

That confidence is growing, and with it, a louder, bolder willingness to call things out. From social media threads to newspaper headlines, people are no longer afraid to challenge cultural clangers and highlight food injustice when they see it. These moments may spark backlash, but they also build awareness and push the conversation about who holds the power and why forward.

But power doesn't just influence which cuisines, cultures and communities are celebrated – it also shapes how our food is grown, traded and consumed around the world.

CHANGING PERCEPTIONS OF EAST AND SOUTHEAST ASIAN EATS

by Anna Chan

Despite its continuing popularity in UK, there are still deeply ingrained perceptions that East Asian and Southeast Asian food should primarily be characterised as inexpensive, quick-service options, often relegated to all-you-can-eat buffet establishments or characterised as a 'cheap' takeaway despite its vast diversity and options available.

East Asian and Southeast Asian food also faces derogatory characterisations, labelled as strange, weird, smelly or unsanitary (aka 'dirty', or worse). These harmful stereotypes often stem from cultural ignorance or sometimes just plain racism, with myths around eating habits, food preparation or even MSG (no, it's not bad for you) rooted in discriminatory attitudes that go unchallenged. This has led to real harm, not just to businesses but by exasperating the target communities across the globe, which was only made worse during the Covid-19 pandemic.

However, positive developments have been emerging through several different initiatives to combat this. The growing #ESEAEats movement that started on social media during the pandemic aims to challenge these misconceptions and to reclaim cultural pride and heritage.

As perceptions change and exposure on social media leads people to seek out a wider variety of cultural cuisines, it's important that this rise in visibility and virality is accompanied by a need to challenge stereotypes.

Anna Chan is the founder and director of Asian Leadership Collective.

How does colonisation affect the production of our food today?

If colonisation is the domination of a small group over a larger community, then the food world is still living through a form of neo-colonialism. Western ideals and corporate agendas dominate global food systems, shaping everything from farming to flavour trends.

As we have established, some of the least well-off and most exploited people in the world are the ones who produce our food. Many live in poverty in their home countries. Others leave their ancestral homes behind to work in wealthier nations – some finding jobs, others setting up on their own and some facing insecure or exploitative conditions. Yet they are behind some of our most popular treats, meals and drinks.

Take coffee. Originally a popular drink in the Islamic world in the 14th and 15th centuries, it was quickly identified by European empires as a valuable commodity. Its rapid expansion was fuelled by enslaved labour on colonial plantations. Today, it's the second most consumed beverage after water,[45] with nearly 2 billion cups drunk every day,[46] mostly in wealthy countries.

According to the Fairtrade Foundation, the global coffee market is worth over $100 billion, but more than 80% of the sales are controlled by just three multinational corporations. Meanwhile, 85% of the world's coffee is produced in the Global South in countries like Brazil, Vietnam, Colombia, Indonesia and Honduras. Over 80% of coffee farmers are smallholders, and at least 5.5 million live below the international poverty line.[47] They face unstable prices, climate pressures and limited investment.

The market remains built on an extractive model that prioritises low costs over sustainability and fairness. But there's growing pressure on the industry to support producers and end the era of cheap coffee.[48] While that may not sound like good news for coffee lovers used to cheap brews, it's a vital step towards valuing coffee properly.

A similar story plays out with cocoa. Europe consumes around half of the global supply, yet three-quarters of the world's cocoa is grown in West Africa. Cocoa production is a major driver of deforestation and chemical-reliant monocultures, with deep human and environmental costs.

While cocoa and coffee are long-established favourites, the same extractive patterns now affect ingredients that have been 'newly discovered' by the West. Global demand surges when Western wellness markets identify a food as the next 'superfood', such as quinoa, teff, avocado or matcha. Local communities may benefit in the short term, but this can also bring risks ranging from boom-and-bust cycles to pressure on land and biodiversity.

The UN named 2013 the 'International Year of Quinoa', sparking global interest. Prices and production surged, skewing demand towards the consumer preference for a single white variety and sidelining over 6,000 varieties. A later study found modest benefits for local producers and little of the damage that had initially been feared, but also no long-term transformation in the livelihoods of the producers.[49]

A similar pattern has emerged with Ethiopia's teff, a highly nutritious grain that has been cultivated for millennia. Despite its global potential, teff is classified as a neglected and underutilised species (NUS), which means it plays a vital role in local diets and livelihoods but remains largely absent from global markets.[50] But as interest grows, so do the risks: monoculture, loss of crop diversity and growing external control over how these foods are grown, sold and profited from.

As demand rises globally for certain ingredients, some traditional community foods become too expensive for local people to enjoy themselves. Oxtail, once considered a humble cut born out of necessity and resourcefulness in Afro-Caribbean cooking, is now a luxury item. Its rising cost means that it's less accessible to some people in the communities that created this cornerstone dish through resilience and ingenuity. This shift reflects a broader pattern where cultural heritage is commercialised without benefiting the people who own it.

At the heart of this is the erasure of Indigenous food knowledge and sovereignty. Small-scale producers and Indigenous communities often know the land best. They've farmed it sustainably for generations. Yet their approaches are still dismissed or rebranded as 'innovative' when taken up by others. As philosopher Julian Baggini has argued, a truly sustainable food future must embrace plurality – what works in one region or culture may not work in another.[51]

Navaratnam (Theeb) Partheeban's Nuffield Scholar report highlights how Indigenous methods are quietly shaping the future of farming, even when they go unrecognised.[52] He also points out how key figures who contributed to global food systems are often written out of history, like the Black cowboys who transformed cattle culture in the American West or Edmond Albius, the boy born into slavery on Réunion Island who discovered how to hand-pollinate vanilla, thereby revolutionising the vanilla industry. Their stories are rarely told, yet their legacies are everywhere.

The generational knowledge of small-scale producers and Indigenous communities is going to be crucial to delivering food sovereignty and better outcomes for the environment. However, many of them remain excluded from policymaking. 'The food systems of the world's 476 million Indigenous Peoples are often branded as "backward" or unproductive,' write Krystyna Swiderska and Philippa Ryan. 'But evidence shows they are highly productive, sustainable and equitable.'[53]

There's a new risk called 'green grabbing', where land is taken from Indigenous people for climate and conservation projects. The European Commission warns this could become the biggest land grab in history. Campaigners like Indian scholar Vandana Shiva are championing food sovereignty to return control to those who work the land and protecting their rights and cultures.

This also means rethinking land justice in wealthier countries. Many marginalised communities continue to be disconnected from land. Farming is expensive, access to land and capital is limited, and people from marginalised and minoritised communities are excluded from the industries that feed us. As Theeb notes in his report, 'Many barriers are systemic and were created in the past but are still very relevant and active today.' Tackling them means going beyond gestures to invest real time, money and effort into equity and inclusion. It means platforming diverse voices, acknowledging historical injustices and building support systems that allow everyone to thrive.

Food sovereignty, here and elsewhere, isn't just about farming. It's about rebalancing power and creating a food system that works for everyone. Just as producers fight for their fair share, so do communities whose food cultures have long been commercialised without recognition or equity.

In truth, many of these inherited power imbalances feel increasingly out of touch with the way the world works today. We live in multicultural societies shaped by migration, exchange and collaboration – and the food we eat reflects that beautifully. So why do the structures and systems that govern it remain so outdated? That's where the conversation about decolonising food truly begins.

How can we decolonise food and drive diversity?

As systemic inequalities are being called out across industries, so are the injustices baked into our global food conversations. As Dr Anna Sulan Masing says, 'Decolonising is about understanding power – the systems, structures and imbalances that shape our world, past and present. To decolonise the plate is to look at historical systems and see how they play out on your plate *right now*. Who holds power in what we eat? Who grows it, cooks it, profits from it?'[54]

The colonisation of our plates and meals has been going on for centuries. Annie Gray says, 'Go far enough back, and you see that British food itself (and French) is part of a process of colonisation, since it is all ultimately Roman, while Spanish and Italian food is (or was) heavily influenced by Middle Eastern ideals as the Islamic Caliphate ruled Spain and bits of Italy until the medieval period.'[55] While there is no denying this, the current debate is about ongoing power imbalances and injustice. There's growing scrutiny of how we treat producers, protect Indigenous knowledge and fairly represent food cultures from racially and ethnically diverse communities, especially when those cultures are commercialised for profit.

The pushback started in earnest in the UK in 2018, with food writers and academics like Masing and Zoe Adjonyoh commenting on embedded colonial attitudes. Jamie Oliver's 'jerk rice' and Marks & Spencer's 'Bengali turmeric curry kit' hit the headlines in the UK when both met with backlash from the communities they claimed to represent. Jerk is a traditional Jamaican barbecue method, and rice can't be jerked. Meanwhile, there's no such thing as a Bengali turmeric curry.

These weren't isolated complaints – they reflected deeper frustrations from people from diasporic and mixed-heritage communities whose food and identity are often misunderstood or misrepresented. And the pushback is no longer coming just from campaigners or academics. People from racialised and minoritised backgrounds are speaking out and demanding accountability too.

These people often find themselves caught in a contradiction. Their food stories are marketable – full of flavour, history and cultural cachet – but their day-to-day realities are harder. In many parts of the world, nationalism and prejudice are rising. Professor Neil Chakraborti, a hate crime researcher at the University of Leicester, notes that political events and economic events have led to a misguided sense of nationalism.[56] The mainstreaming and normalising of prejudice have legitimised and fuelled hatred against those who are deemed different.

The food and drink world is not immune to racism. Recent research highlights how exclusion and hostility still persist in rural areas.[57] Every culture jokes about another one's food, but for minority and migrant communities this can tip into discrimination, like who's seen as 'a good fit', who's allowed opportunities and through which channels. It also plays out through microaggressions, those everyday slights and assumptions – like purposely mispronouncing someone's name, questioning their credentials or exoticising their food – that quietly signal who belongs and who doesn't.

Many sectors of the food industry, from hospitality to media and publishing, remain white-led and Eurocentric in their make-up and outlook. This lack of diversity creates a feedback loop that limits leadership opportunities, narrows cultural understanding and reinforces stereotypes. Without a wide range of voices in the room, assumptions go unchallenged. Complex food cultures get flattened into clichés and tropes like granny's kitchen, mummy's recipes and the 15-minute cookbook formats.

Attempts to cherry pick and 'mainstream' popular aspects of global cuisines, while often well-meaning, can end up reducing them to caricature. Think of the ubiquitous 'Asian salad dressing', a catch-all blend that claims to capture the food traditions of nearly 50 nations. Flip the idea and imagine a 'European salad dressing', and its absurdity becomes obvious.

This kind of cultural shorthand flourishes when teams lack people with deep experience – everyday cultural knowledge that comes from understanding a community – or if those people are unable to speak up. Without those perspectives, nuance is lost and oversimplification becomes the norm.

But changing that isn't easy. Careers in food, media and hospitality often rely on unpaid internships, informal networks and financial safety nets – luxuries not available to many from marginalised or immigrant backgrounds. For generations, more 'stable' careers in law, medicine or engineering have also been seen as more lucrative, stable and prestigious career routes by migrant communities with an eye on social mobility.

Where diversity does exist, it often thins out at the top. Leadership roles remain elusive. Hiring bias, 'cultural fit' and assumptions around merit can all hold people back. As Pooja Sachdev, co-author of *Rewire: A Radical Approach to Tackling Diversity and Difference*, puts it, 'The idea of meritocracy overlooks systemic barriers and inequities and fails to acknowledge disparities in starting points. It's a myth that can do more harm than good.'[58]

The problem starts at the source: in farming, these barriers are even steeper. Agriculture is expensive to enter and poorly paid, with low prestige and limited support, particularly for people from racially diverse communities, many of whom carry inherited trauma from histories of land-based exploitation. In the UK, farming is the least ethnically diverse profession, even though it's central to the food that multicultural communities enjoy.[59]

An absence of leaders from diverse backgrounds also means a lack of representation across organisations and industries. This makes it harder for those who do make it in to feel a true sense of belonging. And there are hurdles to overcome even before that. Hiring decisions are often tainted with biases like 'similarity bias' (favouring those 'like us' or who we feel will 'fit in'), again perpetuating exclusion for anyone from a 'different' background.

In hospitality, representation is more visible at junior levels. But when it comes to awards, leadership and investment, the numbers drop. Only four Black chefs have received Michelin stars in the UK. In 2024, Adejoké Bakare became the first Black woman to win one, at her London restaurant, Chishuru. Meanwhile, surveys by Be Inclusive Hospitality show ongoing racism, microaggressions and lack of management support across the sector.[60]

Publishing, television and retail face their own issues. Stories and recipes from African, Caribbean, East and Southeast Asian and South Asian communities are often filtered through white tastemakers or reduced to tokenistic moments of representation. As chef Maria Bradford concludes, 'The barriers that restrict social mobility have restricted the growth of the Afro-Caribbean food scene. But also, publishers have not always understood how to approach African cooking.'[61]

Supermarkets reflect this imbalance. Only 2% of over 7,400 brands on UK shelves are Black-owned, and only three are available nationally in supermarkets, according to start-up incubator Psalt.[62] Cultural ingredients, if available, are often grouped together in a 'world food' aisle – helpful to navigate, perhaps, but it's a loaded label that reinforces a sense of otherness. It's worth considering whether products might be better integrated by their category, e.g. flour, sauces, tins.

Even in diverse societies, power is unevenly distributed, and the structures that shape recognition, investment and influence are out of sync with the society, the community and the way we live and eat today.

Which brings us to what happens when food is adopted without credit, context or care. That's where the debate over cultural appropriation begins.

OTHER BARRIERS THAT PEOPLE FACE IN THE FOOD WORLD

While race and cultural identity are central to this chapter, they aren't the only barriers at play. Here are just a few more to acknowledge and address within the context of what we eat and drink.

Class and socio-economic background: Unpaid internships, low salaries and fees and lack of access to capital lock many people out, especially those without access to 'The Bank of Mum and Dad' or additional income. The food world often accidentally rewards those with connections, flexibility and an additional source of income.

Gender and sexism
- **In hospitality:** Women make up a significant chunk of the workforce, from kitchens to front of house, yet top jobs and recognition still go to men. As the open letter and comments from female chefs in response to Jason Atherton's throwaway comment about sexism showed, kitchens and restaurants can still be macho spaces that aren't welcoming to women.[63]
- **In food media and writing:** Food media skews female in many visible roles like writers, stylists, editors and content creators. These roles are often linked to domesticity and involve part-time, unstable, unpaid or lower-paid work that is more likely to be undertaken by primary caregivers rather than traditional breadwinners.

Ageism: The industry often idolises fresh, new and trendy talent who are digital and social natives, marginalising older experts and professionals. Fresh talent can also be exploited, especially with underpaid or unstable opportunities, with the promise of career advancement.

Personality and visibility: Today's food world is driven by branding, networking and visibility, especially on social media. But not everyone wants, or is able, to live their life online. Introverts and those who prefer to let their work speak for itself can be overlooked in favour of louder, more self-promoting voices. The pressure to be 'always on' can also exclude those who are anxious, time poor or simply have a different style of communication.

Disability and neurodivergence: From inaccessible kitchens to inflexible work cultures, food spaces often overlook disabled people, both as workers and as eaters.

Sexuality and identity: LGBTQ+ workers still face discrimination in many areas of the industry. Hospitality can be especially tough in kitchen cultures where expressing identity isn't safe or embraced.

What is cultural appropriation?

Cultural appropriation isn't a separate issue to decolonising the plate – it's part of the same power dynamic, says Sulan Masing.[64] It's one of the most hotly debated – and most misunderstood – topics in food. It's often confused with cultural exchange and inspiration. In some quarters, people think it means a blanket ban on anyone working with the ingredients and recipes of a culture that's not their own. So when we talk about cultural appropriation, what are we really talking about?

At its core, cultural appropriation in food is when elements of a culture are borrowed, used or commercialised by someone outside that culture without recognition, deep understanding or benefit to the original community. The problem comes when dominant cultures profit from, dilute or misrepresent historically marginalised ones, stripping away history and heritage. The key word is in the name. Appropriation implies taking something that isn't yours, and it has negative connotations. It implies stealing, snatching, looting and plundering.

The issue isn't about who's 'allowed' to cook what. There's no intellectual property on flavour, and creativity has always driven cuisine forward. Borderless cooking – using global ingredients in surprising ways – can be a brilliant way to innovate, foster connection and reduce waste. But when you're borrowing from a culture, especially one that's been historically exploited, mocked or misrepresented, sensitivity matters.

As a concept, cultural appropriation is easy to mischaracterise and misunderstand. It's often also confused with a row about origin or authenticity. But 'authentic' is tricky to pin down. Are we talking about the way something was cooked 200 years ago? The way it's made in one region? One household? In reality, food is constantly evolving, shaped by migration, trade, climate, creativity and lived experience. What's authentic for one person may feel unfamiliar to another. That's why authenticity can't be policed.

It's also why people from within a culture often evolve their own dishes in ways that might seem unrecognisable to outsiders – and that's more acceptable. When a dish is part of your upbringing, your rituals, your language and your memories, you're not borrowing it – you're in a relationship with it.

That connection gives people more room to experiment, reinterpret and reimagine. It's the difference between using an easily available ingredient to recreate your grandmother's recipe and lifting someone else's tradition without credit or care. Creativity from within a culture comes from lived experience. It carries a different weight and meaning than profiteering from someone else's food from the outside.

That's why when cultural food is commercialised, especially by people outside that culture, it should be done thoughtfully, respectfully and with integrity. That's the key difference between cultural appropriation and appreciation. The checklist below unpacks this further.

It's the same tension captured in that brilliant scene from the TV show *Mo* on Netflix, where the lead character, Palestinian comedian Mo Najjar, reacts to 'chocolate hummus' with mock outrage. It's sharp, it's funny and it hits a nerve because for many people, when something that may seem as simple as a dip is dismissed, distorted or rebranded without care, it's not just a recipe that's lost – it's respect. When someone says, 'What's the big deal about chocolate hummus?', a lot more than chickpeas and cocoa are at stake. It's about culture, heritage and the right to be seen and valued.

HOW TO SPOT THE DIFFERENCE BETWEEN APPROPRIATION AND APPRECIATION

It's not always easy to draw the line, but there are important distinctions. Here's a quick guide.

Cultural appreciation:
- Is curious and humble, not careless and arrogant
- Is built on sharing, not extraction
- Involves deep research, respect and relationship with the origin community or culture
- Credits, uplifts and benefits the original community
- Leads to platforms, partnerships and pay.

Cultural appropriation:
- Takes without acknowledgement of source or context
- Profits without benefit to the original culture
- Flattens, distorts, confuses and reduces meaning or tradition
- Reinforces existing power imbalances
- Often comes from a place of ignorance or shallow engagement.

How to avoid cultural appropriation

So how can we navigate global food cultures without crossing the line into appropriation? There are four key areas to remember: mindset, respect, representation and response.

Mindset

In this context, mindset means the bias, assumptions and filters we use. Looking for commonalities and seeking familiarity is a basic human instinct – it helps us makes sense of the world, find method in the madness and identify and target an audience. We all carry bias, but when it's left unchecked, it can shape the way we engage with food and culture in ways that reinforce stereotypes or flatten diversity.

Some common biases that show up in food are:

* **Affinity bias:** Favouring people who share our background, interests or experiences, often without realising it.
* **Perception bias:** Making assumptions about individuals based on stereotypes or generalisations about the group they belong to.
* **Groupthink:** Aligning with the majority view to maintain harmony or avoid conflict, even when you privately disagree.

These biases are shaped by where and how we're raised, what we're taught and who's around us. In food, they can sneak into everything from how we label dishes to what we think others will 'like'.

Bias shows up in how we interpret flavour. In the movie *When Harry Met Sally*, Harry's famous playful line, 'Waiter, there is too much pepper on my paprikash', illustrates how quickly we judge food through our own lens. What's authentic, delicious or comforting to one person can seem overpowering, strange or even 'wrong' to another.

This cuts both ways. Fuchsia Dunlop once noted how leading Chinese chefs reacted to fine dining in America with bemusement: 'a visceral dislike of rawness' and 'crusty sourdough bread uncomfortably tough and chewy'.[65] In West African cuisine, oil floating on top of a dish is a mark of abundance and generosity, not poor technique. As food writer Freda Muyambo of *My Burnt Orange* says, 'When we see the oil rise to the top, we know we have done well. Even when it's not used in cooking, oil is added on top.'[66] In South Asian kitchens, it signals a dish that's been properly 'bhunao-ed', i.e. slow-cooked until the spices are fully integrated.

Understanding these cultural cues requires curiosity and humility. Not every method, label or shortcut transfers neatly between cuisines, and trying to squeeze them into formats that fit a dominant palate can strip food of its story and soul. The food and drink world thrives on reinvention and creativity, but with that comes responsibility.

When flavours and formats are adjusted to suit perceived mainstream preferences – which, in the Global North, usually means a white, Western audience – it can lead to distortion and misrepresentation, such as:

* Curry pastes sold where the original cuisine never used curry paste.
* 'Mexican pasta' that no Mexican would recognise.
* Dishes stripped of key ingredients or context but still carrying the original name.

There's a difference between *inspired by* and *marketed as*. And that distinction matters.

Where tastes of the global majority are being commercialised, you don't have the automatic right to tweak what others hold dear. That's part of unlearning cultural superiority and arrogance. Changing this approach is what people mean when they say 'decolonise your plate'. Here's how to spot and avert it:

* **Ask yourself:** Would I be okay if someone did this to *my* food or culture? What if a cheat's version of strawberries and cream was made with pears and mascarpone?
* **Flip it:** 'Asian salad dressing' is everywhere. But would 'European salad dressing' make any sense?
* **Put it in context:** If you wouldn't call a dish 'coq au vin' if it didn't feature red wine and was a stir-fry, should you call something 'butter chicken' if there's no butter or creamy tomato sauce?

The context and heritage of each individual recipe, ingredient, technique and even the setting matters. Europe alone has 44 countries and countless regional food traditions. The same applies to Asia, Africa, the Caribbean and beyond. Not all methods translate. Pasta isn't rinsed like noodles. A burnt crust of rice is prized in Persian tahdig but might be judged a mistake elsewhere. A rustic wooden chair might say Manhattan chic to some or village shabby to others. These differences are what make culture and heritage unique.

Respect and representation

Once we start to challenge our biases, the next step is respecting the roots of what we're working with – and representing them with care. It begins with how food and drink products are created and commercialised. There are no shortcuts here. Due diligence, research and cultural context matter. A little knowledge can be a dangerous thing, particularly in a world where taste and cuisine hierarchies still dominate.

While it's widely accepted that it takes years to master the techniques of French cuisine, a holiday in Kerala or Korea is used as shorthand for expertise in Indian or 'Asian' cooking. Cuisines from South Asia, East and Southeast Asia, Africa and Latin America are routinely treated with less rigour, depth and respect than their European counterparts. As Professor Krishnendu Ray notes, the global prestige of a cuisine is often tied to a country's economic and military power, and the wealth of its diaspora.[67] The more powerful the nation, the higher its dishes are priced and the more they are respected.

If extensive travel or formal training isn't possible, consulting a range of trusted voices becomes essential. Professor Priya Deshingkar says, 'While food evolves over time and space, passing off sloppily hybridised or wrongly labelled food is deeply insulting to cooks and chefs who have a contextualised understanding of their cuisine but are rarely consulted by the food industry.'[68]

When people are consulted, they should be paid and credited accordingly. Expecting free or cheap labour that doesn't align with the resulting commercial benefit is another form of exploitation. This hits particularly hard for people from communities that have not only long been exploited but continue to face barriers to progress.

This is also where the idea of the 'white saviour' can creep in – when someone from a dominant background positions themselves as a rescuer, liberator or spokesperson for another culture. However well-intentioned, it reinforces unequal power dynamics and centres the storyteller, not the story. The goal isn't to 'give a voice' to marginalised communities – it's to step back, listen and help amplify voices that already exist.

It's worth noting that many food writers and restaurateurs do engage deeply and respectfully with food cultures not their own while showcasing creativity. To name just a few:

* Thomasina Miers has built the Wahaca restaurant group on years of passion for Mexican food.
* Tim Anderson shares Japanese cooking with care and humour.
* Rachel Roddy writes with warmth about Italian food from her home in Rome.
* Felicity Cloake's *How to cook the perfect...* column in the *Guardian* consistently credits cultural sources and experts before offering her own take.
* Samyukta Nair works with expert chefs to create luxurious and contemporary offerings beyond her Indian roots.

But representation doesn't end with recipes. How dishes are presented – on menus, product labels, social media and packaging – shapes perceptions. There are plenty of watchouts, and respect cuts both ways. These aren't rules for the Global North alone – they apply to everyone. If we want our food and cultures to be honoured and understood, we have to extend the same care to others. Here are five key areas to watch for.

1. Language matters
* **Avoid vague, catch-all origins.** Dishes labelled simply 'Asian' or 'Mexican' often rely on a splash of soy or a dash of chipotle, ignoring the depth and diversity of entire culinary traditions. Think 'Asian salad' (but with no relation to any country) or a 'Mexican wrap' that's Tex-Mex at best.
* **Ditch Western frames.** Calling khichdi 'Indian risotto' or pide 'Turkish pizza' forces non-European dishes to fit European expectations. If you're introducing something unfamiliar, explain it, don't rename it.
* **Understand the words you're using.** This is especially important when the words aren't in English. For example, katsu means cutlet, not curry. Satay means stick, not peanut sauce.

* **Avoid tautologies.** 'Naan bread', 'lentil dal' and 'chai tea' all repeat themselves. It's like saying 'bread bread' or 'tea tea'. You wouldn't say things like 'baguette bread' or 'spaghetti pasta', for instance.

2. Respect culinary context

* **Use ingredients with understanding.** Ingredients are rich with heritage and specific in their usage. Turmeric, for instance, is a spice, not a seasoning, and kecap manis, an Indonesian sweet soy sauce, gives dishes a particular colour and flavour.
* **Don't omit the key element of a recipe.** If the original dish features key spices, techniques or ingredients, then leaving them out makes that dish unrecognisable. For instance, the beef in a Thai panang curry is always thinly sliced.
* **Know a dish's place and meaning.** Dhansak is a Parsi dish traditionally eaten after funerals. While it can be served at other settings, its cultural context shouldn't be overlooked or misrepresented.
* **Consider cultural geography.** Food, community and setting interact. A pork bagel pop-up in a Jewish neighbourhood may not go down well. No halal options on the menu in a multicultural location equals exclusion.
* **Avoid 'fixing' or 'improving' traditional dishes.** Calling cultural food 'healthy' or 'elevated' can imply that the original is somehow inferior, e.g. Indian and Chinese takeaways 'rediscovered' as healthy fakeaways or adding vegetables to 'elevate' hummus, which ignores the fact that it's already part of a balanced meal when traditionally served with crudités, bread and mezze.

3. Get the naming and framing right

* **Provenance matters.** Is it Korean? Korean-style? Korean-inspired? Language matters. A dish is only Korean if it's replicated in its traditional guise and is something the community would recognise. It's Korean-style if it bears close

resemblance and Korean-inspired if it moves further away from the original.
* **Don't use reductive shortcuts.** If it's your 'cheat's' version or twist on a dish, explain how and why. A 'quick laksa' made with red curry paste and coconut milk may be tasty, but would a Malaysian cook see it as laksa?
* **Avoid vague praise or comparisons.** If a Vietnamese pho is described as 'like a spicy ramen' or injera is called 'Ethiopian naan' as shorthand, you haven't taken the time to educate your audience and improve their understanding. Respect dishes on their own terms and take the trouble to explain what they are.

4. Presentation isn't just visual
* **No upright chopsticks in rice!** In many East Asian cultures, this mimics funeral offerings and is considered disrespectful. Put chopsticks beside the bowl or on a rest.
* **Avoid mismatched cultural symbols.** Using chopsticks for a Thai green curry or dressing a sushi set with cherry blossoms and dragons can confuse, reduce and flatten cultural expression.
* **Be careful with humour.** The *Great British Bake Off* sombrero-and-poncho moment in 2022, where presenters joked about Mexico's existence, is a case study in why stereotypes backfire.
* **Don't exoticise or romanticise.** Words like 'exotic', 'niche' or 'weird but good' turn lived food cultures into spectacle. They 'other' people and their traditions.

5. Respect people, not just dishes
* **Avoid tokenising names and symbols.** Patterns and motifs, like dragon fonts or Sanskrit lettering used for branding, can feel shallow or appropriative without real context.
* **Respect difficult histories.** Jerk, gumbo and soul food are all dishes born out of survival and resistance. They're not trends.
* **Don't use people as props.** Using 'locals' as background characters or set dressing for food shoots often reduces real lives to aesthetic. Who is being seen? And who is being used?

* **Celebrate your sources and inspiration.** If borrowing from or inspired by someone or a community, name check, platform or, better still, enable them to benefit commercially

These issues come with their own vocabulary, and a quick guide to some commonly used terms is included in 'The Language of Food and Identity' section in the appendix.

Response

Food is emotional, bias-driven and deeply personal, so it's inevitable that we'll all get it wrong with culture and identity at some point. Mistakes often happen because of ignorance and a lack of understanding rather than an intention to offend, but how we respond to those mistakes matters just as much as the reason behind them being made.

One of the most effective ways to reduce the risk of cultural insensitivity is to build diverse teams and to actively listen to different perspectives, especially those from the communities whose food and culture is being represented. But people from racially and ethnically diverse backgrounds need to feel safe enough to speak up and empowered to be heard.

This is easier said than done. Many people from immigrant communities have been raised to keep their heads down and to assimilate, not to challenge the system. The barriers to entry, the pressure to succeed in some areas and a hostile political climate can make it feel risky to call out problems, especially in industries where you might be the only person of colour in the room or in an environment where you're grateful for the work and opportunities. That's why creating space for honest conversations, feedback and collaboration is vital.

Of course, no one gets it right all the time. We're only human, after all. But when mistakes do happen, the best response is simple:

* **Acknowledge it.** A sincere, unreserved apology goes a long way. Silence can be misinterpreted for lack of caring or engagement.

* **Listen before speaking.** Take time to understand what went wrong and why people are upset.
* **Don't respond in anger.** Defensive reactions and online bitebacks rarely help. Take a moment. Step away from social media if needed and come back when you've had time to reflect.
* **Make it right.** Whether it's changing a product name, updating a menu, crediting contributors or committing to long-term change, show you're improving with action. Waitrose, for instance, changed the racial slur on its lime leaves labels and lobbied the British Retail Consortium to make this industry standard.
* **Learn and grow.** Errors provide fertile ground to improve knowledge, understanding and be better.

As writer and activist Audre Lorde said in her book *Sister Outsider*, 'It is not our differences that divide us. It is our inability to recognise, accept, and celebrate those differences.'[69] We all have blind spots. What matters is whether we're willing to acknowledge them and build something better together.

We've looked at the people behind the plate – the cooks, growers, cultures and communities who shape our food. But food doesn't just carry history and leave an imprint on us. It leaves footprints on the ground we walk on and a mark on the world we live on. So what about the planet that feeds us? What's the cost of what we eat – and who's paying for it now?

The big takeaways

1. **Food is more than what we put in our mouth:** Every dish holds memory, tradition and identity, but also reflects who has held power over ingredients, trade and narratives.
2. **Colonial legacies linger:** Empire reshaped diets and food systems worldwide. Those structures didn't vanish; they evolved into today's hierarchies, trade and agriculture models and cultural biases.
3. **Cuisines travelled with people:** Forced and voluntary migrations created new ingredients, dishes and culinary traditions.
4. **Migration reshapes British plates:** South Asian, Caribbean, Chinese and African diasporas created high street staples and comfort foods, often while facing prejudice. Their influence continues to shape what British food means today.
5. **Outdated hierarchies endure:** Eurocentric ideas still set the benchmarks for cuisine, medicine and body image, while outdated and discriminatory myths – from the fear of MSG to BMI measures – continue to shape perceptions.
6. **Bias influences views on nutrition:** Western dietary models often dismiss traditional wisdom and cultural ingredients and staples like rice, plantain and coconut oil, taking them out of context.
7. **Representation is unequal:** Food industries from hospitality to publishing remain overwhelmingly white-led, which influences who gets platformed, how cuisines are described and which stories are told.
8. **Decolonising the plate is about power:** It means asking who grows, cooks and profits from food today and whether historical injustices are being repeated.
9. **Appreciation isn't appropriation:** Borrowing becomes harmful when credit, context and benefit are stripped away from marginalised communities.
10. **Sensitivity matters:** Mindset, respect, representation and response are key to celebrating global food cultures without reinforcing old stereotypes or inequalities.

PLANET

Environment, climate, nature

'Can I get a drink of water please?'

'Negative. The last drop was drunk in the year 2040. Tell us, what was water like?'

'We used to have a lot of it. Probably didn't look after it as well as we could have. We used to have water fights ... we'd drink it all the time ... we'd turn the tap on and just wait for it to be the perfect temperature. And then we'd take a clean glass and for some reason we'd rinse it out again.'

'But you had no idea you were destroying the planet?'

'No, we knew...'

Comedian Simon Brodkin in his record-breaking TikTok climate change act, 'What life is like in the year 2284'

The world we live *on* is just as important as the world we live *in*. And future generations might not see the funny side of how we ate and drank today.

As the global population grew, so did the challenge of feeding everyone. We intensified farming, scaled production and created vast food systems to keep hunger at bay. In many ways, it worked. But that progress also came at a cost and now we're dealing with the consequences. Around the world, people are asking how we can reverse the damage and rediscover what our ancestors knew: that nourishing people and protecting the planet must go hand in hand.

How does the planet stay in balance?

For millennia, the Earth has managed to support us and keep the environment within liveable limits, all while quietly regulating itself. Scientists describe this as Earth's 'source and sink' function. The planet has ecosystems that provide resources as 'sources' and absorb waste as 'sinks', helping to keep the system in balance.

Carbon is a perfect example. It flows constantly between the atmosphere, land, oceans and living organisms. It's released into the air through natural processes like volcanoes erupting, wildfires burning, plants decaying and animals burping. At the same time, trees, soil and oceans soak it up. Mangroves, seagrass and kelp forests – often called 'blue carbon' habitats – can store 10 times more carbon than rainforests, locking it away for centuries.[1]

The same balancing act happens with nutrients like nitrogen, phosphorus and potassium (NPK), the essential trio that supports healthy plant life and fertile soil. Nitrogen in the air is converted into a usable form by microbes in the soil. Some plants, like peas, beans and lentils, help the process by fixing nitrogen into the soil as they grow. Organic waste like chicken manure or fish meal returns phosphorus and potassium to the ground.

The problem isn't just how these cycles work – it's that we're disrupting them. We're releasing greenhouse gases like carbon dioxide and methane far faster than the Earth can absorb them, while also overloading soils and waterways with synthetic nitrogen and phosphorus from fertilizers. Carbon dioxide levels are at the highest level in recorded history and rising fast, with worrying implications.[2] Fossil fuels are the main source of carbon dioxide emissions, yet we keep burning more each year.[3]

Methane, a far more potent heat-trapper than carbon, is also surging. Today, around 60% of methane emissions come from human activity.[4] Agriculture is a major source. Cows and sheep alone account for 12–20% of greenhouse gas emissions, through their burps and the forests cleared to feed them.[5] Waterlogged rice paddies emit nearly 8% of human-caused methane.[6]

At sea, bottom trawling, where heavy nets scrape the seabed, not only wrecks ecosystems but also releases carbon long buried in sediments – by one estimate, as much carbon as 88 million cars each year. Over the past 50 years, more than half of the world's underwater kelp and seaweed forests have disappeared, lost to warming seas and habitat destruction.[7]

By overwhelming nature's operating system, we've weakened the planet's ability to manage itself. Which begs the question: how much pressure can Earth really take, and how close are we to the edge?

A planet under pressure

For nearly 12,000 years, since the end of the last Ice Age, we've lived in a period of relative calm and stability known as the Holocene. The climate was stable and ecosystems thrived, allowing human civilisation to grow and flourish. But since the dawn of the Industrial Revolution in the late 1700s, the human impact on the planet has intensified dramatically. This period, which accelerated after the Second World War, is often referred to as the Anthropocene: an age where our activity is pushing Earth to its limits.

In 2009, a group of scientists from the Stockholm Resilience Centre asked a vital question: how much is too much? They developed the concept of planetary boundaries: nine key limits to define a safe operating space. These boundaries measure the stability and resilience of the Earth, helping us to understand where we're pushing too far and beyond the tipping points.

The nine boundaries are:

* **Climate change:** Rising global temperatures and extreme weather.
* **Novel entities:** Synthetic chemicals, plastics and genetically modified materials that didn't previously exist in nature.
* **Biogeochemical flows:** Overloading nutrients like nitrogen and phosphorus, which affects soil and water.
* **Freshwater use:** Unsustainable use of rivers, lakes and soil moisture.
* **Land-system change:** Clearing forests, draining wetlands and turning wild land into farms or cities.
* **Biosphere integrity:** The health and diversity of living organisms and ecosystems.
* **Ocean acidification:** The drop in ocean pH caused by excess CO_2 absorption.
* **Stratospheric ozone depletion:** The thinning of the ozone layer, which protects us from harmful UV radiation.
* **Atmospheric aerosol loading:** Fine particles in the air that affect weather, climate and health.

In 2023, the Stockholm team assessed all nine boundaries for the first time. The results were stark: six have already been crossed, including climate change, biodiversity loss and land use. A seventh – ocean acidification – is dangerously close.

Why does this matter to food lovers? Because the food system is one of the biggest pressures on the planet. Nearly half of all food currently produced globally depends on breaking planetary boundaries, particularly when it comes to land, fresh water, nitrogen use and biodiversity. If everyone lived and ate like the average European, we'd need at least three Earths to sustain us.[8]

At the same time, global food demand is rising as the population grows. The question is: can we meet rising demand without pushing the planet even further out of balance? Many believe we can, but only by making big changes. That means rethinking how we farm, reducing waste at every stage and changing what and how we eat. It means moving away from the extractive practices of the past and using innovation to support, not harm, the natural systems we all depend on.

To understand where this shift started, we need to look at the Green Revolution. A key turning point in modern agriculture, its proponents credit it with feeding the world. Ironically, given its name, it left a trail of environmental damage in its wake that we're still reckoning with today.

How agriculture broke away from nature

For over 10,000 years, people domesticated plants and animals in ways that worked with nature,[9] and around 6,000 plants were cultivated for food.[10] It's striking to think that from all the wild plants available, early humans somehow worked out exactly which ones to domesticate, a feat that researchers describe as an 'astonishing success' of ingenuity and observation.[11] Many of these plants continue to feature in our diets today.

Early farming practices were rooted in cultural knowledge. The milpa (or 'three sisters') system dating back 7,000 years in Mesoamerica planted corn, beans and squash together so each supported the other. The corn provides a structure for the beans to climb, the beans fix nitrogen in the soil, and the squash covers the ground, preventing weeds and retaining moisture.[12]

The rice–fish system in Asia, used for over 2,000 years, created a self-sustaining mini-ecosystem where fish fertilized the soil and kept pests at bay, while the plants provided shade and shelter. Traditional food cultures were also deeply seasonal and ecologically aware. In Bengal and Burma, for example, the hilsa fish was left alone until it reached maturity to protect future stocks.

That interdependence began to fray centuries ago. As farming became commercialised and global trade expanded, food production was increasingly shaped by extraction rather than co-existence. Colonialism displaced traditional systems and shifted land, labour and ecosystems to feed distant markets, creating inequalities in responsibility for climate change that remain today.[13]

As demand for food rose, so did the pressure to squeeze more from the soil. Fertilizers became sought after. The Incas used guano (seabird droppings) rich in nitrogen, phosphorus and potassium (NPK) as early as the 15th century;[14] by the 19th century, European powers were scrambling for guano supplies in a global trade boom.[15] But as reserves dwindled, concern mounted about how to continue feeding a growing population.

By the early 20th century, a breakthrough arrived. This time it wasn't from nature, but the laboratory. In 1909, German chemist Fritz Haber developed a method to synthesise ammonia by reacting nitrogen with hydrogen using fossil fuels. His colleague Carl Bosch later scaled it up for industrial use at German chemical company BASF. The result was the Haber-Bosch process, a revolutionary technique for mass-producing synthetic fertilizer, widely credited with staving off famine.[16] Both men won Nobel Prizes, though Haber's legacy is shadowed by his role in developing chemical weapons in World War One.

After World War Two, concerns around food security were urgent. As Henry Dimbleby writes in his book *Ravenous*, Britain was producing only 30% of the food it needed, relying heavily on its colonies.[17] By the middle of the century, most of the world's fertile farmland was already in use and fears of mass starvation loomed. The pressure was on to squeeze more food out of every inch of soil.

The global rollout of industrial farming

Enter Norman Borlaug's Green Revolution. An American agronomist and Nobel Peace Prize laureate, Borlaug was tasked with meeting the challenge of feeding a rapidly growing population in the mid-20th century, particularly in regions facing famine. By breeding high-yield varieties of wheat, rice and maize and pairing them with irrigation, chemical fertilizers and pesticides, Borlaug ushered in a new era of productivity. It's been called both a blessing and a curse: a blessing because it increased crop yields, lowered food prices and reduced hunger in many parts of the world; a curse because it also locked us into a system of industrialised, input-heavy farming with significant environmental costs.

But the Green Revolution didn't just introduce new seeds and sprays – it also replaced long-standing Indigenous farming methods across the world. Farmers were encouraged, even incentivised, to abandon traditional knowledge systems that had evolved over generations, tailored to local climates, soils and ecosystems. In India and Mexico, for example, ancient polyculture systems gave way to single high-yield crops that were often dependent on imported fertilizers and patented seeds. State policies and foreign aid often made this switch feel less like a choice and more like an expectation.

The new system promised prosperity. Supporters argue these breakthroughs were vital in helping to stave off famine and feed a rapidly growing population, but many smallholders found themselves caught in a cycle of dependency on fertilizer, pesticides and ever-more water. As yields plateau and climate shocks increase, it's proving hard to wean farmers off these methods. As Josiah Meldrum, director at Hodmedod's, notes, the real risk isn't moving away from fossil-fuelled farming, it's sticking with it.[18] These input-intensive systems are contributing to ecosystem decline and raising health concerns, while smallholder farms using low-input, agroecological approaches still feed many people.

The Green Revolution wouldn't have been possible without the fertilizers derived from the Haber-Bosch process. What's less well known is that many agricultural chemicals were originally designed for warfare. Surplus ammonium nitrate from explosives and deadly organophosphates developed as nerve agents as weapons of war were rebranded as fertilizers and pesticides. As the renowned Indian environmentalist Vandana Shiva provocatively puts it, 'We're still eating the leftovers of World War Two.'[19]

Soil, sea and beyond

The long-term impact of all this has been devastating. Half of the nitrogen in synthetic fertilizer never reaches crops – it pollutes our air and water instead.[20] In rivers and lakes, it triggers algal blooms, which spread across the water's surface like a green slick, blocking sunlight and sucking oxygen out of the water. This creates 'dead zones' where aquatic life suffocates – a process known as eutrophication.

In the soil, excess nitrogen leads to acidification, while heavy use of fertilizers depletes organic matter and kills off the complex web of microorganisms that keep soil healthy. It loses its ability to hold water, store nutrients and grow healthy crops. Soil devoid of life, with no worms or insects in it and no birds chirping around it, is a clear warning sign.

One of the lesser-known casualties of extractive farming is soil carbon. Healthy soil is one of the planet's biggest carbon sinks – it stores more carbon than the atmosphere and all plant life combined. But when land is tilled, compacted or steeped in chemicals, that carbon escapes into the air, adding to climate change.

And here's the part that matters to all of us who love food: poor soil health affects not only what farmers can grow, but also what ends up on our plates. Declining soil quality leads to less nutritious crops, lower yields and greater vulnerability to extreme weather.[21] That means fewer fresh ingredients, higher prices and more reliance on synthetic additives to make up for the flavour and nutrition that once came naturally from the ground.

The American broadcaster Paul Harvey once said, 'Despite all our accomplishments, we owe our existence to a six-inch layer of topsoil and the fact it rains.'[22] The documentary *Six Inches of Soil*, which follows a new generation of British farmers working to bring life back to the land, echoes this truth. It's a reminder that soil is more than dirt – it's the living foundation of every meal we eat.

The challenges didn't stop on land. The Blue Revolution followed the Green, beginning in the 1980s with industrial-scale fishing and, later, fish farming. Wild fish stocks were relentlessly depleted after World War Two, peaking in the 1990s.[23] As natural reserves declined, fish farming surged. Much like land-based monocultures, early modern aquaculture systems often ignored the long-term impact on ecosystems, water quality and marine health, and many challenges remain.

Across both revolutions, one principle drove the system: maximum productivity. The relentless pursuit of volume and yield put profits ahead of people and the planet. Major institutions continue to back damaging intensive farming models. The African Development Bank, for instance, is investing billions in agricultural 'modernisation', a strategy criticised for promoting monocultures, threatening biodiversity and making small-scale farmers dependent on multinational seeds, chemicals and export markets.[24]

As Indian geneticist and Green Revolution pioneer M.S. Swaminathan later reflected, 'The Green Revolution became a greed revolution.' What we need, he argued, is an evergreen revolution – one that 'increases productivity in perpetuity without ecological harm', grounded in farming that works with soil, water and biodiversity, not against them.[25]

Swaminathan passed away in 2023 at the age of 98, but his message feels more relevant than ever. The way we eat and drink today is both shaped by this system and helping to sustain it.

CAN SMALL FARMS FEED A GROWING POPULATION?

The answer is both yes and no. It depends on how you look at it.

Globally, smallholder farmers already produce one-third of the world's food[26] – and as much as 70% in low- and middle-income countries.[27] Figures vary depending on definitions and data,[28] but their role is undeniable.

There's no arguing that small farmers form the backbone of rural life and are vital to climate resilience, thanks to their deep local knowledge. But they also face major barriers: poverty and limited access to finance, land, infrastructure and markets. With the right support, like governments sourcing more food for schools and hospitals locally, they could do even more.

In the UK, the debate is often framed as big vs. small. But as Charlie Taverner of the Food, Farming and Countryside Commission says, it isn't a binary choice. Taverner says that for the past 50-60 years in the UK, we've built our food system around cheapness at all costs. That's left scaling up and intensifying as the only viable option for many farmers who are just trying to survive. The future needs both, provided all farming is circular and regenerative.[29]

Farm size isn't everything. Large farms bring efficiencies but also costs, from fossil fuel use to fragile, long supply chains. Small farms can be diverse and resilient, but not all are automatically sustainable. A resilient food system needs both. It must also be inclusive, protecting access to culturally important foods, supporting fair trade and growing a wider range of crops where possible, without losing identity or flavour.

The Commission's *Farming for Change* report shows a fully agroecological UK system could feed the nation.[30] This is farming that works with nature, not against it, using methods that restore soil, protect biodiversity and build resilience. It's climate-smart and rooted in community.

Smallholder and author Chris Smaje agrees but points out it would mean rethinking what we eat. Coffee, bananas and beef burgers on demand wouldn't fit that system. 'You can't always get what you want in life ... and that's not always a bad thing,' he says.'[31] That doesn't have to mean a restricted plate. It could mean rediscovering flavour, seasonality and diversity closer to home.

Shifts towards more seasonal fruit and veg, more pulses, fewer ultra-processed foods and less intensively farmed meat will also be needed. It won't happen overnight. As Smaje reminds us, our current food culture has been shaped by centuries of sourcing what we want, when we want it, on a global market.

But small farms can and should play a bigger role, despite the pressure they are under. As non-profit Growing Culture argues, the idea that they can't feed the world often serves the interests of an industrial food system built on global supply chains and corporate consolidation.[32]

How what we eat (and what we don't) affects the planet

Where food comes from and the impact some of our favourite edibles have in getting to, on and off our plates can leave a bitter taste.

Our tastes and preferences

We're driven by price, taste and convenience, but we're also bamboozled by marketing claims, contradictory headlines and ever-shifting opinions. Whether we're piling meat on the grill, stirring almond milk into our coffee or reaching for a bag of frozen chicken nuggets, what we eat has a direct impact on the environment.

One of the wonders of the modern food system is that you can buy a whole chicken, plucked, shrink wrapped and ready to roast, for less than the cost of a cup of coffee on the high street. Prime cuts of beef and lamb, neatly trimmed and packaged, seem surprisingly affordable. Meanwhile, climate-friendly crops like beans, with their natural nitrogen-fixing power, have quietly fallen off many Western plates.

Animal products, particularly red meat, have a much higher carbon and water footprint than vegetables, grains or legumes. Beef tops the list, followed by lamb. In intensive systems, livestock also produce large volumes of waste that can pollute air and water if poorly managed. Yet animals don't have to be a problem. When integrated into farming systems, they can play a positive role in circular, sustainable agriculture by grazing land that's unsuitable for crops, returning nutrients to soil or upcycling grasses and by-products into food. Research by international experts and academics shows that livestock can be an essential component of sustainable, circular farming systems when managed well.[33]

Examples like silvopastoral systems, which integrate trees, livestock and biodiversity, show that animals can work with, not against, nature. As the saying goes, *it's the how, not the cow*. But even 'better' meat carries costs.

Pasture-fed cattle live longer, producing more methane. As Mike Berners-Lee points out, land used for grazing might store more carbon if rewilded as forests or peatlands. Simply choosing 'better' meat isn't enough if we don't also eat less of it.[34]

Pigs and chickens are slightly different, as they don't produce methane like cows and sheep do thanks to their single-stomach digestive systems. But pigs need high-protein feed, often made from soya grown in Brazil, where deforestation remains a serious concern. Factory farms generate large volumes of slurry (liquid excrement), manure and gases like ammonia. These pollutants can leach into rivers, pollute the air and harm biodiversity if not carefully managed. Storing and spreading waste carefully, or even turning it into renewable energy, can reduce the impact.

In regenerative and organic systems, by contrast, pigs can play a more positive role by breaking up compacted soil, fertilizing land with their manure and restoring biodiversity when moved in rotation. A notable example is Spain's dehesa system, home to the Iberian pig and the famous jamón ibérico. Here, pigs graze under oak trees, feeding on fallen acorns while helping to maintain a healthy, wildlife-rich landscape that needs little meddling.[35]

Chicken, meanwhile, can appear as the 'green' alternative, but the consequences of intensive poultry are stark. The River Wye, which runs 150 miles from the Welsh mountains to the Severn Estuary, is being affected by waste run-off from poultry farming and other pollutants.[36] Simply switching from beef and lamb to cheap chicken isn't an environmental silver bullet.

Turning pescatarian doesn't automatically reduce your impact either. Aquatic food consumption is growing twice as fast as the global population.[37] Overfishing, warming seas, pesticide run-off and harmful algal blooms are putting marine ecosystems under extreme pressure. This matters because marine life plays a vital role in carbon sequestration (the natural storage of carbon in the sea), making healthy oceans a key ally in tackling climate change. Over 90% of global 'blue food' production faces major risks, particularly in Asia and the US.[38]

In the UK, our choices are based on just five species – cod, haddock, salmon, tuna and prawns – which adds to the pressure.[39] Salmon, with its crispy skin and promise of omega-3s, is easy to grab in a weekly shop. Most of what we eat is intensively farmed in open-net cages off Scotland's coast. These farms have been criticised for polluting waters, spreading sea lice and disease, and relying on fishmeal and soya feed, though the industry points to ongoing efforts to improve welfare and reduce impacts through new technologies and feed innovations. Animal welfare activists bemoan the link between increasing salmon farming and declining wild salmon stocks, although this is also contested.

Plans for the UK's first onshore salmon farm have faced fierce opposition, not just over animal welfare but also because it risks moving these environmental problems onto land. According to the Sustainable Restaurant Association, 'There is very little truly sustainable salmon farming. Most of it should be avoided,'[40] although others argue the sector is evolving.

Even at the higher end of the market, sourcing remains opaque. As food writer Catherine Phipps points out, smokehouses often talk about aromatics and small batches but say little about where their salmon comes from.[41] The same could be said of prized cured meats like American country ham, where the craftsmanship sometimes masks the industrial realities behind the pork production.

While high-impact animal products dominate our diets and debates, lower-impact alternatives such as pulses and beans are often overlooked. Shellfish like locally farmed mussels and oysters are low-impact, nutrient-rich choices that even help clean the water as they grow. So is wild venison, which can help control deer populations and protect forest regeneration. We'll return to these practical solutions in the final chapter.

How it's made

How our food is grown and raised matters just as much as what it is and how it's processed. It's not just what's on our dinner plates – it's also what's in the everyday treats that we rarely question. Chocolate bars, biscuits, snack foods and ready meals often have hidden environmental costs baked into every bite.

Many staple crops like soy, maize and palm oil are grown in vast monocultures that depend on fertilizers, pesticides and fossil fuels. While productive, these farming methods are linked to deforestation, soil degradation and biodiversity loss. These crops then become the raw materials behind countless foods, from ready meals and fizzy drinks to biscuits, snack bars and even animal feed. This heavy reliance on a small number of commodities puts further pressure on land, biodiversity and freshwater systems.[42]

Palm oil is a striking example. Indigenous and of cultural significance to West Africa, it was transformed under colonial trade and globalisation into a cheap, processed oil. Today it's found in nearly half of all supermarket packaged goods, from pizzas and biscuits to toiletries and cosmetics.[43] Over 85% of the global supply comes from Indonesia and Malaysia, where rainforest clearance has destroyed the habitats for endangered species like orangutans and pygmy elephants.[44]

Like palm oil, chocolate carries a heavy footprint. The biggest impacts occur at the beginning, during the growing and processing of ingredients like milk powder, sugar and cocoa. These account for up to 97% of chocolate's total environmental burden. Like palm oil, cocoa production, especially in West Africa, is linked to deforestation and biodiversity loss. Certification schemes like Fairtrade and the Rainforest Alliance have helped raise awareness and improve standards, though challenges remain around transparency and enforcement. Among chocolate types, dark chocolate has the lowest carbon footprint, while more processed, sugary products like chocolate confectionery rank the highest.[45]

It's no wonder, then, that research concluded that a diet high in UPFs also tends to be more resource intensive on average, consuming more land, energy and water per calorie produced than diets based on whole or minimally processed foods.[46]

And plant-based convenience foods aren't automatically a free pass. Burgers, nuggets and sausages made from highly refined soy, pea protein or mycoprotein can have lower direct emissions than beef but still involve significant farming, energy use and processing. While some plant-based meat alternatives have 30–90% lower greenhouse gas emissions than beef, their environmental footprint is still often much higher than simply eating whole legumes like beans or lentils (we'll return to pulses in the final chapter).[47]

Even shifting to whole plant foods without consideration bears environmental costs. Popular foods like avocados and almonds are grown as monocultures, often in water-scarce regions. Large-scale production of both relies heavily on managed honeybee colonies because wild pollinators alone can't meet the demand. Dr Justine Butler of Vegetarians International Voice for Animals highlights that honeybees are now intensively farmed, transported and exploited at industrial scale, often with serious consequences for their health and survival.[48] Growers in places like California are actively working on reducing water use and supporting pollinator health. And while these crops have impacts worth noting, they are still far less greenhouse gas-intensive than beef or lamb.

From the farm to the factory, our food's environmental footprint grows long before it reaches our kitchens. How it gets to us in the transport, packaging and retail chains adds another layer of impact.

HOW DO WE MEASURE FOOD'S ENVIRONMENTAL IMPACT?

Understanding the environmental footprint of food is eye-wateringly complicated. How is it even possible to compare beef to beans, or almonds to oats?

This is where life cycle assessment (LCA) comes in. It's a scientific method that adds up a food's impact at every stage of its life: growing, processing, packaging, transport and even what happens to waste. However, LCAs aren't perfect. There's plenty of debate about them, especially when it comes to meat and dairy.

Take methane. Most assessments use a standard called GWP100, which spreads its impact over a century. Some scientists and farming groups

> prefer a newer measure called GWP*, which accounts for methane's shorter lifespan and shows lower impacts when herds are stable or shrinking.
>
> But some critics, including non-governmental organisations (NGOs), argue that GWP could make high-impact systems look better on paper, muddying comparisons and slowing action on climate goals. More thinking and much debate is continuing in this space.

How food gets to us

One of the great benefits of a global food system is that food can come from anywhere, at any time, and be produced using the most creative of means. But these come with environmental costs and are often misunderstood.

Food miles and carbon footprint

The concept of food miles was coined by UK food policy expert Tim Lang in the 1990s. It clocks the distance food travels to get to us, and the subsequent environmental impact. For example, the average avocado travels around 4,820 miles to reach a plate.[49] But distance alone doesn't tell the whole story. We also need to consider how food is produced and how efficiently natural resources are used alongside how it is transported to get the full picture.

If we consider travel, an avocado shipped from Peru by sea (which is how they travel in practice) may have a lower footprint than a tomato grown in a heated UK hothouse. But if that avocado were to travel by air, the picture changes dramatically. Most food travels by land or sea, both relatively low-carbon methods. The problem is air freight, which is common for perishable foods like asparagus, berries and green beans.

Fruit and vegetables can be grown in several ways. Traditional open-field farming relies on seasonal weather and natural soil conditions. Polytunnels extend growing seasons and protect crops from the elements but still require fertilizers and irrigation. Vertical farming has emerged, using stacked indoor systems with controlled light, water and nutrients to grow crops year-round, often close to where they are eaten.

High-tech greenhouses, such as those used in the Netherlands, offer year-round growing conditions with precise control over heat, light and nutrients. While greenhouse farming can be more efficient than open-field production in some climates, it consumes significant amounts of energy (often from fossil fuels) and generates waste. Some of the world's most advanced greenhouses now combine renewable energy, rainwater collection and 'closed-loop' systems to reduce waste and resource use.

Southern Spain, particularly Almería, for instance, supplies much of the UK's winter fruit and vegetables, helping make affordable fresh produce widely available in our supermarkets. The region grows tomatoes, peppers and cucumbers under a vast patchwork of plastic-covered greenhouses dubbed the 'sea of plastic'.

But Almería's intensive farming relies heavily on groundwater extraction in an area already prone to drought. The environmental toll is stark: aquifers are shrinking, plastic pollution is widespread and pesticide run-off threatens soil and biodiversity. Harsh conditions for low-paid migrant workers have also raised serious human rights concerns.

The picture is rarely straightforward. While the intensive agricultural methods that use vast greenhouses on former scrub and marginal farmland may often damage local environments, research suggests that the plastic and glass roofs increase the 'reflectability' of the Earth's surface, actually creating a cooling effect.[50]

In the UK, vertical farms like Crate to Plate and Unbeleafable offer another path: growing salads locally with minimal pesticides and no air miles. Energy use is a challenge, but these systems support local enterprise, diversify farming, provide fresh, healthy food year-round, and reduce food waste by selling leaves that stay fresh longer. If powered by renewables and well managed, they can genuinely lower overall footprints compared with some traditional supply chains, though they aren't yet a perfect solution in every case.

As Louise Gray points out in her book *Avocado Anxiety*, calculating the true carbon footprint of food is a 'notoriously complicated business that leads to a lot of head scratching'.[51] She stresses that the burden shouldn't fall on shoppers: 'You can't expect people to be calculating in the supermarket aisle. Producers, retailers and government need to take the lead. For consumers, the choice has to be easy, affordable and desirable.'[52]

It's not just land and energy use we need to think about. As climate pressures mount, water – where it's drawn from, how much is used and where it ends up – is also an urgent challenge.

Water footprint

Every asparagus spear, almond and avocado we eat carries another invisible cost: the water used to grow it. Some foods are far thirstier than others, and many are produced in regions where water is already running dangerously low.

Water footprint is the amount of water consumed and polluted during all stages of production. One-quarter of the world's crops are grown in areas where water supply is 'highly stressed, highly unreliable or both'.[53] Rice, wheat and corn – which together provide more than half of the world's food calories – are especially vulnerable: 33% of these three staples are grown using water supplies that are already highly stressed or variable.[54] And that pressure is intensifying. Climate change and competition for water are threatening supplies and putting global food security at risk.

It's not just the staples and UPFs we need to think about. Trendy and nutrient-dense ingredients are also major water users and are often grown in drought-prone areas for export. In Peru, vast groundwater reserves along the hyper-arid Pacific coast have helped turn the country into a major agro-exporter. Avocados and green asparagus – two of Peru's most cultivated export crops – are among the most water-intensive foods grown per hectare.[55] Producers are responding with measures such as drip irrigation and sustainability certification, but long-term groundwater depletion remains a concern.

California, the largest food-producing state in the US, faces similar pressures. It supplies a significant share of the country's milk, beef, fruit, vegetables and nuts, but it's also one of the driest regions. Climate change has brought more frequent droughts, floods and wildfires. Agriculture draws heavily on the overstretched Colorado River, and crops like almonds and alfalfa effectively export scarce water to international markets. Growers have invested heavily in drip irrigation and groundwater regulation, which are gradually coming into fruition.[56]

Closer to home, Spain produces around a quarter of the EU's fruit and vegetables, much of it destined for export. Agriculture accounts for over 80% of the country's water use, and years of drought and rising demand are pushing resources to the brink. Yet Spain has also been at the forefront of irrigation modernisation and water reuse schemes, with greenhouse vegetable systems in Almería now using far less water per kilo of produce than many open-field systems elsewhere.

These examples show that water-intensive foods often shift resources from regions of scarcity to regions of relative abundance, raising questions about how sustainable that trade really is. But they also show farmers and governments grappling with solutions from new irrigation technologies to regulation and certification. The challenge is whether these efforts can keep pace with climate change and rising demand.

Packaging and transport

Many of the foods we buy, especially convenience foods and ultra-processed products, come heavily packaged in plastic. Food packaging is now the largest single use of plastic globally, according to the United Nations Environment Programme.[57]

Plastic was a game-changer. 'It revolutionised the packaging sector by extending the shelf life of fresh food, enabling essential health applications, contributing to lighter and safer shipping and reducing emissions,' says Plastics Europe, the trade body for Europe's plastics industry.[58] Lightweight, cheap and durable, it made food easier to move, store and protect.

But it's also been described by environmentalists as 'fossil fuel inside us'. Plastic packaging – often used once and discarded – is a potent pollutant and less than 10% of it recycled globally.[59] The bulk of mismanaged waste occurs in low- and middle-income countries.[60] And not every kind of packaging can be recycled. Containers made from mixed materials – think crisp packets or ready-meal trays – are rarely processed by recycling systems.

Much of this waste ends up in landfills or the ocean, where it languishes for hundreds of years. It absorbs chemicals and breaks down into microplastics and nanoplastics. These have been detected in a wide range of foods, including drinking water, beer, honey, seafood, bivalves, sugar and cooking salt.[61] As Jack Marley, former Environment Editor at The Conversation, says: 'They have been found in remote Arctic ice and on top of mountains. They have also been discovered in our blood, breast milk and semen. What we do to the environment, we ultimately do to ourselves.'[62]

The burden isn't equally shared. Coastal and Indigenous communities, which are often the ones that are most exposed to plastic pollution, are frequently excluded from decisions about how to tackle it.[63] Meanwhile, after three years of negotiations, UN talks to tackle plastic pollution have collapsed.[64]

Shipping food around the world adds its own environmental burden in terms of emissions and ocean health. Cargo ships release ballast water and oil residues and create noise pollution that disturbs marine life; lost packaging and shipping materials contribute to ocean plastic; and most ships still burn and spill heavy fuel oil, a high-pollution fossil fuel.

Refrigerated transport is also energy intensive. It's part of what's known as the cold chain – the temperature-controlled supply system that keeps perishable food fresh as it's on the move. This includes chilled warehouses, refrigerated lorries, air freight, supermarket fridges and even home delivery coolers. Many cold chains rely on hydrofluorocarbons (HFCs), powerful greenhouse gases that are thousands of times more warming than carbon dioxide. Cold-chain logistics are estimated to account for about 4% of the global greenhouse gas emissions.[65]

Factors such as population growth, increased living standards and a surge in online shopping due to post-pandemic shifts have spurred a consistent rise in demand for these services.[66] As more fresh and frozen foods are shipped further and faster, the climate cost grows. Even how food reaches our homes – by car, van or delivery service – adds up, especially when it involves extra trips or layers of packaging to keep items cold.

We've talked about the vast amounts of land, water and energy that are used to grow our food and then get it to us. But shockingly, one-third of it never gets eaten, and there is more inbuilt waste in food production.

What we don't eat

The food wasted at every step to get from field to fork carries a massive environmental cost. Around one-fifth of all food produced for human consumption is lost or wasted.[67] That's food grown with precious land, water, fuel and fertilizer, only to be discarded.

Food waste is built into the system from the start. Crops are left unharvested due to costly or unavailable labour, cancelled orders or because they don't meet supermarket standards. Food spoils during storage and transport. Overproduction is common across farms and factories, often because it's cheaper to produce too much than risk running short.

By the time food reaches retailers, more is lost to stock management issues, over-ordering and packaging damage. Bulk-buy promotions and oversized packs, which are designed for convenience or perceived value, often push us to take more than we need. UK shoppers spend £17 billion on food that is thrown away, which is an average of £1,000 a year for a household of four people.[68] By weight, households are responsible for 60% of food wasted in a single year in the UK. The rest comes from farms (15%), manufacturing (13%), hospitality (10%) and retail (2%).[69]

A less visible form of food loss occurs in what we feed animals. Up to 40% of the world's farmland and over 30% of cereal crops are used for animal feed, mainly for pigs and poultry.[70] This includes soy, maize and cereals that could, in theory, feed people. Turning feed into meat or milk is an inefficient process, especially for beef and dairy, which require more land, water and emissions per calorie produced than plant-based foods. This includes soy and maize alongside cereals grown specifically for this purpose. By contrast, cattle often graze on grass or co-products from the food chain, and in well-managed systems they can thrive on land that isn't suitable for crops.

Animals help reduce waste by eating by-products that humans don't, like the tough, hard bit of plants we can't or won't eat, like tougher parts of plants, brewers' grain, oilseed cake and food-processing residues. Pigs and poultry are particularly good at turning leftovers and scraps into food. In regenerative and small-scale systems, this can be part of a more circular food model.

And it's not just farm animals. The global pet food industry is a major consumer of animal protein. Many pet foods make use of offcuts and organ meats, but premium brands increasingly use prime cuts of meat and fish as well as grains and seeds, competing directly with human food. With hundreds of millions of pets around the world, mostly in high-income countries, the environmental impact of our furry friends is worth considering too.

In households, food waste is shaped by habits, marketing and culture. We favour produce that looks perfect, items with longer expiry dates and multi-buy deals that seem too good to pass up. Yet much of this food ends up forgotten at the back of the fridge or tossed after a missed expiry date.

While you may think this sort of food waste is a 'rich country problem', a 2023 UN report found similar average levels across high, upper-middle and lower-middle-income countries.[71] The bigger difference is between urban and rural areas. In rural communities, food waste tends to be lower, with leftovers fed to animals, composted or reused. In cities, food is more likely to go straight into the bin.

What happens to the food we don't buy at shops? Supermarkets often donate unsold but still edible food to charities and food banks. While this reduces waste and helps people in need, critics argue it shifts responsibility onto charities while letting retailers claim a sustainability halo. Many supermarkets are now calling for legislation to create industry-wide accountability.

While the system slowly shifts, there's plenty we can do in the meantime, from shopping and eating out more consciously and valuing the food already in our homes to questioning the green claims on packaging that can so often mislead us (we'll look at how to navigate this in the final chapter).

Planet

MAKING SENSE OF DATE LABELS

Dates for usage are about safety or quality, not the environment, but misunderstanding them drives millions of tons of perfectly good food into the bin every year. Here's what date labels really mean.

- **Use by:** This is about safety. Food past its use-by date shouldn't be eaten, especially perishable items like meat, fish or pre-made salads. Even if it looks and smells fine, bacteria can grow that you can't see. It's best to stick to use-by dates for anything with a short shelf life.
- **Best before:** This is about quality, not safety. Food past its best-before date may not be as crisp, fragrant or flavourful as it once was, but it's still perfectly safe to eat. Trust your senses: if it smells fine, looks fine and tastes fine, it probably is fine.
- **Sell by/Display until:** These are mainly for sellers, not shoppers. They're about stock rotation, not safety. You can safely ignore them once you've taken the product home.

What about long-life goods like spiced and dried foods? Spices, dried herbs, dried pulses and tinned foods don't suddenly go off after their best-before date. They may lose colour, flavour or aroma over time, but they don't pose a health risk. A pinch of paprika that's past its best-before date won't harm you – it just might not pack the same punch in your cooking.

Bottom line? Date labels err on the side of caution. Don't let them do all your thinking for you. Sight, smell and taste are your friends. If something looks off or smells strange, bin it. If it's just a little faded or past its prime, it might still have plenty to offer, especially in a soup, sauce or stew. As for tired spices, a dry toast or sizzle in hot oil can bring them back to life.

Setting wrongs right

If we take inspiration from nature, we're reminded that cycles, not straight lines, lead to renewal. The same is true of our food. In a truly rounded and grounded world, precious resources are not treated as disposable. Instead, materials, nutrients and energy are kept in use for as long as possible through smarter design, use and reuse. In food terms, that means making better use of land, water and energy, reducing waste, composting and giving by-products a fresh use.

It also means embracing the caring economy we talked about in the first chapter, i.e. one that puts health, sustainability and community ahead of relentless efficiency. So how can wrongs be set right?

The politics of progress

The politics of climate change is interlinked with our food. One of the central frameworks guiding global action is the Paris Agreement, signed at COP21 in 2015. Nearly every country on Earth pledged to keep global warming well below 2°C (ideally 1.5°C) above pre-industrial levels.

But most experts now agree that we are not on track to meet those goals. Some countries and companies are pledging to reach net zero, which means cutting greenhouse gas emissions as much as possible and offsetting the rest so that the overall result is zero. The UK, France, Norway and New Zealand are among those making it legally binding by 2050, but progress is uneven and the path remains fiercely contested.

Governments have much of the power to deliver change, yet public money still props up environmentally harmful practices. In the UK, campaign group Feedback found that public funds have flowed to some of the world's biggest salmon-farming giants.[72] In the EU, more than 80% of its main farming subsidy scheme, the Common Agricultural Policy (CAP), still supports emissions-intensive livestock production.[73] Globally, fossil fuel subsidies reached an astonishing $7 trillion in 2022 – about 7% of global GDP.[74]

Addressing our reliance on fossil fuels remains contentious and full of contradictions. Former UK Prime Minister Tony Blair argued that phasing out fossil fuels and reducing energy use is unrealistic, and backed carbon capture and storage (CCS) instead. But many scientists insist that there's no path to climate safety that doesn't involve a rapid reduction in fossil fuel use.[75]

Meanwhile, our ability to make lower-carbon choices – like switching to electric heat pumps instead of gas boilers – is held back by wider systems still locked into affordability. In the UK, for example, electricity prices are still tied to the cost of gas, making cleaner choices harder to afford. Food politics is vulnerable to influence too. The EAT-Lancet Commission's Planetary Health Diet, which called for reduced meat consumption in 2019, was met with orchestrated pushback from the meat and dairy sector.[76]

But public appetite for change is growing. Research shows that people around the world are worried about climate change, and 80% want their governments to take stronger climate action.[77] In the UK, people feel overwhelmed by unhealthy food environments, feel misled by marketing and are ready for bold leadership.[78] We want food systems that reflect our values, not just the interests of powerful industries. Food finally made it onto the agenda at COP28 in 2023, a long-overdue step to bring it closer to climate action.

Examples of action elsewhere offer hope. France's Nutri-Score labels, Denmark's plans for a carbon tax on food and Amsterdam's junk food marketing restrictions show what's possible when politics align with public will. In New Zealand, the Whanganui River has been granted legal personhood, embedding Indigenous ecological principles into law.

Alongside these grounded, place-based efforts, a different approach has taken shape that relies on markets, credits and accounting.

The emergence and challenges of carbon markets

You've probably seen claims like 'carbon neutral', 'climate positive' or even 'carbon negative' on everything from beer and vodka to snack bars. As companies race to meet net zero targets and win over climate-conscious consumers, carbon claims have become a powerful marketing tool. But what do they actually mean?

As carbon market expert Yuejia Peng explains, the basic idea is that emitting CO_2 has to carry a price, otherwise there's little incentive to cut it. Carbon markets put a cost on pollution, creating financial reasons to reduce or avoid emissions. Some markets are mandatory, set up by governments; others are voluntary, driven by companies keen to meet pledges or bolster their green credentials.

These claims are often based on carbon offsets, where a company pays to fund emission reductions elsewhere while continuing to pollute. These reductions might involve planting trees, protecting forests or investing in renewable energy. The idea is to balance the books: emissions here, savings there.

Offsets are controversial for two main reasons, says Peng. First, they risk becoming a substitute for real emissions cuts: it's easier to buy credits than to overhaul business models. Second, the quality of credits is often in doubt. How do you know a promised ton of carbon reduced or removed is genuine and permanent?

The offsetting framework was formalised under the Paris Agreement, which established carbon markets as a tool to reduce emissions where it's cheapest and most efficient. This has helped funnel money into renewable energy, forestry and conservation projects, and for some governments it's been an important step in putting a price on pollution. It shows that emissions can be treated as a global commodity with real costs, not an invisible externality.

The reality, however, is more complicated. Even in voluntary offset schemes, human and environmental harms have been widely reported. Research by CarbonBrief shows that more than 70% of carbon offset projects examined had caused harm to Indigenous peoples or local communities (IPLC). Some were displaced from their land, while others were pressured to sign away their rights without fully understanding the terms.[79] Another recurring issue is double counting, where the same carbon savings are claimed by both the country of origin and the buyer, undermining the credibility of the system.

Planting trees, which is a common offset strategy, also carries risks. Studies show that planting fast-growing trees like eucalyptus or pine on natural grasslands can actually *increase* the risk of catastrophic wildfires, as seen in Chile and Portugal. Instead of storing carbon, poorly designed projects can make the problem worse.[80]

'It's not what you plant, it's where, how, and with whom,' Yuejia Peng explains. She notes that some forestry projects have helped Indigenous groups gain land rights and income, but many others fail due to monocultures, poor planning or lack of community involvement. 'There's no silver bullet,' she adds, 'but there are better ways to do this.'[81]

Carbon may now be a currency, but the real work of climate action still happens on the ground and in the sea.

Developments in agriculture and aquaculture

Many farmers are at the forefront of leading change. In Andhra Pradesh, India, an ambitious government-led programme is working to convert 6 million farmers across 8 million hectares of land to chemical-free, regenerative farming by 2031. The right support and incentives can drive fundamental and positive change.

The transition to climate- and nature-friendly food production in the West has its roots in what's known as 'sustainable intensification'. Coined in the 1990s, it was about producing more food from the same land while reducing environmental damage. It recognised that farming couldn't expand indefinitely without devastating ecosystems and it aimed to improve efficiency, not just yields.

Since then, more farmers, policymakers and food businesses are turning to practices that don't just limit harm, but actively regenerate nature by putting something back in. Regenerative agriculture, a movement originally driven by farmers in North America, is gaining ground elsewhere. In the UK, the Groundswell festival – once a small gathering of a few hundred farmers – now attracts thousands of people from across agriculture and related disciplines to discuss soil health, policy, nutrition and best practice.

The regenerative agriculture market is projected to grow to $16.8 billion by 2027,[82] but the term itself remains loosely defined. As the UK's Advertising Standards Authority (ASA) notes, it's effectively a 'pick and mix' of principles: integrating livestock and arable farming; limiting soil disturbance; year-round soil cover maintenance; biodiversity and crop rotations; and living roots in the soil.

There is inherent difficulty in defining the approach, as regenerative farmers will not necessarily employ all these practices, or to the same extent. It gets confused with organic farming, which is certified to a set standard.[83] Both are better for soil, long-term food security and farmer livelihoods.

As the phrase 'regen ag' becomes more familiar, it's open to greenwashing and mis-selling akin to carbon claims. A 2024 analysis by the New Climate Institute found that most of the 30 major agri-businesses studied used the phrase 'regenerative' in their sustainability messaging, but only one-third had measurable targets and many failed to name actual practices.[84] This gap risks undermining the credibility of farmers working to restore soils and ecosystems.

In the UK, the ASA issued guidelines in November 2024 to help communicate regenerative agriculture practices without misleading consumers. Events like Groundswell and farmer-led networks are helping to define what regeneration looks like in practice. Meanwhile, IPES-Food hails agroecology as the most promising way to address climate, nature and justice in the food system. It also offers a helpful breakdown of many of the terms that are often used interchangeably but mean different things in practice (see 'Climate Solutions in Agriculture: Some Definitions' in the appendix).

In the water, sustainable aquaculture and regenerative marine food systems are also gaining ground. Some fish farms are adopting integrated models, pairing species like salmon with seaweed and shellfish, which can filter water, absorb excess nutrients and improve the overall health of marine ecosystems. Shellfish such as mussels and oysters are natural filter feeders, which means they feed by drawing in water and straining out tiny particles like plankton and organic matter. This cleans the water, making them not only low impact to farm but actively beneficial to coastal environments.

Nature-based aquaculture systems that mimic wild habitats are being tested widely, aided by technology like sensors and underwater cameras to reduce waste, avoid bycatch and improve animal welfare. In Finland, for example, the Snowchange Cooperative blends Indigenous knowledge with sustainable fishing and local supply chains.

Another notable example is Esteros Lubimar in Cádiz, Spain, which transformed a drained estuary back into a thriving ecosystem. By restoring natural water flow and encouraging microalgae growth, the area now supports a diverse range of species, including branzino, sea bream and flamingos. This approach demonstrates how regenerative aquaculture can heal nature while providing nutritious food sources.

In the UK, efforts are also underway to build more regenerative marine food systems. Loch Fyne Oysters in Argyll has long championed low-impact shellfish farming that supports cleaner waters and thriving marine ecosystems. Meanwhile, SeaGrown in Scarborough is pioneering seaweed aquaculture in the North Sea, absorbing carbon and excess nutrients while creating habitats for marine life. These models offer a glimpse into a more restorative seafood future.

Together, these examples point to something bigger: a revolution in how we grow and harvest food, one that works with nature, not against it. Behind many of these shifts lie new tools and ideas shaped not just by tradition or policy, but also by technology and innovation.

THE ORGANIC QUESTION

The organic movement has deep roots in soil health. In 1943, farmer and scientist Lady Eve Balfour published *The Living Soil*, comparing organic and chemical farming methods. Her work led to the founding of the Soil Association three years later, setting the standards that still guide organic farming today.

The market has grown steadily since then. UK sales of organic food and drink hit a record £3.7 billion in 2024, more than double what it was a decade ago,[85] though only around 3% of farmland here is organic. Some countries are going further. For example, Denmark aims for a quarter of its farmland to be organic by 2030.[86]

Why choose organic? It's about working with nature: no synthetic pesticides or fertilizers (unless specifically approved), no GMOs, strict rules on antibiotics and animal welfare, and farming practices that build soil health and biodiversity. For many, the appeal is also in what organic avoids. Studies show pesticide residues on organic foods are generally lower, and organic farming supports wildlife and water quality.

Organic convenience foods must also meet stricter standards on what goes in and what's left out – no artificial colours or preservatives, and fewer ultra-processed ingredients.

Is it healthier? The evidence is mixed. Some studies suggest higher levels of antioxidants in organic fruit and vegetables,[87] though results vary by crop. Organic milk and meat consistently contain more omega-3s thanks to diets rich in grass and clover. While evidence is stronger on soil health and biodiversity, the jury is still out on whether organic farming delivers significantly better health outcomes for consumers.[88]

The truth is that nutrition research is complicated. Our health depends on what we eat day to day, but also on sleep, stress, income and lifestyle. Healthier outcomes in organic consumers may reflect these wider factors. Experts agree the bigger priority is simply eating more fruit and veg, organic or not.

Innovation and technology to the rescue

Innovation in food hasn't always been met with trust, and for good reason. Past efforts in the name of progress and profit have contributed to many of the problems we now face. In some cases, reclaiming traditional, nature-friendly methods offers the best way forward rather than a completely new approach. That said, a new wave of innovation is also emerging, one focused on reducing harm, restoring balance and enabling better choices.

Nature tech

Digital farming first entered the fray as precision agriculture in the 1980s and 1990s as a way for farmers to be more efficient with water, fertilizers and pesticide use. By applying just the right amount, in the right place, at the right time, they were able to maximise yields while cutting waste and costs.

Over time, these tools evolved beyond boosting productivity. Today, they're being used to measure and protect the very ecosystems that farming depends on, from soil health and biodiversity to water use and carbon storage. This growing field is now known as nature tech, a new wave of digital tools designed to work with nature.

Nature tech is playing a vital role across agriculture and aquaculture. Climate and nature expert Jen Stebbing explains how this is already happening. AI and sensors track soil health, water use and biodiversity; ecoacoustics help monitor insect life and detect illegal logging; drones map crop health and vegetation; and smart probes measure soil carbon and other key indicators.[89]

BloomX, for example, has developed a mechanical pollination tool that mimics bee buzzing and electrostatic charges to pollinate crops like avocados and blueberries. The tech has boosted yields by up to 30%, particularly in regions where bee populations are in decline. Used in Israel, South Africa, the US and Latin America, the technology offers a more resilient, less extractive alternative to industrial bee transport.[90]

WHAT ARE NATURE-BASED SOLUTIONS?
by Jen Stebbing

The health of the Earth's natural ecosystems underpins much of the world's economic value, so biodiversity and nature losses pose significant problems for corporations and society at large. Nature-based solutions (NbS) are actions that protect, manage and restore ecosystems to address societal challenges, providing benefits for both human well-being and biodiversity.

What is nature tech?

Nature tech in its broadest term, is any technology that is good for nature. We see a lot of nature tech being developed to support the implementation and acceleration of nature-based solutions. Nature tech's official definition is: 'Any technology that enables, accelerates and scales the nature-positive transition.'

What is driving these developments?

Several factors are driving the development of nature tech. Companies need to comply with new regulations and reporting standards, such as the Global Reporting Initiative (GRI) and the European Sustainability Reporting Standards (ESRS) under the Corporate Sustainability Reporting Directive (CSRD). Additionally, frameworks like the Taskforce on Nature-related Financial Disclosures (TNFD) are encouraging businesses to assess and disclose their impacts and dependencies on nature.

Businesses are increasingly aware of the risks related to nature loss and climate change, which can impact their operations. Shifts in market demands, liability concerns and the growing interest of investors in sustainable technologies are also pushing companies to adopt nature tech solutions. These technologies help businesses manage their environmental impact by providing better data and tools.

What are some of the challenges with take-up, integration and implementation?

One of the main challenges with adopting nature tech is the lack of understanding and expertise within companies. Many businesses are not familiar with how these technologies work or how to use them effectively. Additionally, integrating new systems can be costly and time-consuming, especially for companies with limited resources. There can also be challenges with data accuracy, as collecting and verifying nature-related data often requires advanced tools like satellites, sensors and AI. Finally, some businesses worry about whether these solutions will deliver real benefits, making them hesitant to invest.

Jen Stebbing is an independent climate and nature consultant, writing with extracts from Integrating Nature Tech: A Guide for Businesses by Nature4Climate and partners.

On the ground

Reducing methane from cattle is a major target. In Canada, dairy farmers are selectively breeding cows that naturally emit less methane. In France, scientists have developed ways to measure emissions by cow, allowing producers to prioritise lower-emitting animals. The UK's largest dairy co-operative, Arla, is testing Bovaer, a feed additive that can cut methane from digestion by up to 30%.

But while these tweaks show promise and might buy us some ecological time, they don't tackle the deeper questions: why do we produce so much livestock in the first place, and how well are we managing it? India, for example, has the world's largest livestock population and is the top producer and consumer of milk.[91] Religious reverence for cows by Hindus, coupled with bans on slaughter in many states, has led to large numbers of ageing or unproductive cattle being abandoned. These free-roaming animals pose issues for waste management, public health and the environment.

Rice is also seeing traditional cultivation methods being turned on their head. In Vietnam, where paddy fields used to be submerged in water, thereby trapping oxygen, a new method called alternate wetting and drying (AWD) is being used. Fertilizers are being applied by drones, and rice stubble, which was previously burned as a source of pollution, is being collected and used for livestock feed as well as for growing straw mushrooms.[92]

Yet focusing only on carbon emissions risks missing the bigger ecological picture. Traditional paddy fields often produce much more than rice – they support fish, crabs, frogs and other important foods. Rice straw is also a valued resource for building materials like thatch, which offers natural insulation, unlike steel or concrete. Moving away from these systems could leave communities more dependent on high-impact industrial materials, with knock-on effects for livelihoods and cultural heritage.

Meanwhile, investments in plant-based alternatives continue apace, with start-ups and established players alike developing plant-based meat and dairy analogues to appeal to meat eaters and dairy lovers. The benefits could be profound: research suggests these new approaches can deliver the same products with 80–95% reductions in climate impacts, water use and land requirements, although overall impacts will vary depending on the ingredients and processes involved.[93]

At sea

A wave of emerging and disruptive technologies is reshaping what sustainable aquaculture could look like.[94] These include robotics for underwater monitoring and automated feeding; digital platforms and sensors to track fish health, oxygen levels and water quality; recirculating aquaculture systems (RAS) that reuse water and reduce pollution; alternative feeds from algae and microbes, with research underway on grass; and oral vaccines that reduce disease without stressful injections.

Individually, these technologies show promise, but the real breakthrough lies in joining them up – combining equipment, sensors, platforms and protocols into systems that can run efficiently and manage human error. Yet people continue to play a central role. In Scotland, the largest mass escape of farmed salmon in a decade – a major environmental event – was caused not by tech failure, but by something far simpler: someone forgot to secure a hatch.[95]

While these advances open the door to cleaner, more efficient seafood production, they also raise questions. Big companies are best placed to afford these high-tech systems, while small-scale fishermen and farmers may be left behind. Governments, investors and extension services have a role to play in ensuring the tools of transition are shared fairly.

But should we trust tech? As food writer and policy adviser Honor Eldridge notes, it's natural to feel cautious about technology, especially when past promises haven't always delivered. But fear shouldn't stop us from asking the right questions. We should be asking whether technology helps us redesign the food system or just delays the need for real change. We should also be wondering about the risk of new challenges popping up.[96] Generative AI uses a vast amount of fossil fuel-based electricity to function and water to keep cool. A single ChatGPT search can use five times as much energy as a web search.[97]

Behind every technological breakthrough lies a bigger question: who benefits? Much of the innovation we see today is still shaped by the same economic drivers that got us here: a global system designed to maximise short-term profit, often at the expense of people, nature and future generations. Technology can help us do things better, but only if it's part of a deeper shift towards an economy that values care, co-operation and regeneration, not just growth for growth's sake.

Used thoughtfully, innovation can support more resilient, inclusive and nature-friendly food production. But we must be clear-eyed about its limits. Technology is a tool, not a fix, and it's no substitute for the deeper economic and social shifts we urgently need.

SHOULD WE FEAR TECHNOLOGY IN FOOD?

by Honor Eldridge

The digital revolution has had a transformative impact on food and farming. From the emergence of gene editing, the use of AI and cell-cultured meat, every aspect of our food system will be impacted by new technologies in the coming years. Many people claim that these technologies are what will ensure that we can continue to feed the world in the face of growing populations and climate change. Yet other people warn against the adoption and extol the traditional methods.

Should we fear technology in our food system? Or is it merely neophobia and a sense that new foods are a bit yucky that is causing us to reject it solely because it's new? It's worth being cautiously optimistic about these new products and not immediately distrust innovation. The food challenges that we face are considerable, so we need to open up to these technologies. Carefully designed and managed with appropriate regulatory guardrails, these new foods could help get us closer to a sustainable future for food.

Admittedly, technology hasn't always been a force for good. The environmental destruction and public health crisis that resulted from the Green Revolution are a case in point for the damage caused by embracing technology without a full understanding of the long-term consequences. It's reasonable to be cautious.

However, most of these problems were, in fact, caused by capitalism, greed and a system that has allowed the corporate control of our food system. But technology isn't synonymous with capitalism. Technology is a tool. It doesn't come with a philosophical bent. It's not good or evil. It's something that we can choose to embrace or reject. And it's not a homogeneous block. Some are deeply connected to the industrialisation of food, while others can support sustainable approaches. We can pick and choose.

Agroecological and regenerative farmers have already started embracing technology to help them become more environmentally sustainable and economically resilient. Is there room for those of us committed to healthy diets to embrace more technology in our food? It's worth taking it case by case. People's decisions about what they want to eat are deeply personal. Some are driven by environmental concerns, others focus on animal welfare, while some on social justice. Some people do not have those luxuries and are only able to make food choices based on price.

New food products, like cell-cultured meat, for example, can address key food concerns for some people. It might not be the right choice for everyone, but it might be the right choice for someone, and they should have the option to make that choice. These foods are required to go through rigorous food safety protocols to be deemed safe. Once they reach the market and those standards are all met, it's up to each individual to decide for themselves, based on their own priorities, what they want to eat.

Honor Eldridge is a food system expert and author of The Avocado Debate.

Planet

A new generation of food changemakers

Across the UK, a new wave of change is showing that food can be grown, cooked and shared in ways that care for people and the planet. Some people are working inside big companies to shift practices, while others are building fresh solutions from the ground up. Together, they prove that creativity, care and collaboration can spark real change, from grocery shelves to restaurant tables.

While exciting small and mid-sized businesses often grab the headlines, some of the biggest food companies are also investing in change. From committing to regenerative supply chains to cutting plastic packaging, many are experimenting with better ways to do business. Progress is uneven, but their scale means their actions ripple across entire supply chains.

Some of this work began long before the current wave of food innovation. Yeo Valley, once a small family farm, has grown into a household name, proving that food grown with care for people, care for animals and care for the planet can thrive in mainstream retail. Meanwhile, grocery pioneers like Riverford and Abel & Cole have brought farm-fresh organic groceries to thousands of homes.

Others are building on that legacy with fresh approaches. Wildfarmed, founded by DJ-turned-farmer Andy Cato, works with growers to produce flour from pesticide-free wheat grown in biodiverse fields. Their bread is now stocked in supermarkets, with oats and barley next on their radar.[98] Nice Rice backs farmers using water-saving, methane-cutting techniques for one of the UK's most-eaten staples.

New retail models are emerging too. Granville Community Kitchen is making seasonal, local and organic veg boxes affordable and adaptable by cultural cuisine, recognising that access alone isn't enough without relevance and dignity. Online platforms like Wylde Market and Herd Market are reimagining farmers' markets for the digital age, connecting consumers directly with passionate, specialist small-scale producers.

Others are tackling the waste, surplus and inefficiency baked into today's food system. Oddbox rescues surplus and wonky fruit and veg rejected by supermarkets. Rubies in the Rubble turns surplus produce into chutneys. Legghorn reduces poultry waste by giving us a taste for retired breeder hens. These businesses show ingenuity and compassion, but in an ideal world they wouldn't need to exist because the challenges they address would have been fixed at source.

This wave of purpose-driven enterprise is also growing. Many food and drink businesses are BCorp, a certification for businesses that demonstrate purpose and impact. It raised the bar for applicants by creating new criteria requiring them to meet a higher minimum standard across multiple areas. The Guild of Fine Food's Great Taste Awards, best known for celebrating artisan brands and flavour, now also champion start-ups with ethical and sustainable missions through their bursary scheme – and entries for these have been steadily rising. It's a sign that more food entrepreneurs are putting people, planet and profit on equal footing, and being recognised for it.

In hospitality, values-driven innovation is gathering pace. Thomasina Miers, co-founder of the Wahaca restaurant group, has long championed sustainable sourcing, plant-forward menus and waste-conscious kitchens, all inspired by the flavours and spirit of Mexican street food. A founding member of the Sustainable Restaurant Association, she also co-founded Chefs in Schools, a charity that's transforming food and food education in the classroom. Wahaca, voted the UK's most sustainable restaurant group by Which?, now has a 50% vegetarian menu, reduces waste by cooking whole carcasses, and sources British regenerative beef.

Mitch Tonks, through his Rockfish restaurants, works exclusively with Marine Stewardship Council (MSC)-certified seafood and is helping to rebuild local supply chains through seasonal preservation and a zero-waste ethos. And pulses are making a comeback thanks to the work of many chefs, restaurateurs, brand owners and more.

What all these changemakers have in common is that they are working within – and often against – an outdated food system that can be geared towards production and high profits at the cost of ecological balance and social justice. Large corporates and supermarket chains still dominate the market and their record has been mixed. Their scale and visibility, however, mean they can play a crucial role in making a positive impact – and they increasingly are.

Pressures on business continuity and externally from campaigners, consumers and innovators within these businesses are pushing them to act – their own resilience and commercial futures are also at stake. From embracing government initiatives to nudge people towards healthier choices to trialling more plant-forward ranges, the ripple effect is real, even if it's far from fast enough.

As Wildfarmed co-founder Andy Cato explained in response to an audience question at Groundswell, doing things things the right way isn't always easy or popular. Sometimes it means making choices that don't feel perfect, like Wildfarmed's decision to sell white bread made from regeneratively grown wheat. It's less nutritious than wholegrain, but more familiar and affordable for customers. Crucially, it helps farmers scale up better farming practices.

Food grown properly, with care for people and planet, also often comes at a higher price, putting it out of reach for many. These businesses are navigating tightropes every day, balancing impact, integrity and affordability in a system that still makes that balancing act incredibly hard. Their successes offer hope, but they also reveal the deeper work still to do: changing the rules of the game so that positive steps for a better future aren't the exception, but the norm.

So where do we come in? As food lovers, what can we do to support this shift and help it grow? Our final chapter looks at ways we can do our bit for positive, practical change.

The big takeaways

1. **The planet is under strain:** The way we produce and consume food is pushing Earth's natural systems towards dangerous tipping points.
2. **Soil and seas are in crisis:** Intensive farming has degraded soils, reduced biodiversity and released the carbon once stored underground, while industrial fishing and aquaculture have depleted wild stocks and damaged marine ecosystems.

3. **Our tastes carry costs:** Popular choices like beef, chicken, salmon, chocolate, palm oil, avocados and almonds have steep environmental footprints, while pulses, beans, shellfish and wild venison offer a better alternative.
4. **Environmental impact is complicated business**: Calculating the true footprint of food – from production to transport – is notoriously complicated. Producers, retailers and governments must make sustainable choices easier for us all.
5. **Water is a hidden ingredient:** Agriculture consumes 70% of global fresh water. Crops like rice, wheat, almonds and avocados are often grown in drought-prone regions, exporting 'virtual water' from areas of scarcity to where it's already abundant.
6. **Plastic is a packaging paradox:** Food packaging is necessary and is the single biggest use of plastic, yet less than 10% is recycled globally. Microplastics are now found everywhere – including in our own bodies.
7. **Food waste is endemic:** One-fifth of all food produced for human consumption never gets eaten, wasting precious land, energy and resources. In the UK, households account for 60% of waste, but farms, manufacturers, retailers and hospitality all play their part.
8. **Labels matter but can mislead:** Date labels often confuse safety with quality, sending edible food to the bin. Green claims can be just as murky, with marketing sometimes masking more than it reveals.
9. **Innovation is a tool, not a fix:** From methane-reducing cattle feed and cultivated meat to vertical farms and nature tech, technology can cut impacts. We need to be open to its potential, but it mustn't distract from the deeper reforms needed in how things work.
10. **Changemakers are lighting the way:** Across farms, brands, kitchens and communities, people are proving that food can be grown and shared with care for people and planet. Their work shows what's possible and why we must all play a part.

POSITIVE, PRACTICAL CHANGE

'I am a nice shark, not a mindless eating machine. If I am to change this image, I must first change myself.'

Bruce, *Finding Nemo* (2003)

Let's be honest – none of us can single-handedly transform the food system. It's vast, anxiety-inducing and riddled with challenges that are beyond our control. As food writer Jay Rayner aptly concludes in *A Greedy Man in a Hungry World*, 'All this stuff is ear-bleedingly, eyeball-gougingly complicated.'[1]

It's complicated, and as we've seen, there are trade-offs everywhere. When we're bombarded with doomsday headlines about the planet on fire or the perils of processed foods, it can feel easier to switch off or get distracted. But the thing is, every action we take, however small, contributes to something bigger.

As food lovers, we have more power than we think. Armed with what we know now, we can do things differently, starting with small steps that suit our lives. As the saying goes, 'There is only one way to eat an elephant: one bite at a time.'

It might mean going back to what our grandparents knew was good and true. It might mean embracing something new. Most often, it will mean balancing both, doing our best to make better choices within the limits placed on us by the pressures of modern life.

What that looks like will be different for all of us. Time, money, availability and headspace all matter. It's easy to say we should all cook from scratch, eat organic and buy direct from local producers, but that's simply not realistic for everyone.

So where can we start? Here are 10 ways we can make a difference – practically, positively and within our means.

1. Care and engage

Like Bruce the great white shark in *Finding Nemo*, we need to have an epiphany about how we relate to the food we eat.

It starts with something surprisingly simple: caring. Caring about where food comes from and about the people who grow, make, sell and serve it. Caring about how what we eat affects not just our health and well-being, but that of the planet too.

When you care, it's hard not to get curious, start asking questions and notice the stories on and behind the labels. Who's growing our rice? Where does our chicken come from? How much are the people who made our chocolate being paid? We don't have to become experts, but the more we engage, the more we'll notice. And the more we notice, the easier it is to make better choices all round.

While it's easy to get swept up in the whirlwind of a 'superfood', it's a marketing term, not a nutritional truth. All food is super, especially when it's grown, cooked and shared with care. From bags of carrots and tins of beans at home to what we order in a restaurant and whose work we support, every meal is an opportunity to do better.

Caring and engaging aren't about being perfect. They're about being awake to the world around us and doing what feels achievable, bit by bit. It's not all or nothing. It's about building a better relationship with what we eat and drink over time.

2. Take a balanced view

Food conversations today can feel loud, emotional and polarised. From competing voices and inherent bias to half-baked claims on social media, it's easy to lose sight of what's true and meaningful. Taking a balanced, inclusive and holistic view helps cut through the noise.

It means stepping back and seeing the bigger picture and asking what being 'good' really means in practice. For example, a restaurant might boast a menu full of consciously sourced ingredients, but if the people cooking and serving that food are being underpaid or mistreated, is it really a 'good' business? Or if you call yourself a plant-based food-waste warrior while running roughshod over the traditions of diverse communities, are you still part of the problem?

Equally, conversations about the diets of underprivileged communities can take place in privileged spaces with little racial diversity. If people from underrepresented groups are invited to contribute to these conversations without being paid or meaningfully subsidised, it's just another form of exploitation. Bursaries, sponsorships and fair pay for participation are small but powerful steps towards fixing this.

The same goes for how we approach corporate players. It's easy to paint big businesses as the enemy but they have power, resources and influence, along with shareholders, stakeholders and savvy shoppers who are pushing them to change. If they've been part of the problem, they can be part of the solution. Their own resilience and commercial future also depend on it: no company thrives on a planet with broken supply chains, dwindling resources and distrustful consumers. Shutting them out of the room and shouting them down just drives their work underground and makes it harder to have joined-up conversations.

Building a truly inclusive and effective movement means welcoming *all* voices to the table. That's what holistic thinking looks like: bringing together a community of people who care, however different they might seem.

Balance also means staying realistic. With budgets tight and time short, food choices are often limited and women still carry much of the burden of feeding families. True balance means recognising these realities, finding common ground and moving forward without guilt or judgement.

3. Connect with how food is produced and sold

Once we take a holistic and balanced view, we need to connect more closely with how food gets to our plates and where it goes from there. Every time we buy food, we cast a vote for the kind of food system we want to support. As activist Vandana Shiva says, 'Eating is an ecological act, eating is a political act. Eating is a health act. And eating is an act of solidarity.'[2]

We also vote with our wallets. Many of us can afford to pay a little more but often choose not to thanks to a food culture that prizes convenience and bargains, but as we've seen, cheap food comes at a cost. Someone always pays the price. Better buying choices reward the producers, suppliers, retailers and products working towards good food for all.

Shop smart

Supermarkets' actions and business models can sometimes be easy to criticise, but we we rely on them for convenience, affordability and choice. They also provide opportunities for suppliers to sell large volumes of products, secure investment and bring new ideas to a wide audience. Many supermarkets are taking steps to make healthier and more sustainable choices easier for all of us, but they still rely on us to engage and respond to make it worth their while.

Premium supermarkets often set the bar on quality and welfare standards, but value and mid-range retailers are stepping up too, using their scale to drive affordability while improving sourcing standards. Fairness and quality don't always have to come with a higher price tag. Shopping exclusively at premium retailers isn't realistic for everyone, and it's not the only way to support change. Combine supermarkets with farmers' markets, produce box schemes or independent shops when you can to champion and support a wider range of businesses and community initiatives. This helps spread your money more widely, giving more businesses a chance to benefit from your custom while getting you closer to producers and growing your own food knowledge along the way.

Eat seasonal and local

Getting closer to producers often means getting closer to seasonal and local food, which tends to taste better, be more abundant and offer better value when it's in peak supply. It's also one of the simplest ways to cut food miles and reduce environmental impact.

Of course, eating entirely seasonally is tough in the UK, but making the most of what's in season when we can connects us to how our fruit, vegetables, fish and even cheese is produced. Ceri Jones, food educator and author of the cookbook *It Starts with Veg*, recommends eattheseasons.co.uk as a handy guide to what's in season here.

Buying and eating local supports the local economy, traditional foodways and Indigenous knowledge. However, not everything we eat can or should be local. Our palates are global and access to cultural staples from around the world – like turmeric, rice or plantain – is essential for many.

What matters is being mindful of how that food is produced. If that £1 jar of turmeric seems too good to be true, it probably is. Somewhere along the supply chain, something will give. Likewise, applying blanket bans on so-called 'problematic' products like palm kernel oil can do more harm than good. Millions of smallholder farmers around the world rely on crops like palm for their livelihoods. Change is needed, but it comes from demanding better standards, not cutting off vital sources of income altogether.

THREE KEYS TO EATING SEASONALLY
by Angela Clutton

I always break the point of eating seasonally down to three things:

The sustainability angle. Producing things out of their natural season, a long way from where they are consumed, simply takes more energy. Even if those things are in season there and so are being more naturally grown, the energy of storage/refrigeration to protect them while they get them where they are going is significant – more so than the impact of the actual miles.

Then there is deliciousness. Things taste better in their season when given all the benefit of growing in the climate they love, whether that's sunshine for peaches or frost for kale. And back to the storage/transportation issue: produce is cropped before being fully ripe so it doesn't spoil in transit. But fake ripening in transit or on the shelves doesn't do much for flavour.

Lastly, there is the soulful pleasure of feeling the rhythms of the year through your kitchen. I believe that eating seasonally is a key to letting yourself roll with that. There is joy in anticipation. It's important to miss things and then appreciate them even more.

Angela Clutton is a food writer and the author of Seasoning: How to Cook and Celebrate the Seasons.

Grow your own

A kitchen garden, balcony planter or shared allotment may not feed a household, but that's not the point. Growing your own food, even just a few herbs or salad leaves, is less about self-sufficiency and more about connection: to what we eat, how it grows, the seasons and the soil itself. It's also a powerful way to spark an early understanding of food production in children, especially those growing up far removed from land or growing spaces.

Whether it's a windowsill full of basil or a bucket of potatoes on a balcony, growing something edible invites us to slow down, get our hands dirty and appreciate the time and effort behind every morsel. And if you're the type to kill any plant you touch, inspiration abounds for small, forgiving projects that are easy to start and hard to finish off. TV producer Martha Swales, known online as Marf's Kitchen Garden, has brought her little city garden to life in creative ways: planting seeds in washed-out tins of fish, replanting supermarket herbs and sprouting fruits in containers. Her advice for anyone thinking of giving it a go? Just start.

Gardening can be a solitary joy, but it's also a powerful collective act. As the Unearthed exhibition at the British Library in 2025 showed, gardening and growing bring people together across cultures, generations and backgrounds. The Coco Collective community garden in London's Lewisham, for example, reconnects members of the Afro-diaspora to growing heritage plants and ancestral knowledge.

Gardening also helps rethink waste. Kitchen scraps and leftovers can be turned into compost, feeding the soil instead of the bin. If decomposing waste isn't your thing, initiatives like Compost Club collect household food waste in East Sussex and return it later as rich matter for gardens. Elsewhere, community compost schemes share the bounty with local parks, neighbours and shared plots. From window boxes and kitchen counters to parks and community gardens, green spaces that grow food nourish far more than just our diets.

4. Build better food habits for life

Cooking real food at home helps us nourish each other, waste less and stretch our budgets further. A basket of basic ingredients can go a long way, especially when we batch cook, freeze leftovers and make the most of seasonal produce.

It doesn't have to mean hours in the kitchen either. Microwaves, air fryers and slow cookers are helping turn simple, affordable ingredients like cheaper cuts of meat, dried lentils and beans, and frozen vegetables into wholesome meals. Cooking might not always be quick or easy, but it's one of the best tools we have to build healthier habits for ourselves and our families and to have a positive impact on the planet. It's an essential life skill.

But here's the catch: not everyone knows where to begin, and for many, cooking isn't a pleasurable pursuit. Whether we're parents, carers, teachers or friends, we all have a role in helping each other and the next generation build a healthy relationship with food. And it doesn't have to be perfect or fancy. Here's how:

* **Normalise real, everyday cooking.** Food education in the UK is patchy at best, and nutrition barely gets a look in. Practical, life-long cooking skills with versatile and culturally varied demonstrations, such as how to make a tomato sauce, a curry base or a stir-fry, will stand the next generation in better stead.
* **Pass on your skills.** If you do know how to cook, pass it on. Show someone how to toss a salad or stir a pot. Get kids involved early with jobs like peeling, mixing and rolling. As women still carry most of the cooking and domestic load at home, teaching boys and men these skills helps to shift the balance and share the responsibility more fairly.
* **Seek out opportunities to engage.** Organisations like the Country Trust and NFU Education run food education activities across the UK. Many schools, councils and charities offer cooking clubs, community kitchens and growing projects. Get involved if you can or spread the word about them with schools and parents who might not know they exist.

* **Support better children's menus.** Many restaurant chains and independents are improving kids' options, offering smaller versions of adult dishes or meals packed with colour and variety. Choose these when eating out if your progeny permit and tell the business, your friends and followers why you're doing it.
* **Talk about where food comes from.** Whether it's rice from India, avocados from Peru or cheese from Somerset, start conversations about the people and places behind the food on your plate. This builds respect for cultures and communities beyond our own.

Food habits don't stop with childhood. We can all keep learning to make more informed, respectful choices. Food festivals, tours and courses provide opportunities for learning and family fun.

Another thing to consider is that as we age, our food needs change. Whether you're caring for older relatives or working in food or hospitality, think about offering softer foods, smaller portions or meals that are easy to prepare and eat. From tech-powered meal planning to texture-modified foods, new tools are emerging to help meet the needs of us all. We need to stay curious and support businesses and services that are trying to do things differently.

HEALTHY AGEING AND SUSTAINABLE EATING
by Barbara Bray

In the UK, men and women over the age of 65 can expect to spend around half of their remaining years in good health. There are a range of reasons for this, including levels of affluence and where we live, but one factor that is modifiable is what we eat. The better our diet, the greater the chance of increasing the number of years that we spend in good health.

Healthy ageing is defined by the World Health Organization (WHO) as 'the process of developing and maintaining the functional ability that enables well-being in older age'.

This gives us the opportunity to decide what good looks like for us as individuals. One person's daily hill walk could be another's afternoon tea with friends. The same applies to our food behaviours, such as shopping, cooking and eating.

The best diet is one that we can sustain and enjoy. No food is nutritious if it ends up in the bin. Food waste can be harder to manage, especially as meals bought outside of the home are often served in larger quantities than we need, and depending on where you live, single portions of food in supermarkets can be harder to find.

It's easy to fall into a routine of rotating the same six meals each week and reducing the mental load of thinking about what to buy, prepare and eat, but the meals that serve us well are not the same throughout the course of our lives. Mid-life is an opportune time to assess dietary needs and look at how our food behaviours impact our health and the environment. Progress rather than perfection is a helpful place to start.

Barbara Bray is a healthy ageing nutrition expert and founder of Alo Solutions, a food safety and nutrition consultancy.

5. Buy and eat less, but better

As an antidote to all-you-can-eat buffets, piled-high platters and bulk-buy deals, there's a more considered, tasteful way to eat and drink: buy and eat less, but better. For those who can afford to make the switch, this simple shift can have a big, positive impact.

Buying less helps reduce food waste. It encourages us to think more carefully about what we actually need and can use instead of filling our baskets with offers and fresh produce we forget about until it's too late. Wasting less food at home saves money, time and precious resources.

Eating less gives us the opportunity to prioritise better-quality and higher-welfare products when we do buy them. This could mean choosing organic produce, free-range eggs, higher-welfare meat or better-sourced fish. It might also mean backing artisanal and small-batch producers who inject diversity, creativity and quality into our food system. Labels like Great Taste gold stars can be a useful signpost. These small swaps make a real difference when we buy and eat them more occasionally rather than as the everyday norm.

It also helps break the cycle of so-called 'cheap' food. By choosing to buy less but better, it sends a message that we value food produced with care and that we're willing to support the people and practices that make it possible and boost our own health in the process.

Meat

'Buy and eat less, but better' is a message that stirs strong feelings when it comes to meat. Nutrient-dense and protein-rich, animal-based food is essential to nutrition in many countries. But what counts as 'less' is relative, and when life is busy or you're eating on the go, it's not always easy to clock quality. In the UK, we eat roughly twice as much meat as the global average, and a lot of it is processed or preserved by smoking, curing, salting or adding preservatives, which can fall into the ultra-processed Nova category. There are currently no official recommended intake levels.[3]

For health and for the planet at a population level, though, the message is clear: we need to eat less meat. The UK's National Food Strategy recommends a 30% reduction in meat consumption by 2032. The Climate Change Committee calls for a 35% reduction of meat consumption by 2050, recommending eating better-quality meat and more plant-based food.[4]

It's a tough message, given how much we love eating meat and how deeply livestock farming is tied to rural communities and food traditions. But change doesn't have to mean cutting it out altogether. It's about eating more consciously: respecting where meat comes from, choosing better when we can and appreciating the bigger picture, as Rob Percival notes in his piece here.

WHAT MEAT LOVERS CAN DO NEXT
A Q&A with Rob Percival

Why do so many animal lovers happily eat meat?
In the UK, we pride ourselves on being a nation of animal lovers, yet most of the meat in our diets (namely, that provided by pigs and chickens) is sourced from industrial farming systems with routine welfare failings. It seems that we commonly say one thing and do another – our values and behaviour are misaligned. This misalignment is partly caused by cultural traditions, which can be deeply entrenched. Our society (like all others) has allocated animals into 'food' and 'non-food' categories – we treat one group very differently to another, and channel our empathy more readily towards those in the 'non-food' camp.

Beyond this cultural context, our psychology is also important. Recent research has demonstrated that we are adept at withdrawing moral concern from 'food' animals, perceiving them to be less minded, sentient and valuable. This happens beneath the threshold of conscious thought and facilitates more uninhibited consumption.

Why do we enjoy eating meat so much? There is a whole group of people who react very badly (take it as a personal attack, even) when they're told they need to reduce meat consumption.
We are what we eat. That is to say, our identity is informed by our diet. And in the case of meat, it seems that we are especially sensitive to challenge. Research has shown that the very presence of a vegan can trigger a defensive response in meat eaters.

We are perhaps so sensitive because we know that meat can be ethically problematic, even at the best of times. Consuming animal foods requires that we take animal lives, and that can be morally disturbing. The killing of animals is a highly ritualised activity in almost every society – it is an act imbued with deep meaning, and always, always ethically complicated. But that's not true in our society. We just look away and pretend it isn't happening. This strategy works, for the most part. But we remain sensitive. We don't like being reminded of our complicity in harm or confronted with the alternative – the possibility that we could choose to abstain from animal foods and eat plants.

When it comes to planetary impact, are some meats better than others? How do poultry and eggs compare to, say, beef and lamb?

Generally speaking, ruminant meat (beef and lamb) and dairy contribute more greenhouse gases than chicken and pork. That's on a product level. But it's also important to look at the system the animal was farmed in. Most pigs and chickens are industrially farmed, and the overall impact is hugely damaging to nature and the climate. On the other hand, many ruminant animals are free ranging (though industrial dairy is a big business) and so can be better for nature if farmed in an organic or agroecological way. From an environmental perspective, if one eats animal foods, the mantra should be 'less and better' – much less than the average diet today, and much better standards of animal welfare.

Is there a perfect system to rear animals for food?

There is no perfect system, but organic provides the most comprehensive certification of welfare and environmental sustainability. Farmers in the organic camp and beyond are also innovating, employing regenerative and pasture-fed methods, integrating trees into pasture and doing all sorts of clever things that can further improve ecological outcomes.

What would you advise meat lovers to do?

Beyond eating 'less and better' and choosing organic or pasture-fed products, I'd suggest 'eat the lot'. You may be familiar with the concept of nose-to-tail eating, where one consumes, as far as is practical, the whole animal – I suggest we go one further. I propose *obligatory* nose-to-tail eating. If you eat 'meat' at all, and especially if you consider yourself a 'meat lover', you must be prepared to eat the lot: heart, liver, kidneys, connective tissues, edible bits from inside heads, bones and so on.

Do you want to eat animals or not? That is the question. For me, it's either all in or all out. Eat nose-to-tail or go plant-based. There's lots of good nutrition in the offal. And it's better for producers if we buy the whole beast, and more respectful to the animal. The idea that we raise and slaughter an animal only to eat a select few slices of muscle should be seen as absurd and backwards. For those who don't want to eat hearts, offal and gristly bits, going plant-based is an excellent choice.

Rob Percival is the author of The Meat Paradox: Eating, Empathy, and the Future of Meat and head of food policy at the Soil Association.

Seafood

Eating seafood more responsibly is more complicated than it seems, especially in the UK, where our preference centres on just five species: cod, haddock, salmon, tuna and prawns. According to seafood expert Mike Warner, founder of A Passion for Seafood and chairman of the Shellfish Association of Great Britain, this narrow preference creates a paradox: 'We export around 80% of what we catch and import much the same amount of what we like to eat.'[5]

That makes changing habits difficult. Without a deeper national seafood culture, Warner says, people aren't thinking about seasonality, sustainability or trying new species unless they're dining out. Consumption is either static or falling, and encouraging change is a real challenge.

For everyday shoppers, certifications are a good place to start. They aren't perfect – they can miss seasonal nuance or be confusing – but they're still 'good reference points for making better choices at the checkout'.

When it comes to affordable, sustainable options, Warner suggests looking beyond supermarket fresh fish counters, where quality and product knowledge can vary. He advises looking to frozen-at-sea (FAS) products and good-quality, accredited tinned fish for better value and transparency.

What about omega-3? While salmon is often sold as the go-to source, its reputation is largely down to clever marketing. But not all farmed salmon is the same. Newer systems and higher-welfare methods are working to reduce impacts. There are plenty of lower-impact oily fish that are just as rich in omega-3, such as mackerel, herring, sardines, sprats and shellfish like crabs, prawns, oysters and mussels. If you're after an alternative to farmed salmon, Warner recommends trying trout: look for Mòr Atlantic Trout, which is reared in the open sea to high welfare standards, or ChalkStream Trout, a freshwater option with a lower environmental impact.

Ultimately, there's no single simple answer to what makes seafood 'better'. It depends on your values – whether you're prioritising flavour, nutrition, sustainability, seasonality or supporting fishing communities. But with a little curiosity and some trusted guidance, it's possible to eat fish in a way that's good for you and better for the planet.

Bread

'Eat better bread' is fast becoming one of the more contentious messages in the conversations about what we eat, touching on everything from nutrition and food waste to class, culture and affordability. Loaves can be bought for pennies, with long lists of suspect ingredients but also the added vitamins and minerals many people need.

Professor Giles Yeo of Cambridge University has pointed to the inherent classism in parts of the ultra-processed food debate, especially when comparing cheap supermarket loaves – soft, easy to overconsume and highly affordable – with expensive artisan ones that may not actually be much better when it comes to salt, sugar or additives. And of course, it's neither logical nor practical to expect everyone to bake their own.

Chris Young, who leads the Real Bread Campaign at Sustain, is working to raise awareness about what goes into our bread while pushing producers, brands and retailers to do better. He coined the term 'sourfaux' to describe loaves labelled as sourdough but made with artificial raising agents rather than traditional natural fermentation. While this is duplicitous and misleading for consumers, a BBC Radio 4 Food Programme spotlight also highlighted the real damage it causes to those who can't digest the pretend versions.[6]

Bread is also controversial for another reason: we waste it in vast quantities. According to the Felix Project, around 24 million slices of bread are thrown away in the UK every day, making it one of the most commonly wasted foods.[7] A loaf can be sliced and frozen to stay fresh and last longer to reduce both waste and cost.

SOLVING THE BREAD DILEMMA
by Chris Young

Depending on whose figures you believe, around 11 million loaves of 'bread' are made every day and 99% of UK households buy them. The thing is, the stats also indicate that around 85% are additive-laden loaves, manufactured by industrial dough fabricators using the Chorleywood process.

Loaves made by, or for, supermarket in-store 'bakeries' tend to contain cocktails of additives, hidden by a legal loophole that doesn't require ingredients lists to be displayed for unpackaged food. Increasing numbers of those 'bakeries' are now what we call loaf tanning salons, in which prefabricated products (churned out a long time ago in factories far, far away) are merely rebaked to brown and crisp the crust. That's a heck of a lot of UPF! Even some of the 'craft' bakeries use additives.

So what to do?

Seek out a local, independent bakery that doesn't use additives – the Real Bread Map on the Real Bread Campaign website can help you search. While you're out shopping, look for the Real Bread Loaf Mark. Seize the dough by making your own Real Bread at home, by hand or adopted machine. Other elements of our work towards our vision of everyone having the chance to choose additive-free bread include efforts to put Real Bread on the menu of schools and other public-sector institutions; and our Real Bread for All guide to bridging the gap to what people on the tightest budgets can realistically afford.

Back to the supermarkets and other Big Bakers – if you'd like them to make Real Bread available, accessible and affordable to everyone across the land, tell them so!

Chris Young is the co-ordinator of the Real Bread Campaign by Sustain.

Ultra-processed foods

Ultra-processed foods (UPFs) are one of the most hotly debated subjects in today's food world. They cover everything from sliced bread and oat milk to breakfast cereals, fizzy drinks and ready meals. That's part of the problem. The category is so broad it ends up being more confusing than helpful.

The truth is, UPFs are part of modern life. For many of us they make food affordable, safe and convenient, and cutting them out altogether simply isn't realistic. Research from the University of Leeds suggests that perceptions and psychology, not just processing, play a major role in why we overeat.[8] This echoes tactics the food industry has long used, like bliss points and ultra-soft textures to keep us coming back for more.

Like so much else, it comes down to making informed, balanced choices: paying attention to what's actually in the food, when and how often we eat it, and how it fits into our wider diet and lifestyle.

ULTRA-PROCESSED PANIC: WHAT WE CAN DO NEXT
by Professor Giles S.H. Yeo

I'm not a food snob. I'm also not on the payroll of Big Food. What I *am* is a pragmatist, and I think the current conversation around UPFs has gone a bit off the rails.

The term *ultra-processed food* is too broad. It includes too many different kinds of food. Some of those we probably *should* eat less of. The problem is, once you start putting oat milk, sliced bread and fizzy drinks into the same bucket, you're not helping people, you're confusing them.

A whiff of privilege and hypocrisy
There's a level of privilege in some of these conversations. The idea that the best thing to do is cook everything from scratch and eat whole foods – yes, lovely, but it's not always possible. It's a very privileged position to take. Class is also an issue. If you're standing there with your oat milk cappuccino saying we should ban UPFs, what are we really talking about here?

Taking fear out of additives and labels

Additives are broadly going to be safe, particularly today. I'm not going to drink a pint of xanthan gum - that would kill you. But the same goes for drinking a pint of anything ridiculous. If you're eating a pre-packaged food and you want it to last, of course it's going to have stuff in it. A lot of the concern comes down to names. If someone uses a chemical or Latin name - say, for turmeric - suddenly it looks scary. But it's still turmeric.

There's also this idea that a long ingredient list means something's bad. But that doesn't necessarily tell you anything. Chinese five spice - is that one ingredient or five? If I separate those out on a label, suddenly it looks like a long list. It's the same with ingredients like paprika extract - is it actually from paprika or is it engineered? And if it *is* engineered, is that bad? The length of the ingredients list isn't the thing that should concern us first.

The real problem with UPFs

On average, around 50% of our calories come from ultra-processed foods. And half of that is from bread. I've not seen any evidence that bread, in and of itself, is harmful. Is it tasty? Maybe not always. Is it cheap and convenient? Yes. Is it going to kill you? No.

Moving bread to one side, that leaves 25% of our calories coming from other UPFs. Now *that's* where we need to pay attention. The problem isn't necessarily the processing; it's what processing does to the food. Ultra-processed foods tend to be low in protein and fibre, and high in salt, sugar and fat. That's the issue.

It's about how calorically available the food becomes. Take corn on the cob - your body doesn't absorb all of it. But if you mash that into masa for a tortilla, you suddenly get a lot more of the calories from the same food. Processing does that. So when we're talking about UPFs, we need to look at what's *in* the food, not just the process that made it.

And then there's the Nova classification system. Carlos Monteiro had good intentions. The first three categories are quite useful. But Nova 4? That's where everything else that didn't naturally fit went in. It lumps in packaged bread, sweets and bougie croissants. So of course, when you run health studies on Nova 4 foods, you find links to poor health. Half the stuff in there, we probably *should* eat less of. But not *all* of it.

Moving away from unhelpful narratives

There's this phrase that gets thrown around a lot: 'Don't eat anything your grandmother wouldn't recognise as food.' But I think that's unhelpful. We don't live like our grandparents used to. And yes, of course cooking from scratch and eating whole foods is the best thing to do – in theory. But again, that's a privileged position to take. The people who can do it, should. But many people don't have that option. So what should they do?

Some top tips for your next grocery shop

If you're looking at a product and trying to work out if it's a better choice, ignore the long words for a moment. Focus on five things: protein, fibre, salt, sugar and fat.

Let's say you're looking at lasagnes. You're standing there in the frozen aisle and they're all lined up. Don't ask, 'Is this good or bad?' Ask: 'Which one has a bit more fibre? A bit more protein? Maybe a little less salt?'

Make your choice *within* the class of food you're trying to buy. Don't worry about whether it's ultra-processed. Worry about what's actually *in* it.

And finally, think about what you're eating over a week. We have days when we're busy and tired and just need something quick, then weekends where there's more time to cook from scratch. That's life. If you've had a takeaway on Friday and a kid's party on Saturday, fine. Just have something different on Sunday. It's about rhythm and balance over a period of time.

Professor Giles S.H. Yeo of Cambridge University is an obesity researcher and science communicator who has challenged popular views on ultra-processed foods.

Organic food

On the opposite end of the spectrum of UPFs is organic food. One of the greatest injustices is that good food produced with care is often the hardest to access. Organic food can be more expensive to produce, as it's more resource and labour intensive, and it can seem more expensive, as the price of conventional produce doesn't always reflect its true cost.

So what can you do if you want to buy organic but can't afford to switch completely? You can still make some practical swaps and informed choices.

* **Upgrade your pantry staples.** Oils, vinegars, grains, pulses and spices offer great value over time.
* **Go frozen.** Organic berries and greens can be cheaper in the freezer aisle and the range is growing every day.
* **Choose cheaper cuts.** Organic meat cooked low and slow still delivers flavour and nutrition.
* **Use the Dirty Dozen.** The Pesticide Action Network UK (PAN UK) publishes an annual 'Dirty Dozen' list that names the fruit and veg most likely to carry multiple pesticide residues.
* **Soak your fruit.** Research shows that soaking smooth-skinned fruit in a 2% cornflour solution and then a 5% baking soda solution can remove over 90% of some surface pesticide residues. Just 5–10 minutes in each does the trick if you can be bothered.[9]

6. Eat your beans

Pulses – the family of crops that includes beans, lentils, peas and chickpeas – are one of the best and most overlooked alternatives to meat. Two studies published in 2024, from the Food Foundation[10] and researchers at UCL and the University of Oxford,[11] came to the same conclusion: pulses offer the best alternative from a cost, environmental and health perspective.

Pulses are nutrition powerhouses. Ali Morpeth, registered nutritionist and expert on the link between health and climate, says, 'They are packed with plant-based protein and essential nutrients like potassium, iron and folate. Just 120g, or half a large can, of cooked beans provides around a third of your daily recommended fibre. Regularly consuming beans can improve your digestive health, make you feel fuller longer, and help improve your overall health.'[12]

Pulses are also low in fat and have a low glycaemic index, which means they don't cause blood sugar levels to spike. Dr Nadia Radzman,

Cambridge University research scientist and pulses researcher, is spearheading a campaign called Broad'n Mind to raise awareness of the role of fava beans (the dried version of broad beans) in mental health. She says fermented beans like tempeh and doubanjiang (Chinese spicy fermented beans) are a great source of the relaxing neurotransmitter GABA, which can help with anxiety.

This will come as no surprise to many cultures and communities around the world. Pulses are at the heart of many traditional cuisines, featuring in creative and irresistible ways. The dips and salads of the Middle East; the soups, stews and wraps in South America; and the curries, sautés and fermented specialties of South Asia are all fine examples that have captured the global imagination.

Yet pulses have been stigmatised in recent decades. 'Over time, they became associated with poverty and hardship,' says Dr Radzman.[13] In some places, this has led to what researchers call 'bean hesitancy' – a reluctance to embrace them driven by fears of flatulence, unfamiliarity or the belief that they're old-fashioned or hard to cook.

But change is brewing. A global campaign called Beans Is How aims to double pulse consumption by 2028, with over 100 chefs, schools, organisations and brands across 50 countries joining the cause. In the UK, Hodmedod's is reviving historic varieties like Carlin peas, once eaten by medieval monks. Their collaboration with Bold Bean Co. is helping to rebuild a domestic market for beautifully cooked British pulses.

If you're not sure where to start, look to the cultures that never fell out of love with beans – their recipes are pulsing with inspiration. And if gassiness puts you off, try soaking your pulses well and cooking them with digestive spices like ginger, asafoetida or bay leaves. Your gut – and the planet – will thank you.

7. Try something new

Over the past century, the variety of foods we grow, eat and celebrate has dramatically shrunk. Many traditional fruits, vegetables, grains, animal breeds, fish species and artisan foods have disappeared from our shops, our tables and even our memories, taking generations of knowledge, culture and identity with them.

It doesn't have to be this way. Food writer Dan Saladino, author of *Eating to Extinction*, suggests starting close to home to address this: 'Find a food that's rare or endangered where you live; try a different variety of apple or cheese; taste a variety of pea or bean you've never encountered before; create more diversity by saving seeds and growing food; and support the food producers and farmers helping to preserve distinctive and diverse foods in your area.'[14]

Sustainability and diversity often go hand in hand. With fish, for example, there are plenty of overlooked choices such as coley, hake, Alaska pollock and smoked trout. A Which? taste test even found that two-thirds of shoppers would happily swap smoked salmon for smoked trout, which is less intensively farmed. The Marine Conservation Society's Good Fish Guide rates over 130 species on sustainability and is a useful tool for better choices.[15]

Other planet-friendly foods are also hiding in plain sight. Mushrooms, seaweed, mussels and venison are all good examples. Mussels and other bivalves, like clams, oysters and scallops, are low-impact, affordable and good for marine ecosystems. Imani Black, oyster farmer and founder of Imani Minorities in Aquaculture, says: 'The "right producers" are people that are transparent, knowledgeable and want to share as much information about their products, how they are produced/harvested, etc. to let the consumer know everything about their seafood.'[16]

Venison, often seen as a luxury food, is also becoming more available. Lean, healthy and lower in environmental impact than most farmed meats, it's available in affordable formats like mince and meatballs. Just make sure you check where it's from – locally sourced, wild or well-farmed venison is the better choice, as some imported versions can be intensively farmed overseas.

Beyond these familiar foods, there's a world of exciting, culturally rich ingredients to explore. Insects, for example, are already enjoyed in 150 countries – crunchy, spiced, ground and even coated in chocolate. Singapore has approved 16 species for human consumption. You can find edible insects in places like London's Borough Market, but if that's too much, insect protein powder blends palatably into bakes and smoothies.

Further afield, food tech is pushing boundaries with more adventurous innovations. Kera Protein, for instance, has developed a way to transform chicken feathers into edible keratin protein powder, turning waste into a novel source of nutrition. Whether it makes its way onto our plates remains to be seen.

Trying something new doesn't mean giving up your favourites. It's about broadening your food horizons, supporting biodiversity and celebrating a smorgasbord of ingredients in your culinary adventures.

8. Understand labels

From organic certifications to carbon-neutral claims, food labels are everywhere. Some, like organic or Fairtrade, are based on strict, recognised standards. Others, like Red Tractor, set baseline legal requirements but don't always go much further. Then there are marketing-led claims, like 'carbon neutral', which often rely on offsetting or schemes that are hard to verify.

Without clear, consistent rules on what labels must cover – like environmental impact, animal welfare or social responsibility – labelling can end up confusing more than clarifying. As certification schemes generate income for the organisations running them, there's always a risk of a conflict of interest.

That doesn't mean we should ignore labels. They can help us make better choices, but it's worth reading them with a pinch of salt. What's being measured? Who's doing the certifying? What's being left out? Asking these questions can help you spot greenwashing and shop with more confidence. See the green claims glossary from Which? in the appendix for more.

Many of us already worry about getting it right, especially when nutrition labels, country-of-origin information or ingredients lists aren't easy to understand. Ultra-processed foods (UPFs) are a case in point. As Professor Giles Yeo points out, it's not realistic to stand in the supermarket reading lists of every additive or industrial-sounding ingredient.[17] The small size of the font on the labels also doesn't help our cause. But spotting the difference between a short, simple list and a long, complex one can still guide us towards balance.

Provenance, the story of where food comes from, is often hidden in the small print. While some products proudly fly a national flag or name a region, others make it harder to tell. In the UK, labels must show the country of origin for fresh meat, fish, honey, olive oil, wine, fruit and veg, but wording can still be vague. A pork pie labelled 'British', for example, may legally be made in the UK with imported pork, without always making the country it was reared in clear.

Certifications are better than nothing and can offer extra reassurance, but none are perfect. Standards vary, enforcement isn't flawless and small, responsible producers can choose not to certify at all because certification is costly and time-consuming. As Catherine Chong, climate economist and agroecology activist at CLEAR, puts it in her piece below, labels are both a challenge and an opportunity. They can help us navigate a crowded marketplace, but they're no substitute for building trust.

There's a list of some common and respected labels in the appendix (see 'What Food Labels Actually Mean'), but sometimes a chat with a local producer or digging a little deeper into the brands you love will tell you what you need to know.

A CASE FOR CLEAR LABELLING
by Catherine Chong

Consumers rely on the on-pack information to make quick decisions when shopping. If the right information is provided, they can be empowered to shop based on their personal health, social and environmental preferences.

What are some of the common misleading claims?

There are many examples of misleading claims on the positive social and environmental outcomes of food and drink products, relating to the farming, processing, manufacturing, packaging and transporting aspects of the food, for instance carbon neutral or carbon negative.

Broadly speaking, the complexity in accounting for carbon sequestration, whether at farm level or product level, has opened the door for a Wild West of carbon greenwashing. While it's generally advisable to ascertain the legitimacy of the claims by looking up whether the product has been certified by validation and verification bodies (VVB), that doesn't mean the claims made are definitely accurate. There have been several cases of large-scale misrepresentations by a number of VVBs over the last decades.

Are these labels required by law?

When combining national laws, sector-specific regulations and retained EU laws, there are possibly dozens of laws and hundreds of regulatory provisions that directly and indirectly affect food labelling in the UK. Yet there isn't a mandatory requirement to inform consumers on how our food is farmed. The exception is organic. In the UK, the use of 'organic' on food labels is governed by retained EU legislation that stipulates that only food that has been certified by approved organic control bodies, such as the Soil Association and Organic Farmers and Growers, can legally be sold as organic in the UK.

Can we trust standards like MSC, ASC, Red Tractor or RSCPA? Broadly speaking, yes, with the caveat that one needs to be aware of what the standards cover or mean. Sometimes consumers misunderstood the level of production standards, or the potential social and environmental implications.

> **What does CLEAR do?**
>
> The Consortium for Labelling for the Environment, Animal Welfare and Regenerative Farming (CLEAR) was set up in 2021 by over 20 non-governmental organisations (NGOs) when the Agriculture Act 2020 and Trade Act 2021 failed to safeguard farming standards. The mission was to lobby for a method of production labelling where the information on how our food is farmed would be made mandatory information for all food at all points of sale.
>
> Today, CLEAR consists of almost 60 NGOs, representing a wide range of interests and expertise across the environment, animal welfare, labour conditions and human health, actively representing the voice of agroecology in lobbying for food labelling regulations, rules and policies that will support our food system to transition to a more sustainable and regenerative future.
>
> **Does CLEAR have any advice for consumers and citizens?**
>
> Always engage with NGOs that champion the issues that matter to you. The more you engage, the more you learn, and the more they learn about what you care about. The more engaged everyone is in the food system, the more likely it is that we could achieve food sovereignty and a food system transition to a more sustainable and regenerative future.
>
> *Catherine Chong is a climate economist and agroecology activist. For more information about CLEAR, visit clearfoodlabeluk.org.*

9. Make conscious choices

As sustainability expert Trewin Restorick reminds us in his piece below, the full shelves of our supermarkets hide the real pressures faced by the food system.[18] While the scale of the challenge can feel overwhelming, we all have the power to do something.

One of the simplest places to start is by supporting the businesses – restaurants, cafés, shops – that are trying to make a difference. Another is by valuing what you already have, using up leftovers, reducing waste and making the most of every ingredient.

FIVE WAYS TO CREATE A BETTER FOOD SYSTEM
by Trewin Restorick

The size of the challenge can make individual action feel futile, but change is required at all levels. All of us can play a role in driving the transition to a more robust and fairer food system. Here are five things to consider.

1. Change your diet
We can't keep destroying natural environments to feed the world, so we must farm as efficiently as possible to get the most value from our land. Currently, a huge amount of farmland is used to grow crops to feed livestock, which we then eat. Reducing the amount of meat in our diet would allow some of this land to grow crops that we eat directly. This would cut carbon emissions and safeguard nature. Reducing the amount of meat you eat has environmental benefits, can be healthier and is often cheaper.

2. Reduce your food waste
If food waste was a country, it would be the third biggest carbon emitter in the world. Reducing food waste saves money and has significant environmental benefits. Every household can make a difference through better meal planning, thoughtful use of the freezer and being careful with portion sizes. Any edible food that might be wasted can be redistributed to others through food banks or community fridges, helping those who might be struggling to feed their families.

3. Add variety
Some everyday foods, such as avocados and coffee, will be hit most by a changing climate. There will also be increased risks from disease and pests, which could hit a food system increasingly reliant on a small range of staple crops. We can all help to create a more resilient food system by eating a wider variety of food, particularly foods with a lower carbon footprint, such as beans and pulses.

4. Embrace innovation

The need for change requires a new agricultural revolution that extracts more calories from less land without bankrupting the earth and its soils along the way. Innovation will be required from a sector that is inherently conservative and from a public deeply suspicious about changes to the way that food is grown. We need to be more open to different ways of growing food, from eating insects or lab-based meat for protein to new farming methods.

Any new innovations need to be thoroughly scrutinised to ensure that they benefit our health and the environment. For example, transitioning to a vegan diet consisting of a high level of ultra-processed food might not be the most sustainable option.

5. Celebrate local and community solutions

Fundamentally, we need to cherish and value the food we eat by understanding the amount of time, resources and expertise required to feed the world. Growing your own food or getting involved with community gardens and other local growing schemes is a great way to connect with nature and to directly understand the joys and challenges of growing your own food.

Climate change has often been viewed as a challenge for future generations, reducing the desire of politicians, companies and society to act now. This has always been a false assumption. The impact that climate change is having on food systems *now* demonstrates that all of us need to change our diets and habits to address this problem.

Trewin Restorick is an environmental campaigner, entrepreneur and speaker.

Eat out mindfully

The food we eat isn't limited to our homes. Hotels, cafés and restaurants have a big part to play in supporting people and the planet.

The Sustainable Restaurant Association's December 2024 Impact Report highlighted some outstanding initiatives from around the world.[19] These included a hotel in Bali sourcing salt from Indigenous artisans using traditional methods; a restaurant in Lima reinventing heritage recipes with local plants; a Hong Kong chef cooking monthly meals for people in need; and a London pizzeria that's never let cling film through its kitchen doors.

Not every restaurant can go as far as these, but many are doing what they can within their means, balancing rising costs and customer expectations. Their efforts deserve our support, whether that's choosing dishes made with seasonal or local ingredients or backing chefs who champion waste reduction, unloved ingredients and creative sourcing while also treating their people well.

Some restaurants are even setting new trends that can ripple beyond their own kitchens. In London, Fallow is rethinking supply chains by growing mushrooms in an attic and serving beef from retired dairy cows, while Doug McMaster's Silo, the UK's first zero-waste restaurant, remains an inspiration to many chefs and restaurateurs. Everything there – from menus to furniture – is designed around circularity, proving that waste-free dining is possible.

If these innovations make their way home with us in a doggy bag or as inspiration for our own cooking, even better.

Waste not

What we do with what's left really matters. Taking leftovers home from a restaurant isn't just smart – it's a habit worth developing.

Sustainable thinking for food lovers means valuing every mouthful, whether you're eating out or cooking at home. The simplest place to start? Using up what you've already got.

For many of us, this is second nature, ingrained by years of finger-wagging parents and grandparents warning us not to waste food. But a little modern-day motivation – thinking about the environmental cost of wasted food – can make boxing up or freezing extra portions feel even more worthwhile.

If you'd like to get more creative, there's plenty of inspiration out there. Food writers like Max La Manna, Sue Quinn and Conor Spacey have brilliant cookbooks full of waste-busting ideas. What it really takes is a small mindset shift, starting with asking yourself one simple question: 'Could this have another use?'

This kind of circular thinking – from repurposing leftovers and recycling packaging to ditching single-use plastics like cling film and carrier bags – is at the heart of sustainable eating. Composting food scraps for collection is another powerful habit, turning waste into nutrient-rich fertilizer to feed the soil elsewhere if not in your own garden.

Campaigns like Food Waste Action Week, run every March by Love Food Hate Waste, are full of practical tips. One of the simplest? Buy loose fruit and veg. If all apples, bananas and potatoes were sold loose, the UK could save 8.2 million shopping baskets worth of food waste every year simply by helping people buy only what they need.[20]

And it's not just about food. Reusable alternatives like silicone lids, beeswax wraps and reusable straws help reduce plastic waste. Saving energy and water in the kitchen is another simple way to cut waste and reduce our environmental impact. Small habits like using a pressure cooker, using lids on pans to reduce cooking time, turning off the tap while you wash vegetables or waiting until you have a full load to run the dishwasher can save both energy and water.

These everyday actions might seem small, but they all add up to help protect precious resources while saving money at the same time.

10. Use communication effectively

Many food lovers don't just care about what's on their plate – they also want to work in and with food and drink. That's where good communication comes in.

Our perceptions, choices and actions are shaped by the stories we hear and tell. Whether it's a restaurant promoting sustainability, a farmer explaining their practices or a campaign trying to inspire behaviour change, how we craft and share these stories matters.

Too often the message gets lost in translation. Technical jargon, fear-mongering headlines and polarising soundbites can overwhelm or alienate us. So much food and climate communication falls short, failing to make it feel personal, real or relevant.

Social media is often where communication misses its mark. Some overcomplicate the message. Others treat it like a corporate noticeboard instead of the digital entertainment, emotion-led space it's designed to be. And all the while, the loudest voices are often the least informed.

Ultimately, a product that doesn't sell is worth nothing, no matter how ethical or impactful it might be. That's why brands, campaigners and changemakers need to connect emotionally, use plain language and build trust through storytelling, not fear. There are countless examples of farmers, fishermen and brands telling their stories with aplomb online. Farmer Ben Andrews, Ashley Mullenger (aka The Female Fisherman) and Bold Bean Co. are all excellent examples.

If you're someone building a platform for positive, practical change:

* Know your audience – and meet them where they are.
* Make it meaningful, human and relatable.
* Use emotion to engage – will they feel happy, sad, shocked, amused, etc.?
* Combine feelings with facts, but always in plain language.
* Keep learning, because algorithms change and so do people and trends.

Importantly, we need to craft narratives because people don't remember facts – they remember stories. Stories make ideas stick. They spark emotions that create connection. Relevance and relatability build trust.

The responsibility to engage with communications isn't just on brands. It's on all of us, whether we're scrolling, sharing or starting conversations of our own. Experts like Dr Rupy Aujla of The Doctor's Kitchen and Dr Karan Raja, one of the biggest health and science creators on social media globally, are debunking myths online and making science-based advice accessible.

For food lovers who are more interested in the eating and drinking than the marketing, we can:

* Question what we read before we share it.
* Check the source – is it credible, qualified, biased or just clickbait?
* Support voices that share useful, balanced information.

* Call out bad practice, whether it's misleading claims or poor behaviour.

Social media is a powerful tool when used responsibly and well. It's up to all of us to help shape the conversation and keep the focus on progress, not just noise.

NAVIGATING FOOD SCIENCE MISINFORMATION
by Dr Rupy Aujla

Why do people fall prey to nutrition misinformation online?
We aren't taught about nutrition at school, and certainly not at medical school either. There's a vacuum of information. People know the basics of physics, so they can spot flat earthers talking rubbish online. But with nutrition, there's no widely taught, agreed-upon consensus.

Add to that the fallacy of leaning into contrarian views. There's a general distrust of science, government and the medical establishment, which worsened post-Covid. Plus we're shortcut takers by nature. 'Take this supplement, drink this gut shot' – the desire for a quick fix makes misinformation appealing.

How do you know who to trust?
Look at credentials. A proper university qualification – not an online course – is a good start. 'Registered nutritionist' or 'registered dietitian' titles give some confidence, though it's not a blanket safety net as there plenty of dietitians and nutritionists who can't be trusted online. Red flags? If someone is constantly inflammatory, conspiratorial or doesn't align with the general body of evidence.

There are well-read people without qualifications who can be trustworthy too because they follow the science and back up their claims. It's tough to tell the difference, though, even for me!

What are the watchouts when reading food science headlines?

My honest opinion? Ignore food science headlines. One week protein is bad, the next it's the best thing ever. Science doesn't move as fast as media headlines suggest. Even people with master's degrees can misinterpret studies.

Watch out for who funded the study, whether it's peer reviewed, the sample size and if they're mistaking correlation for causation. But realistically, studies aren't easy for the public to access, and even trained eyes can slip up.

You'll hear things like 'seed oils cause inflammation' or 'soy is feminising', quoting rat studies that don't translate to humans. People see 'study' and 'big publication name' and that's enough to convince them. Honestly, focus on consistently eating well every day instead of chasing nutrition trends.

Dr Rupy Aujla is a nutritional medicine expert, author and founder of The Doctor's Kitchen app and podcast.

Some final food for thought

We've covered tough topics, big questions and the not-so-straightforward answers. The truth is that the food system is messy, imperfect and full of challenges. But that's no reason to switch off or give up.

The aim of this book isn't to put you off your food or to make you feel like you're not doing enough. It's to remind you that your love of food is powerful. That food can bring pleasure, connection and hope not just for you, but also for everything and everyone around you.

As culinary historian Jessica B. Harris says, 'Don't be set in your ways. Always be willing to change your mind, always be willing to be surprised, and always look to find joy.'[21]

Let this be the start of a new way to enjoy food with care, curiosity and confidence, in good taste and with a clearer view of what shapes what we eat and drink, and why it matters..

APPENDIX

Who's who in the world: Understanding the terms

The food system, much like the world it feeds, is shaped by power, geography and history. These terms are often used to describe geographies and communities. Here's what they mean.

Old World and New World

These terms came from European exploration in the 15th and 16th centuries.

* The Old World includes Europe, Asia and Africa – the areas known to Europeans at the time.
* The New World refers to the Americas, 'discovered' by colonisers like Columbus despite already being home to rich, established Indigenous cultures.

These terms reflect a Eurocentric worldview and underpin the early foundations of global food trade and power.

Global North and Global South

These terms describe the global divide between wealthy and less wealthy nations, shaped by colonial histories.

* The Global North includes economically powerful countries like the UK, US, Canada, France, Germany and Japan, most of which were former colonisers.
* The Global South refers to countries in Latin America, Africa and much of Asia, many of which were colonised.

This isn't just about geography. It's about a global system that has long favoured certain nations at the expense of others. The terms started to be used more in the late 20th century, replacing earlier language like 'First World' and 'Third World'.

Settler nations

Settler colonial nations are countries where European colonisers didn't just rule, but settled permanently, often displacing Indigenous populations in the process. These include the United States, Canada, Australia, New Zealand and South Africa.

These nations are part of the Global North, despite being geographically 'south' in some cases. They played a double role: as colonisers themselves and as recipients of land and labour taken from elsewhere. Their food systems are deeply shaped by this legacy, from land ownership and trade dominance to cultural food narratives.

Global majority

Coined by British educator Rosemary Campbell-Stephens, the term 'global majority' refers to people who are minoritised in countries like the UK and US, but who make up most of the world's population. It's a powerful reminder that people of African, Asian, Indigenous and Latin American descent are not a minority globally – they are the majority. It reframes conversations about identity, power and representation, including in food, drink and hospitality.

THE LANGUAGE OF DIVERSITY

Language matters when it comes to tackling racial justice in the food system. We recognise that communications play a big role in influencing people's beliefs and attitudes. Our communications should portray and promote diversity as a normal and positive characteristic of food and farming. We should help people to feel embraced, welcome and included.

Deep-rooted structural injustice is embedded in the food and farming system. This means that we will sometimes need to refer to or portray characteristics of people from diverse backgrounds in association with difficult themes. When we do so, it must be for the clear purpose of challenging the root causes of injustice. We must treat any such description or portrayal with respect and special care while avoiding labels, tokenism, stigma or stereotypes. We need to make special efforts to make it easier for people who have suffered injustices to be heard and support them to do so as respected experts.

Sustain's Diversity Style Guide is a helpful list of key terms around fairness and representation and words, acronyms and terms in use by 'authoritative third-sector advocacy groups, media and government agencies'. It can be downloaded from their website.[1]

The language of food and identity: Words you might hear (and what they mean)

It's important to understand the meaning of and difference between key terms that often come up in conversations about food and identity.[2]

* **Cultural appreciation:** Engaging with another culture with curiosity, care and respect. It means doing your homework, crediting your sources, platforming, championing and monetising talent/voices from that community.
* **Cultural appropriation:** Taking elements of a culture, e.g. recipes, dress or language, without understanding, credit or consent, especially by someone from a more dominant or

privileged background. It often involves profiting from what others were historically shamed or punished for.
* **Diaspora:** A community of people who have moved away – voluntarily or forcibly – from their ancestral homeland, often due to colonisation, conflict, slavery or economic pressures. Diasporas maintain cultural ties and often shape new traditions, especially through food. Examples include the South Asian diaspora in East Africa or the Caribbean and African diaspora in the Americas.
* **Erasure:** The silencing or removal of a culture's stories, people or contributions, often through rewriting history, ignoring origin stories or crediting the wrong sources. Black men, for example, were the first cowboys in the US but were written out of history and popular cultural stories.
* **Immigrant:** Someone who moves from one country to another, usually in search of better opportunities, education, work or family life. Immigrants often carry and adapt their food culture, contributing to the culinary life of their new home. Migration is often voluntary, though not always easy.
* **Lived experience:** First-hand, personal knowledge that comes from being part of a particular culture, identity or community. It's not the same as reading about something, but deep research, ongoing learning and community engagement can help fill the gap when you're working with cultures outside your own.
* **Microaggression:** A subtle, everyday comment or action that reflects bias, often unintentionally. In food, it can show up as jokes about food smelling 'funny' or surprise when someone from a marginalised background speaks eloquently about fine wine or truffles.
* **Othering:** Framing a person, group or culture as different, strange or 'not like us'. It's a subtle but powerful way of reinforcing who belongs – and who doesn't. Think 'ethnic aisle', 'exotic' fruits or describing a dish as 'weird but good'.
* **Reducing:** Oversimplifying a cuisine or culture into a stereotype or single flavour profile. Labelling everything from

South Asia as 'spicy' or seeing hot curries as winter warmers, for example, ignores cultural reality and nuance.
* **Refugee:** A person forced to flee their home due to war, persecution or violence. Refugees often leave everything behind, including access to familiar ingredients or tools. Their food traditions can become vital lifelines as ways to hold on to identity and memory and to build communities amidst displacement.
* **Tokenism:** Including a person or dish from a minority group just to appear diverse without any meaningful engagement, representation or support behind it. It's diversity for show, not substance.
* **Whitewashing:** Repackaging food, culture or stories to appeal to white, mainstream audiences, often by removing names, histories or flavours considered 'too unfamiliar'. It flattens and homogenises and, in doing so, can erase culture and identity.

Climate solutions in agriculture: Some definitions

A loose collection of terms describes how sustainable thinking is being incorporated into food systems. Regenerative agriculture, nature-based solutions and nature-positive solutions aren't entirely new ideas, but they are concepts that are quickly gaining traction alongside agroecology in global policy forums and funding. But there are risks of greenwashing (i.e. abusing this language in marketing as a cover for industrial food production).

IPES-Food believes that true food system solutions emerge through global, deliberative, democratic processes, and that agroecology is the best solution that meets those criteria.[3] The Food and Agriculture Organization (FAO) also has an Agroecology Knowledge Hub on their website.[4]

All the following terms here were provided for this book by Robbie Blake, communications manager at IPES-Food.

Appendix

* **Agroecology:** A way of farming that works with nature, using ecological principles to nurture land, nature and people. It relies on local knowledge, promotes diverse crops, and avoids toxic chemicals and high resource use. It has internationally agreed definitions and, as a movement, pushes for a fairer food system.
* **Regenerative agriculture:** A set of farming practices, and a mindset, aiming to restore ecosystems, soil and biodiversity, and capture carbon by using practices like crop rotation, cover crops and minimal tilling (ploughing). It has no agreed definition so far.
* **Sustainable intensification:** Aims to increase food production on the same land while lessening environmental damage. Critics argue it often relies on high-tech solutions and industrial agriculture without addressing deeper issues like inequality or reducing reliance on Big Ag corporations.
* **Nature-based solutions:** Protecting and restoring nature to address societal challenges like climate change and food security. The term is sometimes misused in international negotiations and by fossil fuel companies to justify offset schemes or to mask harmful practices like land grabs.
* **Organic agriculture:** A way of producing food (and clothing and cosmetics) without synthetic chemicals, fertilizers or genetically modified organisms (GMOs), focusing on soil health and animal welfare. Food sold as organic is certified by strict standards according to law.
* **Agroforestry:** Growing trees and crops together to improve soil health, boost nature and provide shade and shelter for plants and animals. It's a sustainable practice that supports both food production and ecosystem restoration.
* **Conservation agriculture:** A farming method that focuses on soil preservation through minimal tilling, crop rotation and keeping the soil covered. Its main goals are to maintain soil health to prevent erosion and degradation, and to increase productivity.

* **Climate-smart agriculture:** Farming practices designed to adapt to climate change, reduce greenhouse gas emissions, and increase productivity and incomes. Critics argue it often focuses on technological fixes and minor tweaks to existing industrial agriculture.
* **Precision agriculture:** Using technology like sensors, GPS, robotics and drones to optimise chemical inputs to be efficient and reduce waste. Like sustainable intensification, it's often linked to large-scale, industrial food production, and can reinforce reliance on expensive technology and Big Ag companies.
* **Zero-carbon agriculture:** Carefully measuring and balancing the amount of carbon emissions produced on a farm from machinery and animals with the amount of carbon absorbed from the atmosphere in soil and trees. It's difficult to measure accurately.
* **Permaculture:** A design system for farming and living that mimics natural processes, focuses on self-sufficiency and biodiversity, and takes a long-term perspective. It promotes food-producing ecosystems that require minimal ongoing human intervention, thereby reducing chemical inputs and prioritising recycling of nutrients and compost production.
* **Biodynamic farming:** A method of farming that goes beyond organic practices by incorporating spiritual and cosmic principles, such as using lunar cycles and specially prepared composts to guide sowing and harvesting.

A green claims glossary from Which?

* **Biodegradable:** Everything is theoretically 'biodegradable' eventually – even plastic decomposes and degrades over time, though it never disappears completely. This term should be accompanied by certification that the product has been tested to break down in a specific time period and/or conditions.

Appendix

* **Carbon neutral:** This usually suggests a company is offsetting some of its emissions, not that it produces no emissions. Offsetting can be a valid way of reducing emissions, but only once actual emissions have been reduced as much as possible.
* **Compostable:** This means something should break down in an industrial compost environment, not at home. But this type of waste isn't typically collected by local authority recycling. Only products carrying the home compostable certification logo will break down in home compost heaps.
* **Eco-conscious, environmentally friendly, green, natural:** There are no legal definitions or regulations associated with the use of any of these terms.
* **Plastic-free:** This can sometimes be marketing jargon. Question whether the product would ordinarily have been expected to contain plastic.
* **Recyclable:** Many things are technically recyclable, but that doesn't mean local authorities will collect them or even that large-scale recycling facilities exist. If no further details are on the packaging, check the rules in your local area at recyclenow.com.
* **Recycled:** Look for a percentage given for recycled content, as it can sometimes be a very small amount. This information should be included on packaging.

What food labels actually mean

Here are some of the most recognised certifications you'll find on food and drink in the UK.

Seafood

* **Marine Stewardship Council (MSC):** Certifies wild seafood from fisheries working to prevent overfishing and protect marine ecosystems.
* **Aquaculture Stewardship Council (ASC):** Certifies farmed seafood such as salmon, prawns and tilapia, covering environmental and social responsibility.

Crops
* **Fairtrade:** The most familiar label for fairer pay and better conditions for farmers growing certain crops, such as cocoa, coffee, tea, bananas and sugar.
* **Rainforest Alliance:** Aims to improve livelihoods and protect land through a Sustainable Agriculture Standard. Covers bananas, tea, coffee, cocoa, fruit, herbs and spices.

Organic food
* **EU Organic:** The European Union's logo certifies that the food was grown with fewer chemicals and natural methods, ensuring at least 95% organic ingredients.
* **Soil Association:** The Soil Association pioneered organic farming in the UK and is the most recognised label, certifying over 90% of the UK's organic processors.
* **OF&G (Organic Farmers & Growers):** OF&G is another leading UK certification body, with more agricultural focus, working closely with UK organic farmers and processors.

Good business
* **B Corp:** Awarded by the non-profit B Lab, it recognises companies that balance profit with positive social and environmental impact, measuring their performance across the whole business model, not just individual products.

Vegan
* **Vegan Society Trademark:** Certifies products as free from animal ingredients and not tested on animals. Covers food, cosmetics, household goods and more.

Restaurants
* **Food Made Good Standard:** From the Sustainable Restaurant Association, this is the only global certification for food service and hospitality businesses, assessing both social and environmental impact.

Appendix

* **Michelin Green Star:** Awarded to restaurants at the forefront of the industry when it comes to their sustainable practices. These establishments offer dining experiences that combine culinary excellence with outstanding eco-friendly commitments, and are a source of inspiration both for keen foodies and the hospitality industry as a whole.

UK-specific food standards

* **RSPCA Assured:** Focuses on animal welfare on farms, including how animals are reared, transported and slaughtered.
* **Red Tractor:** The UK's largest food and farming scheme, covering food safety, traceability and farming practices.
* **LEAF (Linking Environment and Farming):** Recognises farms using integrated, environmentally friendly farming practices that protect soil, water and biodiversity.
* **Pasture for Life:** Certifies meat and dairy from animals that are 100% fed on pasture, supporting higher animal welfare, soil health and biodiversity.

ENDNOTES

PROLOGUE

1. N.A. Mohidem et al., 'Rice for Food Security: Revisiting Its Production, Diversity, Rice Milling Process and Nutrient Content', *Agriculture,* 12/6 (2022).
2. According to the United Nations: 'UN Calls for Urgent Action to Feed the World's Growing Population Healthily, Equitably and Sustainably', UN Department of Economic and Social Affairs [website], un.org.
3. According to the World Wide Fund for Nature (WWF), a global environmental non-governmental organisation (NGO). See W. Baldwin-Cantello et al., *Triple Challenge: Synergies, Trade-Offs and Integrated Responses to Meet Our Food, Climate and Biodiversity Goals* (WWF-UK, October 2020).
4. Joanna Blythman, 'Strange Fruit', *Guardian*, 2 September 2002.
5. James McCulloch, 'The Truth About Food: Miles, Cheap Labour and Emissions', Eartha [website], 19 April 2023, eartha.life.
6. Richard Wrangham, *Catching Fire: How Cooking Made Us Human* (Profile Books, 2010).
7. Lizzie Collingham, *The Hungry Empire: How Britain's Quest for Food Shaped the Modern World* (Vintage, 2018).
8. Eleanor Barnett, *Leftovers: A History of Food Waste and Preservation* (Apollo, 2024).
9. Carolyn Steel, *Hungry City: How Food Shapes Our Lives* (Vintage, 2013).
10. Pen Vogler, 'Consuming History: Three Decades of Change in How and What We Eat', Nesta [website], nesta.org.
11. Todd Datz, 'Pollinator Populations Are Falling, Here's What That Means for Our Health and Economies', World Economic Forum [website], 20 December 2022, weforum.org.
12. 'Fast Facts – What Are Sustainable Food Systems?', United Nations Sustainable Development Goals [website], un.org.
13. Roxana Bardan, 'Temperatures Rising: NASA Confirms 2024 Warmest Year on Record', NASA [website], 10 January 2025, nasa.gov.
14. FAO, *FAO Remote Sensing Survey Reveals: Tropical Rainforests under Pressure as Agricultural Expansion Drives Global Deforestation*, Global Forest Resources Assessment, 6 November 2021, fao.org.
15. 'The Effects of Deforestation', WWF [website], wwf.org.uk.

Endnotes

16. Jane Court, Ainslie Macdonald and Richard Eckard, 'Understanding Methane from Livestock', Agriculture Victoria, Sheep Notes newsletter [website], autumn 2023, agriculture.vic.gov.au.
17. Lifeng Li, 'Water Scarcity, the Climate Crisis and Global Food Security: A Call for Collaborative Action', UN Chronicle [website], 12 October 2023, un.org.
18. Hannah Ritchie and Max Roser, 'Half of the World's Habitable Land Is Used for Agriculture', 2019, published online at OurWorldinData.org.
19. James Dinneen, 'Groundwater Levels are Dropping Fast All over the World', *New Scientist*, 24 January 2024.
20. Daniel Dickinson, 'Three Billion People Globally Impacted by Land Degradation', UN News [website], 2 December 2024, news.un.org.
21. Eliza Grames, 'Butterflies Declined by 22% in Just 2 Decades across the US – There Are Ways You Can Help Save Them', The Conversation [website], 6 March 2025, theconversation.com.
22. 'We All Depend on the Survival of Bees', United Nations Ukraine [website], ukraine.un.org.
23. Stefanie Deinet et al., *The Living Planet Index Update for Migratory Freshwater Fishes 2024 Update* (WWF, 15 May 2024).
24. IPES-Food, TABLE and the Global Alliance for the Future of Food, 'Fuel to Fork: A Podcast Exposing the Fossil Fuels in Our Food', IPES-Food [website], 24 October 2024, ipes-food.org.
25. '2023 Global Brand Audit: The Coca-Cola Company Is Once Again the Top Global Plastic Polluter', #BreakFreeFromPlastic press release [website], 7 February 2024, breakfreefromplastic.org.
26. OECD/FAO, 'Chapter 6: Meat' in *OECD-FAO Agricultural Outlook 2021–2030* (OECD Publishing, 2021).
27. Rob Percival, *The Meat Paradox: Eating, Empathy, and the Future of Meat* (Pegasus Books, 2022).
28. Julian Baggini, *How the World Eats: A Global Food Philosophy* (Granta Books, 2024).
29. 'Ending Factory Farming – End.It', Compassion in World Farming [website], ciwf.org.uk.
30. Tony Mcdougal, 'Poultry Takes More of the UK Consumer Market', Poultry World [website], 12 April 2024, poultryworld.net.
31. Alexa Phillips, 'How Diseased "Frankenchickens" Sold in Your Supermarket Are Making You Ill', The i Paper [website], 5 April 2025, inews.co.uk.
32. As told to the author by Sutton Hoo Chicken.
33. See Better Chicken Commitment at betterchicken.org.uk.
34. Peter van Horne et al., *Impact of the European Chicken Commitment (ECC) Broiler Production System on Economics, the Environment and Food Safety*, Report No. 2025-138 (Wageningen Social & Economic Research, 2025).
35. 'Farmed Fish', RSPCA [website], rspca.org.uk.

36. Vicente Javier Clemente-Suárez et al., 'Global Impacts of Western Diet and Its Effects on Metabolism and Health: A Narrative Review', *Nutrients*, 15/12 (June 2023).
37. B.M. Popkin, 'Nutritional Patterns and Transitions', *Population and Development Review*, 19/1 (March 1993).
38. Dr Chris van Tulleken, *Ultra-Processed People: Why Do We All Eat Stuff That Isn't Food ... and Why Can't We Stop?* (Cornerstone Press, 2023).
39. Melissa M. Lane et al., 'Ultra-processed Food Exposure and Adverse Health Outcomes: Umbrella Review of Epidemiological Meta-analyses', *The BMJ* (2024).
40. Rob Percival et al., 'What Are Ultra-processed Foods (UPFs)?', Soil Association [website], soilassociation.org.
41. Dr Diane Threapleton, Ali Morpeth and Professor Janet Cade, *Commercial Baby Foods in Crisis: Addressing Health, Marketing and Inequalities in the UK — Summary Report*, University of Leeds, April 2025.
42. Nowell H. Phelps et al., 'Worldwide Trends in Underweight and Obesity from 1990 to 2022: A Pooled Analysis of 3663 Population-representative Studies with 222 Million Children, Adolescents, and Adults', *The Lancet*, 403/10431 (16 March 2024).
43. 'Obesity Profile: Short Statistical Commentary', Office for Health Improvement and Disparities, Official Statistics [website], 3 May 2023, gov.uk.
44. 'New CDC Data Show Adult Obesity Prevalence Remains High', CDC Newsroom [website], 12 September 2024, cdc.gov.
45. FAO, IFAD, UNICEF, WFP and WHO, *The State of Food Security and Nutrition in the World 2024: Financing to End Hunger, Food Insecurity and Malnutrition in All Its Forms* (2024).
46. UN International Day of Awareness on Food Loss and Waste Reduction 29 September [website], un.org.
47. Raju Lal Bhardwaj et al., 'An Alarming Decline in the Nutritional Quality of Foods: The Biggest Challenge for Future Generations' Health', *Foods*, 13/6 (14 March 2024).
48. Juan Diego Martinez et al., 'A Modelled Estimate of Food Access within Countries Shows That Inequality within Countries Has Increased Despite Rising Equality between Countries', *Global Food Security*, 41/18 (June 2024).
49. United Nations Environment Programme, *UNEP Food Waste Index Report 2024. Think Eat Save: Tracking Progress to Halve Global Food Waste* (2024), available at https://wedocs.unep.org/20.500.11822/45230.
50. Rebecca Riddell et al., *Inequality Inc.: How Corporate Power Divides Our World and the Need for a New Era of Public Action* (Oxfam International, 2024).
51. 'Extreme Poverty in Developing Countries Inextricably Linked to Global Food Insecurity Crisis, Senior Officials Tell Second Committee', United Nations Meetings Coverage and Press Releases [website], GA/EF/3590, 11 October 2023.

Endnotes

52. J. Dixon et al., *Farming Systems and Poverty: Improving Farmers' Livelihoods in a Changing World*, Report No. 63492 (World Bank Group, 2001).
53. '"Enormous" Profits from Avocado Exports Drive Deforestation, Water Shortages in Mexico', PBS News Hour [website], 8 September 2024.
54. 'Coffee', Fairtrade Foundation [website], fairtrade.org.uk.
55. 'Cocoa Farmers', Fairtrade Foundation [website], fairtrade.org.uk.
56. 'Cocoa's Bittersweet Supply Chain in One Visualization', World Economic Forum [website], 4 November 2020, weforum.org.
57. Emma Giloth and Ariela Levy, 'Managing Migrant Labor Human Rights Risks in US Food Value Chain', BSR [website], 5 March 2025, bsr.org.
58. Department for Environment, Food and Rural Affairs, *UK Food Security Report 2024*, available at www.gov.uk/government/collections/united-kingdom-food-security-report.
59. Economist Impact, *Global Food Security Index 2022: Exploring Challenges and Developing Solutions for Food Security across 113 Countries*, Key Findings, *The Economist* [website], impact.economist.com.
60. 'What Is Happening to Agrobiodiversity?', FAO [website], available at fao.org/4/y5609e/y5609e02.htm.
61. 'Pick Diversity this British Apple Month', Natoora [website], 11 September 2023, natoora.com.
62. Honor May Eldridge, 'Why Our Love for Avocados Is Not Sustainable', Sustainable Food Trust [website], 31 January 2020, sustainablefoodtrust.org.
63. Jennifer Clapp, 'Concentration and Crises: Exploring the Deep Roots of Vulnerability in the Global Industrial Food System', *The Journal of Peasant Studies*, 50/1 (2022).
64. 'Rising Hunger: UN Chief Identifies Wars, Climate Chaos as Aggravating Factors', UN News [website], 13 February 2024, news.un.org.
65. World Food Programme, *Flash Report: Crisis in Eastern DRC, March 2025*, Reliefweb [website], 2 April 2025, reliefweb.int.
66. Rich Nelson, 'Russia, Ukraine, and the Impact on the World's Food Supply', GLG [website], glginsights.com.
67. Jennifer Clapp, 'Concentration and Crises'.
68. Christine Blank, 'UK Restaurants Slammed by Russian Fish Sanctions, Tax Hike', SeafoodSource [website], 4 April 2022, seafoodsource.com.
69. 'Gaza: Starvation Looms for One in Five People, Say Food Security Experts', UN News [website], 12 May 2025, news.un.org.
70. Doug Weir, 'How Does War Damage the Environment?', Conflict and Environment Observatory [website], 5 May 2025, ceobs.org.
71. 'Somalia Faces Worsening Hunger as Drought, Conflict and High Food Prices Risk Pushing 1 Million More People into Food Insecurity', World Food Programme [website], 4 March 2025, wfp.org.

72. 'High Tomato Prices in Morocco Curtail Vegetable's Export to Europe', Food Business Middle East & Africa [website], 10 January 2024, foodbusinessafrica.com.
73. 'FAO Food Price Index Rises in September', FAO [website], 4 October 2024, fao.org.
74. J.J. Johnson, 'A World without Rice Would Be a World without Culture', *Time*, 25 November 2024.
75. Sean Fleming, 'This Is How Rice Is Hurting the Planet', World Economic Forum [website], 18 June 2019, weforum.org.
76. Charlotte Edmund and Rebecca Geldard, 'Extreme Weather Is Driving Food Prices Higher. These 5 Crops Are Facing the Biggest Impacts', World Economic Forum [website], 12 February 2024, weforum.org.
77. Susannah Savage, 'Climate Change Is Pushing Up Food Prices – and Worrying Central Banks', *Financial Times*, 3 July 2024.
78. 'Farmers Grapple with Scarce Insurance Options Amid Climate Threats', Environmental Health News [website], 28 March 2024, ehn.org.
79. Kantar Worldpanel, Grocery Market Share, worldpanelbynumerator.com.
80. Department for Environment, Food and Rural Affairs, 'Theme 2: UK Food Supply Sources' in *United Kingdom Food Security Report 2021* (2021), gov.uk.
81. Nina Pullman, 'Half of Britain's Fruit and Veg Growers "May Go Out of Business within a Year"', Wicked Leeks [website], 19 September 2023, wickedleeks.riverford.co.uk.
82. 'Latest Food Insecurity Tracker Shows Seven Million Adults Going Hungry', The Food Foundation [website], 28 February 2025, foodfoundation.org.uk.
83. Thomas Weekes et al., *The Cost of Hunger and Hardship – Interim Report* (The Trussell Trust, October 2024).
84. Dr Giles Yeo, 'Why Free School Meals Are the Hidden Bedrock of a Better Society', *BBC Science Focus*, 9 August 2024.
85. The Food Foundation, *The Broken Plate 2025: The State of the Nation's Food System* (The Food Foundation, 2025).
86. Daniel Edmiston in collaboration with Shabna Begum and Mandeer Kataria, *Falling Faster amidst a Cost-of-Living Crisis: Poverty, Inequality and Ethnicity in the UK* (Runnymede, 2022).
87. Em Shrider, 'Poverty Rate for the Black Population Fell below Pre-pandemic Levels', United States Census Bureau [website], 12 September 2023, census.gov.
88. Food, Farming and Countryside Commission, *"So, What Do We Really Want from Food?" Citizens Are Hungry for Change: Starting a National Conversation about Food* (FFCC, 2023).
89. UKO and ORC, *Marketing Organic: Consumer Insights Report* (UK Organic and Organic Research Centre, 2024).
90. Tilly Armstrong, 'REVEALED: America's Food Deserts – the 76 Counties in the US That Don't Have a SINGLE Grocery Store', *Daily Mail*, 14 May 2023.

Endnotes

91. Andrés Castañeda et al., *Who Are the Poor in the Developing World?, Poverty and Shared Prosperity Report 2016: Taking on Inequality*, Policy Research Working Paper 7844 (World Bank Group, 2016).
92. FAO, IFAD, UNICEF, WFP and WHO, *The State of Food Security and Nutrition in the World 2023: Urbanization, Agrifood Systems Transformation and Healthy Diets across the Rural–Urban Continuum* (FAO, 2023).
93. Mark E. McGovern et al., 'A Review of the Evidence Linking Child Stunting to Economic Outcomes', *International Journal of Epidemiology*, 46/4 (August 2017).
94. Jennifer A. Pooler et al., 'Food Insecurity: A Key Social Determinant of Health for Older Adults', *Journal of the American Geriatrics Society*, 67/3 (March 2019).
95. Lotanna Emediegwu, 'Update: How Is the War in Ukraine Affecting Global Food Prices?', Economics Observatory [website], 23 February 2024, economicsobservatory.com.
96. As told to the author.
97. EAT-Lancet Commission, *Food Planet Health: Healthy Diets from Sustainable Food Systems*, Summary Report of the EAT-Lancet Commission (September 2025).
98. Tania Singer, 'Economic Growth: How to Build a Caring Economy', World Economic Forum [website], 24 January 2015, www.weforum.org.
99. Francis Fukuyama, '30 Years of World Politics: What Has Changed?', *Journal of Democracy*, 31/1 (January 2020).
100. Paul Polman and Andrew Winston, 'Stakeholder Capitalism Still Makes Business Sense', *Harvard Business Review* [website], 21 August 2024, hbr.org.
101. Dame Vivian Hunt et al., *Diversity Matters Even More: The Case for Holistic Impact* (McKinsey & Company, 2023).
102. C. Ruggeri Laderchi et al., *The Economics of the Food System Transformation*, Global Policy Report (Food System Economics Commission, 2024).
103. Danielle Nierenberg, 'A Manifesto for Disrupting Global Food Politics', *Forbes*, 6 January 2023.
104. Juliana Weltman Glezer, 'Renovation and Reinvention Are Key to Saving Our Food System. Here's Why', World Economic Forum [website], 13 June 2024, weforum.org.
105. Edelman Trust Institute, *2025 Edelman Trust Barometer: Trust and the Crisis of Grievance – Insights for Food and Beverage Sector*, Edelman [website], 22 May 2025, edelman.com.

PLAYERS

1. Elisa Pineda et al., 'Mexico's Bold New Law on Adequate and Sustainable Nutrition', *The Lancet*, 405/10481 (8 March 2025).
2. City of Copenhagen, *The City of Copenhagen's Food Strategy*, maaltider.kk.dk.
3. C40, *C40 Good Food Cities Declaration: How Cities Are Achieving the Planetary Health Diet for All*, Annual City Progress Report (C40, February 2022), c40.org.
4. Matthew Bell et al., *The Economic and Productivity Costs of Obesity and Overweight in the UK* (Frontier Economics, commissioned by Nesta, 1 July 2025).
5. *HMT-HMRC Soft Drinks Industry Levy Review*, Policy Paper, gov.uk [website], 30 October 2024.
6. IPES-Food, *Who's Tipping the Scales? The Growing Influence of Corporations on the Governance of Food Systems, and How to Stop It* (2023).
7. 'Government Launches "Good Food Cycle" to Transform Britain's Food System', press release, gov.uk [website], 15 July 2025.
8. 'Deforestation: Causes and How the EU Is Tackling It', European Parliament [website], 25 October 2022, europarl.europa.eu.
9. Gyorgy Scrinis, 'Ultra-processed Foods and the Corporate Capture of Nutrition: An Essay by Gyorgy Scrinis', *The BMJ* [website], 07 December 2020, bmj.com.
10. Angela Carriedo et al., 'The Corporate Capture of the Nutrition Profession in the USA: The Case of the Academy of Nutrition and Dietetics', *Public Health Nutrition*, 25/12 (24 October 2022).
11. 'UK Government's Nutrition Advisers Are Paid by World's Largest Food Companies, BMJ Analysis Reveals', *The BMJ* [website], 11 September 2024, bmj.com.
12. Scientific Advisory Committee on Nutrition, *SACN Statement on Processed Foods and Health* (SACN, July 2023).
13. '5 Reasons the Obesity Drug Market Remains Strong', *Thoughts on the Market* podcast, 5 June 2025, available at morganstanley.com/insights/podcasts/thoughts-on-the-market.
14. Jennifer Clapp, 'Chapter 2: The Rise of Big Food and Agriculture: Corporate Influence in the Food System' in Colin Sage (ed.), *A Research Agenda for Food Systems* (Edward Elgar, 2022), pp. 45–66.
15. Michael Fakhri, 'Seeds, Right to Life and Farmers' Rights: Report of the Special Rapporteur on the Right to Food', United Nations General Assembly, Human Rights Council 49th session, 28 February–1 April 2022, A/HRC/49/43, 30 December 2021, documents.un.org.
16. A. Wion et al., *Research for AGRI Committee — The Role of Commodity Traders in Shaping Agricultural Markets*, European Parliament, Policy Department for Structural and Cohesion Policies, Brussels, 2024, europarl.europa.eu.

17. Food, Diet and Obesity Committee, *Recipe for Health: A Plan to Fix Our Broken Food System, Report of Session 2024–24* (House of Lords, October 2024).
18. Ibid.
19. Competition Bureau Canada, 'Competition Bureau Makes Recommendations to Promote Competition in Canada's Grocery Industry', Government of Canada [website], 27 June 2023, canada.ca.
20. Byron Kaye and Renju Jose, 'Australia Supermarkets Should Face Hefty Fines for Code of Conduct Breach, Says Report', Reuters [website], 8 April 2024.
21. See Nina Pullman, 'Half of Britain's Fruit and Veg Growers "May Go Out of Business within a Year"', 19 September 2023, and Nick Easen, 'Fake Farms and Ugly Truths', 28 May 2024, Wicked Leeks [website], wickedleeks.riverford.co.uk.
22. Raj Patel, *Stuffed and Starved: The Hidden Battle for the World Food System* (Melville House Publishing, 2012).
23. Tom Crowfoot, 'The World Urgently Needs More Young Farmers, Says This Expert', World Economic Forum [website], 13 May 2025.
24. Department for Environment, Food and Rural Affairs, *Agriculture in the UK Evidence Pack: September 2022 Update*, available at publishing.service.gov.uk.
25. Zia Mehrabi, 'Likely Decline in the Number of Farms Globally by the Middle of the Century', *Nature Sustainability*, 6 (2023).
26. FAO, *The Gender Gap in Land Rights* (FAO, 2018), available at fao.org/3/i8796en/I8796EN.pdf.
27. European Commission, Joint Research Centre, *World Atlas of Desertification: Smallholder Agriculture*, available at wad.jrc.ec.europa.eu/smallholderagriculture.
28. 'Unpicking Food Prices: Where Does Your Food Pound Go, and Why Do Farmers Get So Little?', Sustain [website], 2 December 2022, sustainweb.org.
29. George Monbiot writes regular features for the *Guardian* and also covered this in his book *Regenesis: Feeding the World without Devouring the Planet* (Penguin, 2023).
30. Chris Smaje, *Saying NO to a Farm-Free Future: The Case for an Ecological Food System and Against Manufactured Foods* (Chelsea Green Publishing Co., 2023).
31. 'Blue Transformation: The Role of Seafood in Feeding a Growing Global Population', Marine Stewardship Council [website], n.d., www.msc.org.
32. Ibid.
33. FAO, *The State of World Fisheries and Aquaculture 2024: Blue Transformation in Action* (FAO, 2024).
34. R. Sharma et al., *Review of the State of World Marine Fishery Resources – 2025*, FAO Fisheries and Aquaculture Technical Paper No. 721 (FAO, 2025).

35. Oceana, 'Tracking Harmful Fisheries Subsidies', Research Summary, June 2021, available at https://oceana.org/wp-content/uploads/sites/18/994812/Oceana_Summary6-22.pdf.
36. Miren Gutierrez et al., *Fishy Business: Estimating the Impact of Irregular and Unsustainable Fishing of Distant-Water Fishing Fleets in Ecuador, Ghana, Peru, the Philippines and Senegal* (ODI, 2024).
37. Ibid.
38. A. Oloko et al., 'Gender Dynamics, Climate Change Threats and Illegal, Unreported, and Unregulated Fishing', *Discover Sustainability*, 6/1 (2025).
39. Ibid.
40. 'FAO Report: Global Fisheries and Aquaculture Production Reaches a New Record High', FAO [website], 7 June 2024.
41. Foodrise, *Blue Empire: How the Norwegian Salmon Industry Extracts Nutrition and Undermines Livelihoods in West Africa* (Foodrise (previously Feedback), January 2024).
42. 'New Study Exposes Staggering Wild Caught Fish Numbers', press release, Compassion in World Farming [website], 8 February 2024, ciwf.org.uk.
43. Spencer Roberts et al., 'Feeding Global Aquaculture', *Science Advances*, 10/42 (October 2024).
44. GRAIN, *The Pushback against Aquaculture Inc.* (10 December 2024).
45. Regin Winther Poulsen, 'Fishy Business: How Brexit Failed to Help a Dying Industry', Pulitzer Center [website], 28 May 2024, pulitzercenter.org.
46. Phoebe Lewis, Ainsley Hatt and Sarah Coulthard, 'The UK Is Losing Its Small Fishing Boats – and the Communities They Support', The Conversation [website], 8 August 2025, the conversation.com.
47. Neus González et al., 'Meat Consumption: Which Are the Current Global Risks? A Review of Recent (2010–2020) Evidences', *Food Research International*, 137 (November 2020).
48. Xiaoming Xu et al., 'Global Greenhouse Gas Emissions from Animal-based Foods Are Twice Those of Plant-based Foods', *Nature Food*, 2 (2021).
49. Neus González et al., 'Meat Consumption: Which Are the Current Global Risks?'.
50. Fuchsia Dunlop, 'China: The Birthplace of Fake Meat', *The Economist*, 2 July 2018.
51. 'Plant-based Meat', Good Food Institute [website], n.d., gfi.org/plant-based.
52. 'Investing in Alternative Protein', Good Food Institute [website], n.d., gfi.org/investment.
53. Paul Gilding, *Renewable Food: A Transformed and Renewable Food System Is Now Possible* (University of Cambridge Institute for Sustainability Leadership, 24 July 2025), p. 18.
54. Ai Kawamura, *Singapore Emerging as a Hub for Cellular Agri-food Production and Sales*, Mitsui & Co. Global Strategic Studies Institute Monthly Report, December 2022, mitsui.com.

Endnotes

55. Ben Cornwell, 'Lab-grown Food Could Hit UK Supermarket Shelves by 2027', New Food [website], 10 March 2025.
56. Polly Foreman, 'Plant-based Meat Alternatives Healthier and Better for the Planet, Report Finds', Plant Based News [website], 28 August 2024, plantbasednews.org.
57. Ryan O'Hare, 'Plant-based UPFs Linked with Higher Risk of Cardiovascular Disease', Imperial news [website], 11 June 2024, imperial.ac.uk.
58. Melissa Hogenboom, 'Sourdough v White Sliced: Which Breads Should We Be Eating?', BBC Future [website], 7 July 2025, bbc.co.uk/future.
59. Global Health Advocacy Incubator (GHAI) – Campaign for Tobacco-Free Kids (CTFK), *Marketing Exposed: A Global Public Health Threat for Food Policy* (November 2022), available at https://UPPindustrywatch.net.
60. Food, Diet and Obesity Committee, *Recipe for Health*.
61. Dakota Kim, 'A Constant Barrage: US Companies Target Junk Food Ads to People of Color', *Guardian*, 11 November 2022.
62. 'The Global Trends Driving the Evolution of Healthy Eating', Mintel [website], 10 September 2024, mintel.com.
63. 'Record Number of Fossil Fuel Lobbyists Granted Access to COP28 Climate Talks', press release, Global Witness [website], 5 December 2023, globalwitness.org.
64. 'COP29: States Must Press Azerbaijani Authorities to End Assault on Civil Society', Amnesty International [website], 8 October 2024, amnesty.org.
65. 'Sleepless in Baku: Signs Emerge of COP29 Hotel Price Gouging', Carbon Pulse [website], 9 February 2024, carbon-pulse.com.
66. As told to the author.
67. As told to the author.
68. As told to the author.
69. Mariana Santarelli, Luciana Marques Vieira and Jennifer Constantine, *Learning from Brazil's Food and Nutrition Security Policies* (Institute of Development Studies and the Food Foundation, 2018).
70. Damian Carrington, '"Insanely Tasty Green Food": How the Meaty Danes Embraced a World-first Plant-based Plan', *Guardian*, 31 January 2025.
71. As told to the author by Robbie Blake, communications manager, IPES-Food (International Panel of Experts on Sustainable Food Systems).
72. Suhasini Srinivasaragavan, 'Irish Products Among Cheap EU Dairy Forcing Some West African Farmers Out of Business', TheJournal.ie [website], 27 August 2024.
73. 'Stop the Poison, Support the Seed: Faith Leaders, Civil Society Organisations and Farmers Call for Justice in Africa–Europe Agricultural Relations', press release, SECAM [website], 1 July 2025.
74. 'About the Right to Food and Human Rights', Special Rapporteur on the Right to Food, UN Human Rights Office of the High Commissioner [website], ohchr.org.
75. Nic Newman et al., *Reuters Institute Digital News Report 2025* (Reuters Institute for the Study of Journalism, 2025).

76. Nic Newman et al., *Reuters Institute Digital News Report 2024* (Reuters Institute for the Study of Journalism, 2024).
77. Bee Wilson, 'How Ultra-processed Food Took Over Your Shopping Basket', *Guardian*, 13 February 2020.
78. Rooted Research Collective and Freedom Food Alliance, *Nutrition Misinformation in the Digital Age, 2024–2025* (Rooted Research Collective, 2025).
79. B. Davis et al., *Estimating Global and Country-level Employment in Agrifood Systems*, FAO Statistics Working Paper Series, No. 23-34 (FAO, 2023).
80. EY Global, 'EY Future Consumer Index: When Talk Turns into Action, Be Set for Change', EY [website], 9 November 2023, ey.com.
81. Vanessa Adamson, 'Environment and Buying Sustainably Drives Consumer Focus', AHDB [website], 28 November 2024, ahdb.org.uk.
82. 'Sustainability Still a Priority for Cash-strapped Brits When Eating Out', press release, Nutritics [website], 30 April 2024, nutritics.com.
83. Charles Abraham, 'New Sodexo Research Reveals UK Consumers Value Sustainable Food, but Barriers Still Remain', Sodexo [website], 14 January 2025.
84. Catherine McAndrew et al., *Debt, Migration, and Exploitation: The Seasonal Worker Visa and the Degradation of Working Conditions in UK Horticulture* (Landworkers' Alliance, 2023).
85. 'World Hunger Facts: Seven Things You Should Know', International Rescue Committee [website], 16 August 2024, rescue.org.
86. 'Obesity and Overweight', Fact Sheets, World Health Organization [website], 7 May 2025, who.int.
87. 'Almost One in Ten Children Obese in First Year of School', NHS [website], 5 November 2024, england.nhs.uk.
88. 'Time to Reinstate Food A-level!', School Food Matters [website], 12 May 2021, schoolfoodmatters.org.
89. 'Shortening Stature: Addressing the Decline in Children's Health', The Food Foundation [website], 6 August 2024, foodfoundation.org.uk.
90. Eszter Timar et al., *Places and Spaces: Environments and Children's Well-being*, Innocenti Report Card 17 (UNICEF Office of Research, 2022).
91. Jon Alexander with Ariane Conrad, *Citizens: Why the Key to Fixing Everything Is All of Us* (Canbury Press, 2023).

PEOPLE

1. Lizzie Collingham, 'How the Trade in Newfoundland Salt Cod Laid the Foundations of the Empire' in *The Hungry Empire: How Britain's Quest for Food Shaped the Modern World* (Vintage, 2018), p. 6.
2. Nathan Nunn and Nancy Qian, 'The Columbian Exchange: A History of Disease, Food, and Ideas', *Journal of Economic Perspectives*, 24/2 (Spring 2010).
3. Ibid.
4. Martha Henriques, 'How Spices Changed the Ancient World', BBC Made on Earth [website], n.d., bbc.com.
5. John Keay, *The Spice Route: A History* (John Murray, 2006).
6. John Keay, 'Chapter 12: Blue Water' in *The Spice Route*.
7. Charlie Harris et al., *For All the Tea in China: The English East India Company*, Oxford Centre for Global History, Global History of Capitalism Project, Case Study #33 (University of Oxford, February 2023).
8. Eleanor Barnett, *Leftovers: A History of Food Waste and Preservation* (Apollo, 2024).
9. Lizzie Collingham, 'How the Wheat for the Working Class Came to Be Grown in America' in *The Hungry Empire*.
10. Paul Kane and Molly Groarke, 'British Empire Facts!', National Geographic Kids [website], natgeokids.com/uk.
11. Charlie Harris and Christopher McKenna, *Enclosing the English Commons: Property, Productivity and the Making of Modern Capitalism*, Oxford Centre for Global History, Global History of Capitalism Project, Case Study #26 (University of Oxford, November 2022).
12. Lizzie Collingham, 'How the Trade in Newfoundland Salt Cod Laid the Foundations of the Empire' in *The Hungry Empire*, p. 33.
13. WRM International Secretariat, 'Colonization and Monoculture Plantations: Histories of Large-scale "Grabbings"', WRM Bulletin 260, World Rainforest Movement [website], 23 March 2022, wrm.org.uy.
14. Charlie Harris et al., *For All the Tea in China*.
15. Jada Phillips, *The Sankofa Report: British Colonialism and the UK Food System* (Food Matters, March 2023).
16. Sathnam Sanghera, *Empireland: How Imperialism Has Shaped Modern Britain* (Viking, 2021).
17. 'How to Look for Records of Slavery and the British Transatlantic Slave Trade', The National Archives [website], n.d., nationalarchives.gov.uk.
18. Nathan Nunn and Nancy Qian, 'The Columbian Exchange'.
19. Jada Phillips, *The Sankofa Report*.
20. Lomarsh Roopnarine, 'Chinese Indentured Servitude in the Atlantic World', Oxford Bibliographies [website], 26 April 2018, oxfordbibliographies.com.
21. 'Learn About the Great Hunger', Ireland's Great Hunger Museum [website], n.d., ighm.org/learn.html.
22. 'The Great Famine', UK Parliament [website], n.d., parliament.uk/about/living-heritage.

23. Michael Safi, 'Churchill's Policies Contributed to 1942 Bengal Famine – Study', *Guardian*, 29 March 2019.
24. Gary Oswald, *Africa during the Scramble: The Years without Food* (Sealion Press, 2022).
25. Ibid.
26. Marie Mitchell, *Kin: Caribbean Recipes for the Modern Kitchen* (Particular Books, 2024), p. 167.
27. Joseph E. Holloway, 'African Crops and Slave Cuisines', The Slave Rebellion [website], n.d., slaverebellion.info.
28. Jessica B. Harris, *High on the Hog: A Culinary Journey from Africa to America* (Bloomsbury, 2012).
29. As told to the author.
30. Keshia Sakarah, *Caribe: A Caribbean Cookbook with History* (Quadrille, 2025).
31. Sathnam Sanghera, *Empireland: How Imperialism Has Shaped Modern Britain* (Penguin Books, 2021), p. 96.
32. Lizzie Collingham, *Curry: A Tale of Cooks and Conquerors* (Oxford University Press, 2006).
33. Ibid., p. 141.
34. Maria Bradford, *Sweet Salone: Recipes from the Heart of Sierra Leone* (Hardie Grant, Quadrille, 2023).
35. J. Sundberg, 'Eurocentrism', in Rob Kitchin and Nigel Thrift (eds.), *International Encyclopedia of Human Geography* (Elsevier, 2009), pp. 638–43.
36. Mallika Basu, 'How Samahan Became a Global Sensation', The Juggernaut [website], 4 April 2024, thejuggernaut.com.
37. As told to the author.
38. Lori Barrette, 'Is BMI Accurate? New Evidence Says No', University of Rochester Medical Center Newsroom [website], 8 January 2024, urmc.rochester.edu/news.
39. Sabrina Strings, 'How the Use of BMI Fetishizes White Embodiment and Racializes Fat Phobia', *AMA Journal of Ethics*, 25/7 (2023).
40. Amanda Wahlstedt et al., 'MSG is A-OK: Exploring the Xenophobic History of and Best Practices for Consuming Monosodium Glutamate', *Journal of the Academy of Nutrition and Dietetics*, 122/1 (2022).
41. 'A History of the Restaurant', Something Curated [website], 3 September 2020, somethingcurated.com.
42. Annie Gray, 'Who Decided French Food Was Best?', *Delicious* magazine, September 2023.
43. Mallika Basu, 'Why "Best of" Lists Often Overlook South Asian Cuisines', The Juggernaut [website], 16 June 2022, thejuggernaut.com.
44. As told to the author.
45. '20 Coffee Statistics That'll Blow Your Mind', Nescafé [website], n.d., nescafe.com.
46. 'Coffee Consumption', British Coffee Association [website], n.d., britishcoffeeassociation.org.

Endnotes

47. United Nations Industrial Development Organization and International Coffee Organization, *Sustainability and Resilience of the Coffee Global Value Chain: Towards a Coffee Investment Vehicle* (UNIDO and ICO, June 2024).
48. Sjoerd Panhuysen and Frederik de Vries, *Coffee Barometer 2023*, coffeebarometer.org.
49. F. Andreotti et al., 'When Neglected Species Gain Global Interest: Lessons Learned from Quinoa's Boom and Bust for Teff and Minor Millet', *Global Food Security*, 32 (2022).
50. Ibid.
51. Julian Baggini, *How the World Eats: A Global Food Philosophy* (Granta, 2024).
52. Dr Navaratnam Partheeban OBE, *Encouraging and Supporting Black and People of Colour in Agriculture* (Nuffield Farming Scholarships Trust, August 2023), nuffieldscholar.org.
53. Krystyna Swiderska and Philippa Ryan, 'Indigenous Peoples' Food Systems Hold the Key to Feeding Humanity', International Institute for Environment and Development [website], 23 October 2020, iied.org.
54. As told to the author.
55. Ibid.
56. Ibid.
57. 'Intimidation, Slurs and Threats – Study Uncovers Racism in Rural England', University of Leicester news [website], 1 September 2025, le.ac.uk.
58. As told to the author.
59. 'NFU Launches Groundbreaking AgriFuture Scholarship Programme', NFU [website], 30 January 2025, nfuonline.com.
60. See the Be Inclusive Hospitality website at bihospitality.co.uk.
61. As told to the author.
62. Daniel Woolfson, 'Startup Incubator Scheme for Black-owned Food and Drink Brands Add Psalt Launches', The Grocer [website], 15 February 2021, thegrocer.co.uk.
63. David Ellis, '"Help Us to Create a More Inclusive Future": 70 Female Chefs Pen Letter Following Jason Atherton Sexism Row', *The Standard*, 19 February 2025.
64. As told to the author.
65. Fuchsia Dunlop, 'Culture Shock', *Gourmet*, August 2005.
66. As told to the author.
67. Joe Pinsker, 'The Future is Expensive Chinese Food', *The Atlantic*, 13 July 2016.
68. As told to the author.
69. Audre Lorde, *Sister Outsider* (Penguin Classics, 2019).

PLANET

1. Stephanie Robinson, 'Sinks and Sources – Awesome Mangroves', WWF [website], 30 September 2013, wwf.panda.org.
2. Kevin Krajick, 'A New 66 Million-Year History of Carbon Dioxide Offers Little Comfort for Today', State of the Planet: News from the Columbia Climate School [website], 7 December 2023, news.climate.columbia.edu.
3. Alex Morrison, 'Fossil Fuel CO_2 Emissions Increase Again in 2024', University of Exeter News [website], 13 November 2024, news.exeter.ac.uk.
4. 'Methane Emissions', European Commission [website], n.d., energy.ec.europa.eu.
5. Arthur Nelson, 'FAO Draft Report Backs Growth of Livestock Industry Despites Emissions', Climate Home News [website], 14 August 2024, climatechangenews.com.
6. 'Methane Emissions Are Driving Climate Change. Here's How to Reduce Them', UN Environment Programme [website], 20 August 2021, unep.org.
7. 'Monitoring Kelp Forest Ecosystems', Ocean Wise [website], n.d., ocean.org.
8. 'Planetary Boundaries', Sustainability Guide [website], n.d., sustainabilityguide.eu.
9. Kim Henrik Hebelstrup et al., 'Prehistoric Plant Exploitation and Domestication: An Inspiration for the Science of De Novo Domestication in Present Times', *Plants (Basel)*, 12/12 (June 2014).
10. UN GE.21-19855(E), Human Rights Council, 49th session, 28 February–1 April 2022, Agenda item 3, Promotion and protection of all human rights, civil, political, economic, social and cultural rights, including the right to development.
11. Michael D. Purugganan, 'Evolutionary Insights into the Nature of Plant Domestication', *Current Biology*, 29/14 (2019).
12. George Edwin Fussell and Kusum Nair, 'The Americas', Britannica [website], last updated 10 August 2025, britannica.com.
13. Simon Evans and Verner Viisainen, 'Revealed: How Colonial Rule Radically Shifts Historical Responsibility for Climate Change', CarbonBrief [website], 26 November 2023, carbonbrief.org.
14. Pedro Rodrigues and Joana Micael, 'The Importance of Guano Birds to the Inca Empire and the First Conservation Measures Implemented by Humans', *Ibis (International Journal of Avian Science)*, 163/1 (2020).
15. Ciara Giaimo, 'When the Western World Ran on Guano', Atlas Obscura [website], 14 October 2015, atlasobscura.com.
16. Matt Blois, 'The Industrialization of the Haber-Bosch Process', *Chemical and Engineering News*, 101/26 (11 August 2023), cen.acs.org.
17. Henry Dimbleby, *Ravenous: How to Get Ourselves and Our Planet into Shape* (Profile Books, 2023).

Endnotes

18. From his LinkedIn post, 'Yeah, But If We Do That We'll All Starve', April 2025, linkedin.com.
19. 'Miscellany', Lapham's Quarterly [website], n.d., laphamsquarterly.org/energy/miscellany/leftovers.
20. 'What's the Problem with Fossil Fuel-based Fertilizer?', Union of Concerned Scientists [website], 5 December 2023, ucs.org.
21. House of Commons Environment, Food and Rural Affairs Committee, *Soil Health: First Report of Session 2023–24*, HC 245 (5 December 2023).
22. See sixinchesofsoil.org.
23. Nicholas P. Sullivan, 'The Blue Revolution: The Transformation of Commercial Fishing in the 21st Century', World Ocean Forum, 4 March 2022, available at medium.com/world-ocean-forum/the-blue-revolution-bee4d19b3d8d.
24. AFSA, *The Costs to Smallholders of AfDB's Feed Africa Initiative: A Closer Look at the 40 Country Compact*, Executive Summary, Alliance for Food Sovereignty in Africa [website], 21 February 2024, afsafrica.org.
25. Geoff Tansey, 'From India's Green to Greed to Evergreen Revolution: M S Swaminathan Discusses a Lifetime's Work', Geoff Tansey Blog [website], 22 April 2016, geofftansey.wordpress.com.
26. Jai Shroff, 'Why Smallholder Farmers Are Central to New Food Security Interventions', World Economic Forum [website], 28 September 2022, weforum.org.
27. Alvaro Lario, 'Why Small-scale Farmers Can Teach Us a Lot About Climate Change', World Economic Forum [website], 13 February 2024, weforum.org.
28. ETC Group, *Small-scale Farmers and Peasants Still Feed the World* (ETC Group, 2022).
29. As told to the author.
30. Food, Farming and Countryside Commission, *Farming for Change: Mapping a Route to 2030* (FFCC, 2021).
31. Chris Smaje, 'Q: Can (small-scale) farming feed Britain (or Tokyo, or the world)? A: Yes ... (probably)', The Small Farm Future Blog [website], 28 February 2024.
32. A Growing Culture, 'Can Small-scale Farmers Feed the World?', Local Futures: Economics of Happiness [website], 16 August 2022, localfutures.org.
33. Tim A. McAllister et al., 'Livestock – An Essential Component of a Circular Bioeconomy', *Animal Fronteirs*, 15/4 (August 2025).
34. 'Addressing the Climate and Ecological Emergencies while Supporting Farmers', Small World Consulting [website], n.d., sw-consulting.co.uk.
35. 'The Dehesa: Spain's Natural Treasure', Museo del Jamón [website], 11 February 2025, museodeljamon.com.
36. Rosalind Malcolm, 'Industrial Chicken Farms Are Trashing Britain's Rivers – and Planning Reforms Could Make Things Worse', The Conversation [website], 3 April 2025, theconversation.com.

37. 'FAO Report: Global Fisheries and Aquaculture Production Reaches a New Record High', FAO [website], 7 June 2024, fao.org.
38. 'More than 90% of Global Aquatic Food Production Faces Substantial Risk from Environmental Change, Finds New Research', EAT [website], 26 June 2023, eatforum.org.
39. 'What Sustainable Seafood Species Can You Eat in the UK? Meet the Nation's Fishy Favourites', Marine Stewardship Council [website], n.d., msc.org.
40. 'Is There Such a Thing as Sustainable Salmon?', The Sustainable Restaurant Association [website], 3 October 2024, thesra.org.
41. Mallika Basu, 'Is Salmon Still on the Menu?', In Good Taste, Substack, 7 March 2025, mallikabasu.substack.com.
42. Fernanda Helena Marrocos Leite et al., 'Ultra-processed Foods Should Be Central to Global Food Systems Dialogue and Action on Biodiversity', *BMJ Global Health*, 7/3 (28 March 2022).
43. 'New WWF Data Shows UK Supermarkets Off Track to Meet Critical Environmental Targets', WWF press release [website], 3 December 2024, wwf.org.uk.
44. '8 Things to Know About Palm Oil', WWF [website], n.d., wwf.org.uk.
45. Shuhan Wang and Yahong Dong, 'Applications of Life Cycle Assessment in the Chocolate Industry: A State-of-the-art Analysis Based on Systematic Review', *Foods*, 13/6 (18 March 2024).
46. Silvia García et al., 'Ultra-processed Foods Consumption as a Promoting Factor of Greenhouse Gas Emissions, Water, Energy, and Land Use: A Longitudinal Assessment', *Science of the Total Environment*, 891 (15 September 2023).
47. Indu Gurung et al., *Rethinking Plant-Based Meat Alternatives* (The Food Foundation, August 2024).
48. Dr Justine Butler, 'Almonds and Avocados – The Plight of the Honeybee', Viva [website], 5 April 2024, viva.org.uk/blog.
49. Based on data from foodmiles.com.
50. Fred Pearce, 'Could the Global Boom in Greenhouses Help Cool the Planet?', Yale E360 [website], 20 June 2024, e360.yale.edu.
51. Louise Gray, *Avocado Anxiety: And Other Stories About Where Your Food Comes From* (Bloomsbury Wildlife, 2023).
52. As told to the author.
53. Liz Saccoccia and Samantha Kuzma, 'One-quarter of World's Crops Threatened by Water Risks', World Resources Institute [website], 16 October 2024, wri.org.
54. Ibid.
55. Xavier Esteve-Llorens et al., 'Environmental Footprint of Critical Agro-export Products in the Peruvian Hyper-arid Coast: A Case Study for Green Asparagus and Avocado', *Science of the Total Environment*, 818 (20 April 2022).
56. 'The Water Footprint of Food', Foodprint [website], 10 August 2018, foodprint.org.

Endnotes

57. 'Everything You Need to Know About Plastic Pollution', UN Environment Programme [website], 25 April 2023, unep.org.
58. 'Plastic Packaging', Plastics Europe [website], n.d., plasticseurope.org.
59. 'Global Plastic Recycling Rates "Stagnant" at Under 10%: Study', Science X [website], 13 April 2025, phys.org.
60. 'Plastics', OECD [website], n.d., oecd.org.
61. Khaled Ziani et al., 'Microplastics: A Real Global Threat for Environment and Food Safety: A State of the Art Review', *Nutrients*, 15/3 (25 January 2023).
62. Jack Marley, Imagine weekly newsletter from The Conversation [website], available at theconversationuk.cmail19.com/t/r-e-thlyqjk-nmtytrikk-ty/.
63. Arielle Samuelson, 'Indigenous Peoples Snubbed at Plastic Pollution Summit', *HEATED*, 5 December 2024.
64. Stuti Mishra, 'UN Plastic Pollution Talks End in "Abject Failure" as Negotiators Reject Draft Treaties', *The Independent*, 15 August 2025.
65. UNEP and FAO, *Sustainable Food Cold Chains: Opportunities, Challenges and the Way Forward* (UNEP and FAO, 2022).
66. Hung-Jui Lin et al., 'Quantifying Carbon Emissions in Cold Chain Transport: A Real-world Data-driven Approach', *Transportation Research Part D: Transport and Environment*, 142 (May 2025).
67. 'Food Waste', European Commission Food, Farming, Fisheries [website], n.d., https://food.ec.europa.eu/food-safety/food-waste_en.
68. WRAP, *Household Food and Drink Waste in the UK 2022* (WRAP, 2025).
69. Xameerah Malik et al., *Food Waste in the UK* (The House of Commons Library, 12 April 2024), researchbriefings.files.parliament.uk.
70. Vilma Sandström et al., 'Food System By-products Upcycled in Livestock and Aquaculture Feeds Can Increase Global Food Supply', *Nature Food*, 3 (2022).
71. 'World Squanders Over 1 Billion Meals a Day – UN Report', UN Environment Programme press release [website], 27 March 2024, unep.org.
72. Amelia Cookson, 'Fishy Finances – Could Your Money Be Propping Up "Big Salmon"?', Foodrise [website], 1 April 2025, foodrise.org.uk.
73. A.J. Kortleve et al., 'Over 80% of the European Union's Common Agricultural Policy Supports Emissions-intensive Animal Products', *Nature Food,* 5/4, (April 2024).
74. 'World Oil and Gas Subsidies Worth $7 Trillion', Energy Live News [website], 18 March 2025, energylivenews.com.
75. Jack Marley, Imagine weekly newsletter from The Conversation [website], 30 April 2025.
76. Clare Carlile, 'PR Campaign May Have Fuelled Food Study Backlash, Leaked Document Shows', *Guardian*, 11 April 2025.
77. See peoplesclimate.vote.
78. Food, Farming and Countryside Commission, *Let's Talk About Food: The Power of Community-led Food Conversations* (FFCC, March 2025).

79. Daisy Dunne and Yanine Quiroz, 'Mapped: The Impacts of Carbon-offset Projects around the World', CarbonBrief [website], 26 September 2023, interactive.carbonbrief.org.
80. Nicola Stevens and William J. Bond, 'A Trillion Trees: Carbon Capture or Fuelling Fire?', *Trends in Ecology & Evolution*, 39/1 (January 2024).
81. As told to the author.
82. 'Regenerative Agriculture Market Set for Significant Growth, Reaching $16.8 Billion by 2027', MarketsandMarkets Research Pvt. Ltd via Globe Newswire [website], 9 December 2024.
83. 'Organic and Regenerative – What's the Difference?', Soil Association [website], n.d., soilassociation.org.
84. NewClimate Institute, *Navigating Regenerative Agriculture in Corporate Climate Stategies: From Key Emission Reduction Measure to Greenwashing Strategy* (NewClimate Institute, September 2024), available at newclimate.org/resources/publications/navigating-regenerative-agriculture-in-corporate-climate-strategies.
85. Soil Association, *Organic Market Report 2025* (Soil Association, 2025).
86. See organicdenmark.com.
87. M. Barański et al., 'Higher Antioxidant and Lower Cadmium Concentrations and Lower Incidence of Pesticide Residues in Organically Grown Crops: A Systematic Literature Review and Meta-analyses', *British Journal of Nutrition*, 112/5 (2014), 794–811.
88. M. Barański et al., 'Effects of Organic Food Consumption on Human Health; the Jury Is Still Out!', *Food & Nutrition Research*, 61/1 (2017).
89. Nature4Climate, Nature Tech Collective, KPMG, Climate Collective and Serena, *Integrating Nature Tech: A Guide for Businesses* (2024), available at nature4climate.org/wp-content/uploads/2024/10/nature-tech-report.pdf.
90. Ibid.
91. 'World without Cows – Resource Wiki', available at docs.google.com/spreadsheets/d/187DtNZPdPdI5e_NKPydN0KLrO4PY14ueC-gCKi9NX3c/edit?gid=0#gid=0.
92. Aniruddha Ghosal, 'Vietnam Farmers Are Revolutionising How They Grow Rice in Bid to Save the Planet', *Independent*, 23 April 2024.
93. Paul Gilding, *Renewable Food: A Transformed and Renewable Food System Is Now Possible* (University of Cambridge Institute for Sustainability Leadership, 24 July 2025).
94. Kangning Yue and Yubang Shen, 'An Overview of Disruptive Technologies for Aquaculture', *Aquaculture and Fisheries*, 7/2 (2022).
95. Rob Hutchins, 'Largest Escape of Farmed Salmon in a Decade Finally Exposed', *Oceanographic* [website], 3 January 2024, oceanographicmagazine.com.
96. Adam Zewe, 'Explained: Generative AI's Environmental Impact', MIT News [website], 17 January 2025, news.mit.edu.
97. Ibid.
98. Emma Gillbard, 'Wildfarmed Expands into Oats and Barley Markets', *Farmers Weekly* [website], 8 July 2025, fwi.co.uk.

Endnotes

POSITIVE, PRACTICAL CHANGE

1. Jay Rayner, *A Greedy Man in a Hungry World: Why (Almost) Everything You Thought You Knew About Food Is Wrong* (William Collins, 2013).
2. 'Shorts: Vandana Shiva', Farmerama [website], n.d., available at farmerama.co/uncategorized/shorts-vandana-shiva/.
3. The Food Foundation, *Meat Facts* (2025), available from foodfoundation.org.uk/publication/meat-facts.
4. 'Government's Food Strategy "A Missed Opportunity" for the Climate', Climate Change Committee [website], 13 June 2022, theccc.org.uk.
5. As told to the author.
6. BBC Radio 4 The Food Programme podcast, 'Sourfaux', 6 June 2025.
7. 'Top 5 Food Waste Facts', The Felix Project [website], 17 March 2025, thefelixproject.org.
8. Graham Finlayson and James Stubbs, 'Ultra-processed Foods Might Not Be the Real Villain in Our Diets – Here's What Our Research Found', The Conversation [website], 15 August 2025, theconversation.com.
9. Xinyi Du et al., 'Efficacy of Household and Commercial Washing Agents in Removing the Pesticide Thiabendazole Residues from Fruits', *Foods*, 14/2 (2025).
10. Indu Gurung et al., *Rethinking Plant-based Meat Alternatives* (The Food Foundation, August 2024).
11. 'Beans and Peas Are the Best Meat Alternative', UCL News [website], 3 December 2024, ucl.ac.uk.
12. As told to the author.
13. Ibid.
14. Dan Saladino, *Eating to Extinction: The World's Rarest Foods and Why We Need to Save Them* (Jonathan Cape, 2021).
15. See mcsuk.org/goodfishguide.
16. As told to the author.
17. Ibid.
18. Ibid.
19. The Sustainable Restaurant Association, *Food Made Good Global Impact Report 2024*, thesra.org.
20. 'Food Waste Action Week 2025 – Buy Loose, Waste Less', Love Food Hate Waste [website], n.d. lovefoodhatewaste.com.
21. MacKenzie Jean-Philippe, '*High on the Hog*'s Jessica B. Harris Is Helping Spotlight the Cultural Importance of Black Food', Oprah Daily [website], 11 June 2023, oprahdaily.com.

APPENDIX

1. You can download *Sustain's Diversity Style Guide* (2023) on their website, sustainweb.org.
2. The definitions for *diaspora*, *immigrant* and *refugee* have been sourced from the International Rescue Committee, 'Migrants, Asylum Seekers, Refugees and Immigrants: What's the Difference?', 4 July 2024, rescue.org; International Organization for Migration, 'Key Migration Terms', ion.int; and European Commission, EMN Asylum and Migration Glossary.
3. IDS and IPES-Food, *Agroecology, Regenerative Agriculture and Nature-based Solutions: Competing Framings of Food Sustainability in Global Policy and Funding Spaces* (IDS and IPES-Food, October 2022).
4. See fao.org/agroecology/overview/en/.

INDEX

#ESEAEats 100

Abel & Cole 157
Academy of Nutrition and Dietetics (US) 51
ackee and saltfish 92
activism 39, 76, 83, 133, 164, 184
Adjonyoh, Zoe 104
Advertising Standards Authority (ASA) (UK) 147–8
affinity bias 112
African Development Bank 129
African food 92–3, 95, 98, 107, 112
Afro-Caribbean food 102, 107
ageing, healthy 169–70
ageism 108
agricultural workers 27, 54
  women 27, 57–8
agriculture 106–7 *see also* rice farming; smallholders
  biodynamic 200
  and climate change 21–3
  climate-smart 200
  conservation 199
  digital 150–1
  early 8–9, 125
  high-tech 67
  industrial 13, 26, 50, 172
  intensive 19, 137, 159
  mechanisation in 58
  organic 132, 147, 149, 199
  precision 150, 200
  regenerative 58, 132, 147–8, 156, 199
  sustainable 131
  water use in 16–17, 28 *see also* crops, water-intensive
  zero-carbon 199

agrobiodiversity loss 30
agrochemicals 17, 54
agroecology 130, 148, 156, 198–9
agri-food chain 53
Albius, Edmond 103
Alexander, Jon 80
alfalfa 138–9
algal blooms 128, 132
Al-Jahiz 8–9
Allen, Abby 35
Almería 137, 139
almonds 17, 135, 138–9
alternative proteins 59, 64–8, 82, 134–5, 153–4, 156
Amazon, the 16
Amazon (company) 55
American food culture 95
American Revolution 87
Anderson, Tim 115
Andhra Pradesh 147
animal feed 141–2
Anthropocene 123
antibiotic resistance 20
antimicrobial resistance 64
apples 30, 35, 41
aquaculture 20–1, 46, 59, 61–2, 128–9, 133, 159
  and digital technology 154
  nature-based 148–9
  regenerative 63, 148
  sustainable 154–5, 182
Argentina 16, 33
Arla 153
artificial intelligence (AI) 78, 151, 154–5
asparagus 6, 138
Atherton, Jason 108
Aujla, Rupy 191

avocados 6, 15, 28, 30, 135–6, 138, 151, 187
Aye, Mimi 97
Ayurveda 96

baby food 25, 68, 97
Baggini, Julian 103
Bakare, Adejoké 107
Balfour, Lady Eve 149
bananas 15, 30, 41, 79, 92
BASF 126
BCorp 158
Be Inclusive Hospitality 107
beans *see* pulses
Beans Is How 181
bees 17, 135, 151
Bendale, Eeshani 96
Bengal famine 89
Berners-Lee, Mike 131–2
Better Chicken Commitment 20
Beyond Meat 65
Bezner Kerr, Rachel 22
Big Food *see* food corporations
biodiversity 9, 17, 29, 46, 54, 58, 61, 82, 102, 129–32, 137, 148, 150–1, 157, 183
biodiversity loss 13, 23, 27, 39, 58, 124, 134, 159 *see also* agrobiodiversity loss
biogeochemical flows 124
biosphere 124
Bite Back 2030 74
Black, Imani 182
Black Eats LDN 95
Blair, Tony 144–5
Blake, Robbie 74
'bliss point' 23–4
BloomX 151
Blue Revolution 128–9
Blythman, Joanna 7, 24, 77
body mass index (BMI) 96, 120
BoerBurgerBeweging 46
Bold Bean Co. 181
Borlaug, Norman 126–7
Bosch, Carl 126
Boston Tea Party 87

Bovaer 153
Bradford, Maria 95, 107
branding 12, 34, 48, 55, 108, 117, 142
Bray, Barbara 169–70
Brazil 16, 24, 33–4, 73, 75, 101, 132
bread 48–9, 70–1, 157, 159, 175–8
Bread and Flour Regulations (1998) 49
Break Free from Plastic campaign 18
Brexit 46, 74
British Empire 88–90, 93–5
Broad'n Mind 181
Butler, Justine 135
butterflies 17

California 135, 138
Calliste, Josina 90–1
Campbell-Stephens, Rosemary 195
cancer 23, 25, 64
capitalism 7, 27, 74, 156
carbon 122
    in soil 128
carbon capture and storage (CCS) 145
carbon dioxide 16, 22, 26, 122–3
carbon emissions 146, 153, 187, 201
carbon footprint 131, 136–8
carbon markets 145–7
carbon offsets 146
carbon sequestration 20, 132
carbon sinks, loss of 16, 128
carbon tax 145
CarbonBrief 146
cardiovascular disease 25
Carême, Marie-Antoine 97–8
caring economy 39, 144
Caribbean 86–7, 89
Caribbean diet 92–3
Carson, Rachel 50
cassava 92
Cato, Andy 157, 159
cattle 19, 131, 141 *see also* livestock
Chakraborti, Neil 105
Chan, Anna 100
ChatGPT 155
Chefs in Schools 158
chicken consumption 18

Index

chickens *see* poultry
child labour 28
children 79–80, 167
    advertising to 70
children's menus 169
Chile 45, 147
chillies 93
Chinese food 65, 94, 97, 120, 181
Chinese workers, indentured 89, 93
chocolate 28, 71, 133–4
Chong, Catherine 185–6
Chorleywood process 70, 176
Chow, Cheryl 97
civil society organisations (CSOs) 72–5, 83
Clapp, Jennifer 32, 53–4
Clarkson, Jeremy 58
climate change 15–19, 21, 28, 33–4, 57, 60, 80, 124, 138, 188
    politics of 144–5
Climate Change Committee 171
climate policy 46
Cloake, Felicity 115
Clutton, Angela 166
coastal communities 60, 62–3, 140
Coco Collective, London 167
cocoa 17, 27–8, 34, 71, 79, 86, 101–2, 134
cod 63, 86, 92
coffee 9, 27–8, 33, 79, 86–7, 101–2, 187
cold chain 10, 72, 140
Collingham, Lizzie 88, 93–4
colonialism 79, 88–92
    influence on food 93–9, 119
colonisation 27, 86–7, 91, 195
Columbian Exchange 9, 86, 92
Columbus, Christopher 9, 86
commodity markets 32
Compost Club, East Sussex 167
composting 48, 142, 144, 167, 190, 200
conflict 29, 31–3, 87–8
Conrad, Ariane 80
Consortium for Labelling for the Environment, Animal Welfare and Regenerative Farming (CLEAR) 186

convenience foods 12, 139
    organic 150
    plant-based 134
Copa-Cogeca 46
COP21, Paris 144
COP28, Dubai 73, 145
COP29, Baku 73
COP30, Belém 73
COPs (cereals, oilseeds, protein crops) 55
corn *see* maize
cost-of-living crisis 2, 34, 36, 74
Covid-19 72, 74, 100
cowboys, Black 103, 197
Crate to Plate 137
crop science 14
crops
    commodity 44
    staple 6, 8, 26, 31, 133, 138, 187
    water-intensive 17, 28, 138–9, 159
cultural appreciation 111, 196
cultural appropriation 109–20, 196–7
    avoiding 115–18
cultural erasure 102, 197
curry powder 94

da Gama, Vasco 87
dairy 18, 65–6, 76, 135, 141, 145, 153, 173
dairy analogues 153–4
DDT 11, 50
decolonisation 104–7, 109
deficiency diseases 50
deforestation 16, 23, 28, 46–7, 64, 73, 102, 132, 134
dehesa system 132
Democratic Republic of Congo 31
Denmark 75, 145, 149
desertification 17
Deshingkar, Priya 114
diabetes 23, 25, 64
diasporas 3, 93, 95, 105, 114, 120, 167, 197 *see also* migration
diet-related illnesses 23
digital technology 12, 55, 76, 150–1, 154–5, 157
Dillon, Sheila 77

Dimbleby, Henry 46, 126
diversity, cultural 104–6, 112, 115, 163, 171, 196
drought 17, 28, 32, 34–5, 57–8, 89, 137–9, 160
drying food 8, 10
dumping, economic 76
Dunlop, Fuchsia 97, 112
Durrant, Rachael 74–5

East Africa 63, 92, 94
East Asian food 100
East India Company (EIC) 87
EAT-Lancet Planetary Health Diet 38, 45, 145
Economics Observatory 38
ecosystems 13, 16–17, 23, 57, 59, 122–9, 147–8, 151–2, 159, 199–200
    coastal 17
    marine 17, 20, 60, 62, 123, 132, 148–9, 159, 182
Eldridge, Honor 154–6
enclosures 9, 88, 90–1
Escoffier, Auguste 97–8
Esteros Lubimar, Spain 149
Ethiopia 32, 102
eugenics 97
Eurocentrism 77, 95–6, 105, 120, 194
European Chicken Commitment 20
European Union (EU)
    Common Agricultural Policy (CAP) 144
    Corporate Sustainability Reporting Directive (CSRD) 152
    Deforestation Regulation (EUDR) 46–7, 73
    Green Deal 46
    Sustainability Reporting Standards (ESRS) 152
eutrophication 128
exceptionalism 95
export markets 54, 62, 129
exports 12, 26–7, 30–2, 47, 76, 89, 138–9, 174
    restriction of 33

factory farms 19
Fairtrade 71, 134
Fairtrade Foundation 101
famine 14, 89, 126–7
farm diversification 58–9
farmers 57–9, 82 *see also* smallholders
    protests by 46, 57
farming *see* agriculture; vertical farming
farmworkers 28, 79
fast food 12, 37, 95, 98
fat 12, 25, 69, 178–9
    saturated 23, 51, 66
fatphobia 96
Feedback (campaign group) 144
feedback loops 6, 105–6
Felix Project 175
fermentation 8, 64–5, 68
fertilizers 54, 126
    nitrogen 22, 128
    synthetic 10, 13, 17, 123, 126
fibre, dietary 25, 66, 69, 179–80
Finland 149
fish 17, 32, 182
fish farming *see* aquaculture
fish feed 62
fish stocks, declining 62
fishing 59–63, 82
    industrial 17, 20, 60, 63, 123, 128, 159
fishing gear 20
fishing rights 61
floods 28, 33, 57, 80, 138
food
    endangered 182
    environmental impact of 131–42, 159
    organic 149–50, 173, 179–80, 185
    seasonal 165–6
Food and Agriculture Organization (FAO) 37, 47, 198
food chains 9 *see also* agri-food chain
food choices 79, 83
food corporations 24, 53–6, 82, 158
food distribution 69–72, 140

Index

Food and Drug Administration (FDA) (US) 55–6
food education 80, 168
food engineering 23–4, 64, 178
Food, Farming and Countryside Commission (FFCC) 37, 74, 130
    Food Conversation Project 74
Food Foundation 36, 180
food imports 35
food insecurity 32, 36–8, 79–80
food labels 45, 49, 143, 159, 183–6, 201–3
food manufacturers 69–72, 82
food markets, global 34
Food Matters, Sankofa Report 88
food media 108
food miles 136–8
food packaging 12, 190 *see also* plastic packaging
food policy 44–9, 82
food preservation 8
food producers, small-scale 103
food processing 10, 69–72, 82
    workers 54
food retail 34–6 *see also* supermarkets
food science 10, 51–2
food security 29, 138
food self-sufficiency 29
food sovereignty 27, 75–6, 103
food system 26, 82
    broken 15–42
    development of 8–14
    global 6–7, 53–6
    people in 78–9
    transformation 40–2
food taxes 44–6
food trade 7, 8–9, 11, 27, 33–5, 41, 44, 47, 54–5, 79, 86–7, 92–3, 110, 119, 125–6, 134
food waste 26–7, 141–2, 159, 175
    avoiding 187, 189–90
fortified foods 24, 50, 56
fossil fuels 15, 18, 22, 26, 123, 126–7, 130, 134, 137, 140, 144–5, 154
    lobbyists 73

France 144–5, 153
'frankenchickens' 19
free range 19–20
French food 97–8, 104, 114
freshwater use 124, 134
Friedrich, Bruce 65
fruit growing 136–7
fufu 92

Gaza 32
gender inequality 57–8, 61
Gene Revolution 11
genetic engineering 67
genetic modification (GM) 11, 54, 124
Gjedsted Bügel, Susanne 51
Global Food Security Index 29
global majority 86, 91, 113, 195
Global North 24, 27, 39, 58, 61, 67, 113, 194–5
Global Reporting Initiative (GRI) 152
Global South 27, 54, 58, 60–1, 64, 73, 79, 98, 101, 194
globalisation 11–12, 27, 31, 33, 47, 98, 102, 130, 134
GLP-1 52–3
Good Food Cycle (UK) 46
Good Food Institute (GFI) 65
governments *see* food policy
grain trade 54–5
Granville Community Kitchen 157
Gray, Annie 97–8, 104
Gray, Louise 137–8
green claims 200–1
green grabbing 103
Green Revolution 11, 126–9, 156
greenhouse gases (GHGs) 16, 22, 64, 122–3, 140, 173
greenhouses 136–7
greenwashing 39, 148, 183, 185, 198
Groundswell festival 147–8
groundwater depletion 16–17, 28, 137–8
groundwater regulation 139
groupthink 112
grow your own 167, 188
Growing Culture 130

guano 126
Guild of Fine Food 158
Guyana 93

Haber, Fritz 126
Haber-Bosch process 126–7
Harris, Jessica B. 193
Harvey, Paul 128
heart disease 23, 64
herbicides 13
Herd Market 157
HFSS (high in fat, sugar, salt) foods 44–5
Hodmedod 71, 181
Holocene 123
hospitality sector 105–9, 120, 158
hydrofluorocarbons (HFCs) 140

Ikeda, Kikunae 97
Imani Minorities in Aquaculture 182
immigrants 106, 118, 197
Impossible Foods 65
indentured workers 89, 92
India 11, 17, 33, 93, 127, 147, 153
Indian food 92–4
Indian workers, indentured 92–3
Indigenous communities 9, 73, 87–8, 91–2, 102–4, 140, 145–7, 149, 165, 194–5
Indigenous cuisines 98, 134, 188
Indigenous farming 103, 127
Indigenous fishermen 61–2
Indonesia 63, 134
Industrial Revolution 10, 88, 91, 123
industrialisation 7, 9–10
inequality 3, 13, 26–8, 39, 42
inflation 33, 35, 69
insects, as food 65–6, 182–3
integrated multi-trophic aquaculture (IMTA) 62–3
IPES-Food 54, 74–5, 148, 198
Irish Famine 89
irrigation 139
Israel 32

Jamaica 92–3, 105
Jarvis, Andy 21–2
Jefferies, Jenny 38
Johnson, JJ 33–4
just-in-time systems 35

Karma Cola 71
Kazim, Leyla 77
kenkey 92
Kera Protein 183

La Manna, Max 189
land conversion 16, 124
land ownership 88, 90–1, 195
Landworkers' Alliance 74, 79
Lang, Tim 136
Legghorn 158
legumes 26, 131, 135
Lei Win, Thin 21–3, 78
life cycle assessment (LCA) 135–6
livestock 16, 18–19, 65, 131, 187
    and climate change 123, 144, 153, 173
Loch Fyne Oysters 149
Lorde, Audre 119

maize (corn) 31, 92, 133–4, 138, 141
Malaysia 134
malnutrition 25, 37–8, 50, 56
Mamdani, Zohran 99
Marine Conservation Society 182
marine degradation 17
Marine Stewardship Council (MSC) 158
market concentration 30–1, 41
marketing 12, 24–5, 46, 55, 70, 74, 78, 82, 131, 142, 145, 160, 163, 174, 183, 198
Marley, Jack 140
masala chai 93
Masing, Anna Sulan 104–5, 109
Mauritius 93
meat 64, 66
    carbon footprint 131
    cultivated (lab-grown) 59, 67–8, 188 *see also* alternative proteins

Index

price of 19
red 131
wild 64
meat analogues 64
meat consumption 16, 18, 46
    reducing 171–3, 187
mechanisation 7, 58
media 76–8, 83
Meldrum, Josiah 127
methane 16, 22–3, 34, 123, 131–2, 135–6
    reduction 153, 157, 160
Mexico 6, 28, 45
microplastics 18, 140
Miers, Thomasina 115, 158
migrant communities 105–6, 118
migrant workers 72, 137
migration 28, 94, 120 *see also* diasporas
Milan Urban Food Policy Pact 45
millet 26, 58
milpa (three sisters system) 125
misinformation 191–3
Mitchell, Marie 91
Monbiot, George 59
monocultures 9, 17, 27, 58, 87, 102, 127, 134–5
monosodium glutamate (MSG) 97, 100
Monteiro, Carlos 24, 178
Morocco 33
Morpeth, Ali 180
Moskowitz, Howard 23–4
Myambo, Freda 112
mycoprotein 64

Nair, Samyukta 115
nanoplastics 140
National Council for Food and Nutrition Security (CONSEA) (Brazil) 74
National Food Strategy (UK) 46, 171
nature-based solutions (NbS) 151–2, 199
nature tech 150–2
neo-colonialism 101–4, 119

Nesta 12
Nestlé 53
net zero 144–5
New Climate Institute 148
New World 88, 194
New Zealand 145
Nice Rice 157
nitrogen 122–6, 128, 131 *see also* fertilizers, nitrogen
nitrous oxide 16, 22
non-governmental organisations (NGOs) 72–5, 83, 136, 186
Norway 62–3, 144
nose-to-tail 173
Nova food classification 24, 51, 171, 178
novel entities 124
nutrient deficiencies 24–5, 56, 70
nutrients 8, 16–17, 24, 26, 50–2, 56, 59, 68–9, 122, 131, 138, 144, 171, 180
nutrition labels *see* food labels
nutrition science *see* food science
nutritional value 24
nutritionism 24, 50–1
Nyemb-Diop, Kera 96

obesity 23, 25, 37, 45
    in children 80
ocean acidification 124
ocean warming 20, 60, 123, 132
Oddbox 157
Old World 194
olive oil 34
Oliver, Jamie 74, 105
Opium Wars 87
oranges 34
organic movement 149–50 *see also* agriculture, organic; food, organic
organophosphates 127
Oswald, Gary 89
overconsumption 55, 80, 175
over-farming 17
overfishing 17, 60, 63–4, 132
oxtail 102
oxtail stew 93
ozone depletion 124

Pacific Ocean 60
packaging *see* plastic packaging
Packham, Chris 7
palm oil 26, 47, 133–4
Paris Agreement 144, 146
Partheeban, Navaratnam (Theeb) 103
Patel, Raj 56
Peng, Yuejia 146–7
perception bias 112
Percival, Rob 172–3
permaculture 200
Peru 136, 138
Pesticide Action Network UK (PAN UK) 180
pesticides 11, 13, 22, 50, 54, 76, 127, 132, 134, 137, 150, 180
pet food 142
Phillips, Riaz 92
Phipps, Catherine 133
phosphorous 122–4, 126
pigs 19, 132, 173
pilau 92
planetary boundaries 123–4
plantain 92, 96
plantations 9, 87, 91, 101
plastic packaging 18, 22 139–40, 159
Plastics Europe 139
Plastics Pact (UK) 49
pollination, mechanical 151
pollinators 17
pollution 32, 139
    air 23, 131–2
    soil 23, 128
    water 17–18, 20, 23, 128, 131–2
Polman, Paul 39
polytunnels 136
Popkin, Barry 24
Portugal 147
potassium 122, 126, 180
potatoes 26, 34, 86, 93
poultry 19–20, 131–2, 173
poverty 27, 36–8, 80
prejudice 105, 120
price wars 34–5
processed food 23, 50 *see also* ultra-processed foods (UPFs)

protectionism 47
protein 64 *see also* alternative proteins; meat
Psalt 107
public health campaigns 46
pulses 71, 130, 133, 158, 160, 180–1, 187

Quinn, Sue 189
quinoa 102

racial injustice 91
racism 37, 105
Radzman, Nadia 180–1
rainfall 17, 34
Rainforest Alliance 134
rainforest clearance 16, 134
Raj, the 93
Raja, Karan 191–3
rationing, wartime 10
Ray, Krishnendu 98, 114
Rayner, Jay 162
ready meals 12, 23, 53, 70, 133–4, 176
Red Tractor 183
refined grains 23, 41
refrigerated transport 140
refrigeration 10, 67, 166
Restorick, Trewin 186–8
Reuters Institute, *Digital News Report* 76
rice 8, 26, 31, 33–4, 86, 92, 96, 120, 138
rice farming 11, 126, 160
    and climate change 6, 22–3, 123
    innovative 153
rice–fish system 125
Riverford 157
Roddy, Rachel 115
roti 93
Rubies in the Rubble 157–8
rum 93–4
Russia 31–2
Russia–Ukraine war 37

Sachdev, Pooja 106
Sakarah, Keshia 93

Index

salmon 62, 132–3, 174
salt 23, 25
samosas 92
Sanghera, Sathnam 88–90, 93
Scientific Advisory Committee on Nutrition (SACN) (UK) 51–2
Scramble for Africa 89
Scrinis, Gyorgy 24, 51
seafood 20–1, 174–5 *see also* aquaculture; fishing; shellfish
seafood industry 60
SeaGrown 149
seasonal work 58
Seasonal Worker Visa Programme 28
seaweed farming 61–2, 149
seeds 22, 54
    hybrid 22
    laws on 74
sexism 108
shellfish 59, 61–2, 133, 148–9, 160, 174
Shiva, Vandana 103, 127, 164
shrinkflation 35
similarity bias 107
Singapore 65, 182
Singer, Tania 39
slave trade 92
slavery 87–9, 91–2, 101
slurry 132
Smaje, Chris 59, 130
smallholders 13, 27, 54, 58, 101, 127, 129–30
smoking food 8, 133, 171
snacking 69
Snowchange Cooperative 149
social exclusion 37
social media 76–8, 83, 190–2
soil acidification 128
Soil Association 149
soil deterioration 17
Somalia 33
sorghum 8, 58
South Asian cuisine 94, 98, 112, 114, 120, 181
Southeast Asia 16
Southeast Asian food 100, 114
soy 26, 34, 44, 47, 132–3, 141

Spacey, Conor 189
Spain 137, 139
Spector, Tim 77–8
spice trade 9, 86–7
Stebbing, Jen 151–2
Stockholm Resilience Centre 123–4
Strings, Sabrina 96
subsidies 44, 58
Sudan 31
sugar 10, 12, 23–6, 33, 41, 49, 51, 86, 93, 134
sugar plantations 87
sugar trade 9, 86–7
sugar tax 44–5
sugarcane 27, 86
'superfoods' 102
supermarkets 10–11, 34–6, 55–6, 63, 158, 165
supply chains 7, 14, 31–2, 71
    global 87
    government control of 10
sustainable intensification 147, 199
Sustainable Restaurant Association 133, 158, 188–9
Swales, Martha 167
Swaminathan, M.S. 129

takeaways, Indian and Chinese 94
tariffs 47
Taskforce on Nature-related Financial Disclosures (TNFD) 152
Taverner, Charlie 130
tea 9, 79, 87, 93
Tea Act (1773) 87
teff 102
three sisters system (milpa) 125
tokenism 107, 117, 196, 198
tomatoes 33, 86
Tonks, Mitch 158
Tony's Chocolonely 71
tree planting 146–7
Trinidad 93
Trump, Donald 47
Trussell Trust 36
Tubb, Catherine 66–7

Ukraine 31–3 *see also* Russia–Ukraine war
ultra-processed foods (UPFs) 24–5, 44, 51–2, 65, 70–1, 134, 139, 176–9, 183–4
Unbeleafable 137
United Nations (UN) 7, 15, 44, 47, 59, 102
    Climate Bureau 73
    Convention on the Law of the Sea (UNCLOS) 61
    Environment Programme 139
    Food Systems Summit 47
    Framework Convention on Climate Change 73
    Sustainable Development Goals (SDGs) 13
    UNICEF 80
United States Department of Agriculture (USDA) 55–6
urbanism 24
US 17, 19, 25, 28, 34, 37, 58, 63, 70, 132, 138

value chain 7
van Tulleken, Chris 25, 52, 56, 77
vanilla 103
vegetable growing 136–7
Vegetarian Society of Denmark (DVF) 74
venison 133, 182
Verma, Chaitali 99
vertical farming 136–7
Via Campesina 73–4
Vietnam 33
vitamins 49, 50
Vittles 77

Wahaca 158
Waitrose 119
Warner, Anthony 14
Warner, Mike 174
water footprint 138–9
weather events, extreme 33–5 *see also* drought; floods
weight loss drugs 52–3

West Africa 34, 60, 62, 92, 134
West African cuisine 112
Western diet 24, 41
wheat 31, 33, 44, 138
whitewashing 98, 198
Wildfarmed 71, 157, 159
Wilkinson, Daniel 28
Wilson, Bee 24, 77
Wong, James 97
Woods, Deirdre (Dee) 74
World Bank 47
World Economic Forum 34, 40
World Food Programme 33, 47
World Health Organization 170
World Trade Organization (WTO) 44, 47
World War One 10
World War Two 10
Wrangham, Richard 8
Wren, Gavin 48–9, 77
Wye, River 132
Wylde Market 157

Yeo, Giles 36, 51, 177–9
Yeo Valley 157
Young, Chris 175–6

ACKNOWLEDGEMENTS

Two cookbooks and lots of recipe, feature and newsletter writing later, this has been the most ambitious publishing project I have undertaken. I have had to lean on some clever in-the-know friends, old and new.

Grateful thanks to:

My publisher, Kristin Jensen, who spotted the opportunity for me to write a book like this well before I did, for her creative genius and endless patience.

Emma Marijewycz for her energy, enthusiasm and efficiency in overseeing the publicity.

Jane Matthews, book designer with the mostest, for her patience and diligence in bringing good taste to life on the cover and inside pages.

Iqbal Wahhab OBE for unwavering belief in my ambitious project ideas and me, the quiet hand-holding and introductions to the best allies in the business.

Fran Bailey for dragging my reluctant self to Groundswell and Harriet Cherry and the team for the warm welcome and learning opportunities there.

Josiah Meldrum, who took me on a beantastic tour to explain crop cover and agroecology, thank you for taking the time to review chunks of this book and never turning me away.

Caroline Dewing for sanctuary and company to help steer a new path, followed by eagle-eyed copy inputs through Future Agenda, her think tank and advisory firm.

Also, for the introduction to Christèle Delbé, who in her own words has been a sustainability expert since it was something only hippies cared about. I'm very grateful you connected me to University of Cambridge Institute for Sustainability Leadership (CISL) and the world of knowledge it opened to me.

Adrian Greet, my tutor on the CISL Sustainable Food Production and Processing course and firm champion, this wouldn't have been possible without your cheerleading and wisdom.

Berenice Pardo Zolezzi at CISL for co-ordinating CISL's support for my initiative, and Georgina Harding and Sarah Bailey for seeing it through.

Nicki Sturzaker and John McAreavey for the generous invitations to Edinburgh, chivvying and space to get cracking.

Everyone I reached out to at the outset to start plotting content who took the time to speak to me:

* Juliane Caillouette-Noble, Sustainable Restaurant Association
* Michael (Mike) Harfleet for the guidance, ever-present wisdom and for introducing me to Tom Harfleet, his son and a creative catalyst for good businesses
* Kate Hofman, founder of Making Pesto and sustainable business champion
* Sareta Puri, Sustain
* Geoff Tansey, Food Systems Academy
* Diedre Dee Woods, Landworkers' Alliance

Jenny Jeffries for being an unfailing advocate and for all the guidance, copy review and inputs.

Charlie Taverner at the Food, Farming and Countryside Commission, Trewin Restorick, Sathnam Sanghera and Dr Annie Gray for taking time to contribute, aid my understanding and review chunks of copy.

Barry Murphy, former partner, Global Sustainability Team at PWC, for sense-checking the 'Planet' chapter.

The reader who anonymously reviewed my sections on animal welfare and farming systems. You didn't want to be named but I will be eternally grateful.

Acknowledgements

Ali Morpeth, Simon Day, Alex Hayes and Kate Cawley for your constant support, sharing your expertise and welcoming me into your networks to help me get a nuanced and balanced picture of the challenges and opportunities.

Katy Jackson of the British Library for letting me trial the book content with food lovers at our sellout Food Matters for Food Lovers course during the Food Season.

To my expert contributors for seeing the value in my project and taking the time to craft supplemental words:

* Dr Rupy Aujla
* Robbie Blake
* Barbara Bray
* Josina Calliste
* Anna Chan
* Catherine Chong
* Angela Clutton
* Honor Eldridge
* Yuejia Peng
* Rob Percival
* Trewin Restorick
* Jen Stebbing
* Catherine Tubb
* Anthony Warner
* Mike Warner
* Thin Lei Win
* Gavin Wren
* Professor Giles S.H. Yeo
* Chris Young

And to everyone else I reached out to who replied to me, breathing their expertise into the pages:

* Abby Allen
* Mimi Aye
* Imani Black
* Maria Bradford
* Professor Neil Chakraborti
* James Collier
* Professor Rachel Durrant
* Louise Gray
* Dr Anna Sulan Masing
* Annabelle Nash, Sutton Hoo Chicken
* Dr Kera Nyemb-Diop
* Riaz Phillips
* Pooja Sachdev
* Chris Smaje

Trudi Ryan for giving me confidence and clarity to forge ahead with my 'food as a force for good' purpose and to Sarah Dean for the kind introduction.

Orlando Martins, Oliver Burton, Gavin Ellwood, Vicki Marinker, Pinky Lilani, Nilesha Chauvet and Jeremy Sice (to name just a few) for the inspiring thoughts and provocations that led me here.

Lea Turner for LinkedIn and Lauren Dudley for Instagram/TikTok training, advisory and connections.

Claire Conrad, my literary agent of over two decades, and Hilary Murray, my talent agent, and team Arlington Talent for always being there.

Mike McKibben for the wisdom and willing ears about all my behind-the-scenes career developments.

Team Good Food, particularly Lulu Grimes for the ongoing sage advice and the introduction to my willing Planet Friendlier accomplice, Keith Kendrick.

Team Waitrose, especially Alison Oakervee, for the friendship, recipe commissions, spice and sustainability love.

Lucia Hobart and Will Mundow for keeping my business and finance show on the road and the kindness as I navigate authorship and self-employment.

My friends, followers and supporters from my years in the communications industry, in the food world, online and at the Guild of Food Writers – your words of support, likes and shares mean more than you realise.

Sally Hishmurgh and Anita Borvanker, whose love I tested by forcing an early review of the book draft on, and for the endless brainstorms. It's less depressing now, promise!

And finally, hugest of thanks to my two teens, family and friends like family, whose love and patience I routinely put to the test, for seeing me through the highs and lows, chaos and calm. I am nothing without you.

READER OFFER

Readers of this book are invited to deepen their understanding of sustainable food systems with a 15% discount on the Cambridge Institute of Sustainability Leadership's (CISL) eight-week online course, Sustainable Food: Production and Processing.

Offer valid until 31 December 2040. Use the code INGOODTASTE at checkout.

Find out more at https://www.cisl.cam.ac.uk/education/learn-online/sustainable-food-production-and-processing

Nine Bean Rows
23 Mountjoy Square
Dublin, D01 E0F8
Ireland
@9beanrowsbooks
ninebeanrowsbooks.com

NINE
BEAN
ROWS

First published 2026
Text copyright © Mallika Basu, 2026

ISBN: 978-1-7384795-3-5

Editor: Kristin Jensen
Designer: Jane Matthews
Indexer: Jane Rogers
Printed by L&C Printing Group, Poland

This product is made of material from well-managed FSC® -certified forests and other controlled sources.
All rights reserved.
No part of this publication may be copied, reproduced or transmitted in any form or by any means without written permission of the publishers.
A CIP catalogue record for this book is available from the British Library.
For EU product safety concerns, contact info@ninebeanrowsbooks.com.
10 9 8 7 6 5 4 3 2 1